THE CONSCIOUSNESS OF JESUS

THE
CONSCIOUSNESS
OF JESUS

by
Jacques Guillet, S.J.

Translated by
Edmond Bonin

NEWMAN PRESS
New York / Paramus / Toronto

A Newman Press edition, originally published under the title *Jésus devant sa vie et sa mort*, © 1971, Editions Aubier Montaigne, Paris, France.

NIHIL OBSTAT:
Msgr. William F. Hogan
Censor Librorum

IMPRIMATUR:
✠ Thomas A. Boland, S.T.D
Archbishop of Newark

April 28, 1972

Library of Congress
Catalog Card Number: 72-81573

Published by Newman Press
Editorial Office: 1865 Broadway, N.Y., N.Y. 10023
Business Office: 400 Sette Drive, Paramus, N.J. 07652

Printed and bound in the
United States of America

Contents

Foreword

It would be naïve and idle to try justifying the weaknesses of this book by the breadth of its ambitions. But perhaps it is not useless to explain its occasionally sinuous course and somewhat unusual manner by the goals it has set itself. For it pursues several, at the risk of attaining none.

The first goal is to examine the gospels in the light of the questions—already old and yet ever actual—put by Rudolf Bultmann, for example. The New Testament makes Jesus a divine personage, the Son of God. Does that not mean giving him a mythical countenance, and must we not smash this idol in order to rediscover faith? Thus there arise problems concerning Jesus' personality and the way it reveals and communicates itself; and although this book treats of them explicitly only in a few essential places, they are constantly present.

To answer these questions, we must necessarily pass through Jesus' own consciousness. Words like *consciousness* or *awareness* are dangerous and readily suspect, but it would be difficult to strike them out entirely. The gospels were certainly not written to make us analyze Jesus' sentiments, his intentions or his thoughts. Still, we must make sure that Jesus really lived out the event related in the gospels, and that they really tell us about his life and death. Short of that, we no longer have any palpable relationship with him, and the Christian faith is abandoned to imagination or speculation, to the myths of thought or fantasy. The greater part of this book is devoted to ascertaining that Jesus *did* so live the gospel event—whence the title we have chosen.

Such an attempt presupposes minimal information about the story of Jesus and the evangelical tradition. For methodological

1

as well as exemplary purposes, we have tried in each chapter to correlate the historical and critical development with meditation on the person of Jesus. This procedure entails a certain lack of coherence and unity: at times we have multiplied references and expanded arguments, but most often we have been content merely to mention some outstanding article or book. The work seems to oscillate, without choosing, between personal synthesis and scientific study. To tell the truth, although the technical apparatus is present in order to establish the weight of the facts, it is meant especially to help the reader pursue this investigation on his own. Treating the gospels for what they are—documents and testimonies—is an indispensable step toward hearing their message.

Aix-en-Provence,
Easter 1971

1
Jesus' Consciousness and the Faith of His Disciples

What relation is there between Jesus' consciousness and the faith of his disciples? The answer is apparently simple and free of all ambiguity: the faith of the disciples rests on the consciousness of Jesus. He knew he was the Son of God, he revealed it to his disciples and proved it by rising from the dead. The disciples in turn proclaimed this event and this faith, they established communities and transmitted their message in the gospels: "These [signs] are recorded so that you may believe that Jesus is the Christ, the Son of God, and that believing this you may have life through his name" (Jn. 20, 31). Indeed, for nineteen hundred years Christians have been living on the gospels and drawing from them this certitude which grounds their faith: Jesus is the Son of God, the Savior of the world, because he said so and because the Father corroborated his statement by raising him from the dead.

The normal, and no doubt necessary, passage from Jesus' consciousness to the faith of Christians is effectuated by the declarations which appear in the gospels and in which Christ tells us about himself and his work. From beginning to end, John's gospel is constructed on this principle: Jesus' assertions concerning what he is—"I am [the Messiah] (4, 26) . . . the living bread (6, 51) . . . the light of the world (8, 12) . . . the gate (10, 7) . . . the shepherd (10, 11) . . . the resurrection (11, 25) . . . the Way, the Truth and the Life" (14, 6)—are echoed by the diverse responses of man; but though the reactions are varied, ranging from deliberate rejection to total adherence, the crux of the matter is always faith, either extended or refused, and faith is always a reply to these words of Jesus, an acceptance of what he means, a reference to his consciousness.

3

The fourth gospel is visibly systematic—so much so that we certainly have a right, without impugning its message, to ask whether it does not generalize and specify contents which were far from being so definite in the beginning. Indeed, in the synoptic gospels, Jesus' statements about himself are much rarer and noticeably less explicit. Nevertheless, by reason of their place, their solemnity, and the echo which they find or the refusal which they provoke, they converge with the Johannine perspectives. For Mark as well as for John, "the Good News about Jesus Christ" (Mk. 1, 1) was written in order to lead up to Jesus' proclamation before Caiaphas: "I am [the Son of God]" (Mk. 14, 62), which is answered successively by the Sanhedrin's verdict: "blasphemy" deserving of death (14, 64) and the Roman officer's profession of faith: "In truth this man was a son of God" (15, 39). By different procedures and in their own way, Matthew and Luke concur with Mark and John, so that, for the four gospels, the Christian faith rests upon a statement of Jesus asserting his unique character, his divine origin, answering the question that is raised as soon as he appears: "Who can this be?" (Mk. 1, 24; 4, 41; cf. Jn. 8, 25). For he alone knows the answer.

In truth, if the gospel texts did not exist, we would have to invent them, so to speak; or, more exactly, if we did not possess these categorical words, there would be no Christian faith. For if Jesus is truly the Son of God, the only-begotten Son equal to the Father, God born of God, he is the only one who can tell us so. No man on earth is capable of discovering this truth, of inferring or proving it. One must know from experience who God is in order to be able to say, "This man is God." Only God can say, "I am the Son of God," in the sense in which Christians understand it. To say, as the Lycaonians did when Paul and Barnabas passed through their country, "These people are gods who have come down to us disguised as men" (Acts 14, 11) is possible only in paganism, in a religion where the deities are mere personifications of cosmic forces, those of nature or of the city. By calling Paul and Barnabas gods, the Lycaonians proved that they did not know what God is. Unless, therefore, Jesus communicates what constitutes his particular experience, unless he tells us both what he is and what he is living, we shall never be able to say actually what he is and believe in the Son of God. Unless Jesus reveals

God to us in his person, we shall meet only a man like ourselves.

But here a formidable difficulty blocks our path. Jesus has to tell us that he is the Son of God if we are to know it. But what can the statement "I am the Son of God" mean? In order to convey an intelligible meaning to us, it must designate a reality which men can experience or at least be able to imagine. Yet, if we imagine him, can we seriously believe that this Son of God who reveals himself thus is anything more than a man? God is the Wholly Other, completely different from man; he cannot have sons as men have children. Does not someone who proclaims himself the Son of God thereby show that he is not God?

This difficulty is not new; it dates from the time of Jesus himself and, as the evangelists tell us, is what provoked the refusal by the Jews and the death of Jesus. But today it is expressed in new forms. The most imposing of these and the most seductive, too, because it eschews any negation and any categorical refusal and is convinced of its fidelity to the Christian faith, is that of Rudolf Bultmann. According to Bultmann, to say that Jesus is the Son of God in a special sense that would make him a being who is both man and God, is to make a statement related to myth.[1] Myth is a permanent temptation for man in regard to God. Since God is totally different from the world; since he is neither visible nor tangible nor perceptible under any form, however spiritualized one might imagine it to be; and since God nevertheless speaks to man in faith and calls upon him to react, it is inevitable that man should fashion for himself a certain image of this God and of his activity in the world—inevitable that he should create myths. In so doing, man obeys not only his need to imagine, not only his poetic fancy, but the practical need to construct a usable world, an objective universe: the very force which has produced technology and science. This need should not be condemned, for it is indispensable if man is to make the world habitable and exploitable. Obliging him to forgo this demand for objectivity would be absurd. All the same, science must recognize its limitations. Founded upon experience and aspiring to objectivity, it can know the human person only from outside, through what is common and interchangeable in man. To presume to reach the other—the secret of the person—through these techniques is to destroy the person, and that is where sin lies. One of the signs of man's total subjugation to sin is precisely his spontaneous tendency thus to utilize the other as an object and to destroy the person.

What science does with the world, mythology does with God. Mythology is a form of science, a "logy" like psychology or cosmology, and this name betrays it. There is a legitimate science of the world and of experience, but science sins when it attempts to reduce the person to an object. By objectivating myth, by fitting it into an organized system and couching it in rigorously precise language, mythology commits an analogous sin—but infinitely graver—the moment it presumes to reach God. God is the Other *par excellence,* the Wholly Other. Whoever we meet along our way, we always want to say what he is, give him a name and a label so that we may utilize him to our advantage, and ask him the reductionistic question *"What? Was? Quoi? What is this thing?"* Instead of that, we should welcome him as an event and a presence, as a call which is addressed to us and awaits our answer, as a challenge which springs up in our existence, a *which,* a *dass,* a *que,* a fact to acknowledge and receive.

For Bultmann, there is some mythology in the New Testament—no longer the naïve mythology of those popular religions which invest cosmic forces with imaginary personalities and populate the world with deities, but a complex mythology, sprung from the diverse currents which intermingled at this time in the meeting of Greece and the East. Two of these currents in particular marked the New Testament profoundly: apocalyptic mythology, with its world of angels and celestial visions, and its feverish expectation of cosmic upheavals; and, on the other hand, gnostic mythology, strongly influenced by Greek speculation, where the persons who acted were concepts and ideas—creations more intellectualized but no less mythological than the archaic legends. The figure of the Son of Man, for example, is related to the apocalyptic myths, while that of the Son of God, the divine Being come upon earth for a time, springs rather from gnostic constructions.

However large the presence of these mythologies may loom in the New Testament, their influence remains limited and can be identified and isolated, so that the authentic message is always living and visible. Demythologizing[2] is possible and, through the constructs of the mind, faith perceives, in the gospels and the apostolic writings, the Word of God. For Bultmann, this is a key statement which rests on a twofold foundation: faith and textual criticism. As an authentic heir of Luther, Bultmann maintains that the believer, because he believes, because he receives from God this gift which nothing in him prepares him for, hears God addressing him through the words of Jesus, without his ever being able to find in the texts of the New Testament a demonstrative argument on which his certitude would rest.[3] On the other hand, and without this fact's constituting a foundation for faith, which cannot rest on any datum of the human order, we must recognize that the New Testament itself blazes the trail for demythologization. Paul and John—the latter, radically—demythologized the apocalyptic eschatology of the first Palestinian communities. Conversely, if we go back to the origins of the evangelical tradition, an attentive study of the texts enables us to rediscover the figure of Jesus, the preacher of the kingdom of God in the lineage of the prophets of Israel, before mythological representations seized him in order to shape him into an apocalyptic figure or a divine man.

A vigorous thinker and a radical critic, Bultmann tears up by the roots the difficulty which stopped us: How can Jesus tell us that he is the Son of God, and how can we be sure that he attaches to this statement the same meaning we do? Bultmann says that this determination to know *who* Jesus is, to have an answer to the question *what?* is a mythological preoccupation. Before him, Luther called it an idle inquiry: "Christ has two natures. How does that concern me? What matters is that he saves me." And just as Luther gladly sacrificed a theology whose formulas he did not find in scripture, so Bultmann, studying the gospels, notices that the "mythological" expressions do not generally go back to Jesus himself, but are the product of a later development, of a language formed in the Christian communities. Serious investigation of the texts shows that Jesus never attributed to himself the quality of Son of God, that he did not present himself as the Messiah, and that, although he spoke of the coming of the Son of Man in the style of the apocalypses, he had no intention of identifying himself with the Son of Man, but only of announcing the imminent coming of the kingdom of God. Without justifying it, obviously, and without serving as a foundation for it, criticism is in accord with faith: the gospels do not permit us to say who Jesus is; they record some of his sayings, in which faith recognizes the Word of God; they report an event, the death of Jesus, in which faith accepts God's salvation. But between the person who lived in Galilee and died in Jerusalem, and the event in which God offers us his forgiveness, there lies an unbridgeable distance, the distance between history and faith, between the world and God. The "Christ according to the flesh" holds no interest for faith.[4] Jesus stood in the direct line of the prophets who effaced themselves behind their message. What they are means nothing; what matters is that God speaks through them. What places Jesus above the prophets is not what he was, but the fact that in his death God tells men that he saves them.

This is a perfectly clear position, a coherent position also— too coherent, in fact, for it commits one to a far-reaching logic. If God saves us in Jesus' death and not in his person, why does he do so in that particular event instead of some other? What value does that death possess, therefore, unless it is the death of that particular man? What does an event mean unless it is lived consciously? What is Jesus' death worth unless it is the death *lived* by Jesus? Otherwise, it is just one more death among millions of others. It may be an example for mankind, an imperishable memory, or a decisive date; but can it be the event in which God saves us? And what salvation can there be for humanity in the mere fact of an exceptional death? Short of holding that everything depends on an arbitrary and irrevocable decree of God's, who decided to make Jesus' death and the announcement of salvation coincide in time, it is necessary that some communication be established between him who dies and him who believes, between the consciousness of Jesus and that of the believer.

Bultmann himself does not shy away from this exigency, especially when he strives to retrace the development of the pristine message and its relation to Jesus' preaching, as Bultmann understands it. The heart of this preaching is a call to decision in faith and obedience. But in its absolute radicalness, independent of any general consideration and any particular circumstance, this call cannot be justified except by the coming of him who is there, by the presence of the Word of God in Jesus. "Jesus' call to decision implies a christology." [5] There is a relation between what

Jesus is and the act of faith which he demands. Bultmann's followers, moreover, have intensified this exigency. For the most part, they hold that the preaching of the nascent Church—the kerygma, according to the consecrated terminology—must necessarily lead back to the historical Jesus, and that the essence of this preaching is to assert the identity between the Christ of faith, in whom God saves the world, and Jesus of Nazareth.[6] They insist, however, on maintaining the distance which separates the early preaching of the Church from the teaching of Jesus. Though Jesus displays an exceptional awareness of his mission, he says nothing about himself as a person; so that the Christology which springs from his authentic sayings is only an "indirect Christology," to quote Hans Conzelmann.[7]

"Indirect Christology"—this term seems to present a good starting point for our study. Not that it is clear: as Conzelmann himself understands it, we could question its coherence. Is the fact that Jesus "opens up immediacy to God in every relationship" sufficient to warrant speaking of Christology, even indirect? When Jesus underlines these relationships, he ought also to know exactly what he is doing and whence that certitude comes to him. Else, his message does not come to him from what he is but from another, from outside; he is only a prophet, the greatest of all, the one who has been further than all; he is not the one in whom we shall be able to believe as we call him "the Christ"; there is no Christology, not even indirect.

Still the investigations of Bultmann and his followers, as well as the expression "indirect Christology," contain a profound and momentous truth.

First of all, there is the massive fact that, according to the synoptics, Jesus never once on his own took the floor to say who he was. Formal statements concerning his person always come from someone other than he: from the Father at Jesus' baptism and at the transfiguration (Mk. 1, 11; 9, 7), from the unclean spirits (1, 24; 3, 12), from Peter at Caesarea (8, 29), from the crowd when he entered Jerusalem (11, 9-10), from the high priest before the Sanhedrin (14, 61), from the centurion on Calvary (15, 39). In an author who is writing to present "the Good News about Jesus Christ, the Son of God" (1, 1), this constant fidelity to such a definite policy implies a fundamental conviction and an essential datum. John's gospel, on the other hand, though it is not afraid to multiply statements by Jesus concerning himself, concurs with the synoptics in its own way. There, Jesus' assertions, beginning with the words "I am...," usually appear at the end of a discussion or dialogue brought about by a deed of his. Of course, it is Jesus who stands up in all his grandeur and makes the light shine forth; but he does not do so immediately: rather, he waits for the question to pose itself, as it were, and then he offers the key to the discussion that has been launched. Sometimes even, the interlocutor may be the one to raise the question, as the Samaritan woman did, for example, when she said, "I know that Messiah—that is, Christ—is coming; and when he comes he will tell us everything" (Jn. 4, 25). Jesus had only to answer, "I who am speaking to you, I am he" (4, 26). This situation is very reminiscent of the synoptics. The other instances are more clearly "Johannine," and Jesus leads the dialogue from the start. But it always is a dialogue, a meeting in which man finds himself gradually brought to recognize or reject in Jesus the presence and action of God: " 'Work for food that endures to eternal life, the kind of food the Son of Man is offering you. . . .' 'Give us that bread always. . . .' 'I am the bread of life' " (Jn. 6, 27-34). " 'This sickness will not end in death. . . .' 'If you had been here, my brother would not have died. . . .' 'I am the resurrection' " (Jn. 11, 4-25). " 'We are descended from Abraham. . . . Are you greater than our father Abraham? . . .' 'Before Abraham ever was, I Am' " (Jn. 8, 33-58). This is not a pedagogical device, a stratagem that consists in waiting for the right moment in order to create a big effect and impress the listener. Rather it is genuine pedagogy which truly sets man in motion and leads him to the heart of existence.

Indeed, behind the literary data, which seem to be just as conscious in the synoptics as in John, there lies a fundamental datum which derives from the very nature of the gospel fact, as it is grasped by faith. The believer cannot confess that Jesus is the Son of God unless he has received this revelation from Jesus himself. (That was our starting point.) But he cannot receive this revelation through Jesus' words only, nor even through his words and his deeds as they shed light on one another. In this double condition, contradictory as it seems, lies the paradox of Christian revelation. On the one hand, Jesus alone can say what he is; and, on the other, he cannot say anything concerning himself before men have spoken and said what they think about him.

In order to reveal himself, it is not sufficient that Jesus speak, nor even that he act: what he says must be understood, it must have meaning, and it must have the same meaning for both the speaker and the listener. Revealing himself cannot consist in uttering a set form of words and having someone repeat them, as a teacher inculcates a lesson: "Repeat after me: 'I am the Son of God.'" The formula which is repeated has to have the meaning that the Revealer attaches to it. When the two interlocutors are men and when the words used necessarily have the same meaning for both, the only problems that arise have to do with intelligence and pedagogy. But when it is the Son of God who comes to say what he is and to have men repeat it, the situation is completely different. Jesus could speak certain words, explain them in order to avoid misinterpretations, and have them repeated so as to be sure that he has been understood. He is certainly capable of that: what other teacher was ever so skillful at reaching his audience? But would he really be revealing himself? He would open boundless horizons to human thought and would leave us in conversation with just that—human thought, and no more.

We can understand, therefore, why Jesus reveals himself only by taking up the very expressions used by his interlocutors. It is necessary that the men who see Jesus act should themselves formulate the words to express what they see and what they believe. Then Jesus, a man who speaks their language and the God who sounds their hearts, will know what they mean when they speak; and we ourselves, coming after them, will in our turn know and be able to understand what they meant: men found these words and gave them this meaning, and Jesus told them it was the right meaning. The words of revelation must be discovered by men, not dictated by Christ, so that we may rest assured that this is not merely a lesson learned by rote, so that we may understand that man can formulate a judgment concerning Jesus which is accurate and states the truth. But at the same time, these words which men have found and formulated in their own language must denote what Jesus alone can say, since he alone knows who he is. Here is the paradox of revelation: if men are really to say who Jesus is,

they have to say it without his making them do so; and what they
say of their own accord in order to express their own thinking
must be the authentic echo of what Jesus knows about himself.
How is that possible?

If it is possible, if the gospels afford us a glimpse of such a
process—Jesus stimulating his disciples and enabling them to
render in their language the confession which is destined to become that of the Christian faith—then the term "indirect Christology" is rigorously valid: Christ is at the origin of an utterance
which, before any theological synthesis, already expresses the
faith of the Church. Then also, by allowing us to rediscover the
origin of this utterance, by causing it to be born of an experience
and to reach a real person, the gospels open up to us the road
which leads us out of the impasse where myth held us. If we can
detect a continuity between the confessions of the nascent
Church, the experience of the disciples and the consciousness of
Jesus, then the demythologizing of the New Testament escapes
the dangers of personal adventure and human wisdom; it is communion in spirit with the faith of Peter and the Twelve, with the
experience of the Christians of Jerusalem, Corinth or Rome.

But if an indirect Christology can flow naturally from the
synoptic gospels, and if it is authentic, if it truly expresses what
Jesus thought and wanted, then direct Christology, as formulated
in John's gospel, is equally legitimate. If Peter can confess that
Jesus is the Christ, it is because Jesus himself knows it and brings
Peter to this act of faith. In their account of this process, the
synoptics show us rather the visible aspect, the growth of the disciples and the blossoming of faith. John, instead, takes us back to
the source, to Jesus' words and deeds, which were constantly dictated by and directed toward this goal. By multiplying first-per-
son declarations, John could very easily generalize an exceptional
procedure and make explicit from the first meetings a style of
speaking which Jesus did not utilize until his last hours—with the
result that the fourth gospel might baffle a superficial reader. Still
we must remember that John himself, at the beginning of his account, describes an early phase in which the disciples confess their
faith before Jesus has really begun to speak. Thus we hear Andrew say to Simon, "We have found the Messiah," and Philip tell
Nathanael, "We have found the one Moses wrote about in the

Law, the one about whom the prophets wrote: he is Jesus, son of Joseph, from Nazareth" (Jn. 1, 41.45). But, above all, we must understand John's purpose. By having Jesus make these explicit declarations so early and articulating around them the discussions with his adversaries and the movement which led the believers to faith, he doubtlessly commits an anachronism; but he knows what he is doing: he wants to show that in all their dealings, whether tending toward belief or toward rejection, those who met Jesus had to reply to the more or less explicit message which he addressed to them, and basically this message was always the same —always the expression of what he was, always an "I am. . . ."

Thus, the four gospels, completing one another, give us the answer to the paradox which obstructed our path. Men must find within themselves some way of saying who Jesus is without having to repeat it, and that is the direction of the synoptics. What men say in order to express their own thinking must, furthermore, be the authentic echo of what Jesus knows about himself, and that is the schema of the Johannine revelations. Lastly, these two movements must coincide and, through both of them, there must appear the outline of a real existence, of a living man.

NOTES TO CHAPTER 1

1. R. Bultmann, *Jesus Christ and Mythology* (New York: Charles Scribner's Sons, 1958), pp. 16-17.
2. If Bultmann prefers *demythologizing* to the simpler term *demythifying* (*Entmythologisierung*), that is because he wishes to destroy, not myth, which is a necessary stage in religious thinking, but mythology—the myth which has become logos, a scientific construct which opposes to faith the assurance of its mass and its objectivity. See André Malet, *The Thought of Rudolf Bultmann* (White Plains, New Jersey: Irish University Press, Inc., 1970).
3. "We can believe in God only in spite of experience, just as we can accept justification only in spite of conscience. Indeed, de-mythologizing is a task parallel to that performed by Paul and Luther in their doctrine of justification by faith alone without the works of law. More precisely, de-mythologizing is the radical application of the doctrine of justification by faith to the sphere of knowledge and thought. . . . There is no difference between security based on good works and security built on objectifying knowledge." R. Bultmann, *op. cit.,* p. 84.
4. Bultmann readily quotes St. Paul (2 Cor. 5, 16): "Even if we did once know Christ in the flesh, that is not how we know him now." See his *Faith and Understanding,* trans. by Louise P. Smith (New York: Harper & Row, Publishers, 1969), Vol. I, pp. 132 and 217. But Bultmann strains the meaning of this text. Paul in no way intends to reject "Christ in the flesh." What he rejects is the pretention of those who boast of having known Jesus "according to the flesh"; he opposes spiritual knowledge to fleshly knowledge, not the fleshly Christ to the spiritual Christ. See Xavier Léon-Dufour, *The Gospels and the Jesus of History,* trans. by John McHugh (New York: Desclée Company, 1968), pp. 54-55.
5. R. Bultmann, *The Theology of the New Testament,* trans. by Kendrick Grobel (New York: Charles Scribner's Sons, 1951), Vol. I, p. 43. In his preface to the French translation of Bultmann's *Jesus Christ and Mythology,* P. Ricoeur stresses that there is perhaps a certain distance between Bultmann's "effective exegesis [and] the representation which he forms of it in his theoretical writings" (p. 24). The former would give more consistency to the texts than the latter would allow us to suppose.
6. This is in particular the object of J. M. Robinson's *Le kérygme de l'Eglise et Jésus de Nazareth* (Geneva: Labor et Fides, 1961). The reader will find a brief survey of the various authors and their positions in G. Minette de Tillesse, *Le secret messianique dans l'évangile de Marc* (Paris: Cerf, 1968 [Lectio Divina, 47]), pp. 456-464.
7. "All parts of Jesus' teaching are stamped with an indirect christology. Jesus does not teach expressly who he is. But he acts in his proclamation as one who opens up immediacy to God in every relationship. After his death, this indirect christology is transposed into the direct christology of the community's faith." Hans Conzelmann, *An Outline of the Theology of the New Testament,* trans. by John Bowden (New York: Harper and Row, Publishers, 1969), p. 127.

2
The Gospel Itinerary

Since it seems feasible to draw up the itinerary of the gospels, we should try to say why it does and under what conditions. First, we must measure the difficulties of the undertaking. It is practically impossible to sketch a biography of Jesus, to rediscover the course he traveled, the stages of his activity. Not only because of the problem of synchronizing the information in the different gospels, but for a more profound and crucial reason: the evangelists themselves were not concerned with these perspectives. They did not necessarily scorn history, but neither did they wish to write the story of Jesus by chronicling every moment of his existence. John's gospel, for instance, has certainly preserved the memory of precise and authentic details;[1] yet it is probable that, desiring to link each of Jesus' great deeds with some feast of the Jewish calendar, he placed them in a very special order from which it would be dangerous to deduce a chronology. Of the four evangelists, Luke surely pays most attention to the succession and concatenation of facts, but he, too, has a way of grouping events in distinct series which makes an exact reconstruction impossible.

It is even more difficult to re-create the inner development of the people in the gospels, the progress or the crises of faith among the disciples, Jesus' vision of the adventure to which he was committing himself, the evolution of his line of conduct, the modifications of his psychology.

Such considerations interested neither the anonymous early tradition nor the evangelists. At every stage of composition, the gospels were written to highlight the actuality of Jesus' deeds in the life of the Christians and their communities. The remembrance of the past and the challenge of the present are intertwined

15

on every page. This is proof that the Risen One living with his disciples is indeed the same as Jesus of Nazareth, but it constitutes a formidable obstacle for anyone who hopes to discern Jesus' consciousness at a given moment of his existence. The Jesus whom the evangelists put before us is the Jesus whom their faith reaches, the risen Jesus. Any attempt to isolate the pre-resurrection Jesus is most aleatory in the eyes of historians and meaningless for believers, whose faith surely cannot rest on such artificial and precarious bases.

Yet it seems to us that an avenue lies open and that, without embarking on such a chimeric adventure as exploring Jesus' consciousness and reconstructing his spiritual itinerary, and without seeking to know what the texts do not tell us, it is not illusory to try to rediscover, in the writings themselves, the presence and the action of Jesus' consciousness. For this presence to be real, it is not indispensable that the words in our gospels should have been integrally and literally spoken by Jesus: one can compile authentic sayings uttered by somebody and still only give a false picture of him. Besides, none of the words in the gospels were uttered as they appear by Jesus, since he spoke Aramaic and since, from the first, the Gospel of Christ, proclaimed and transmitted in Greek, was a translation and therefore an interpretation. But if, on the one hand, Jesus' words as they resounded in Capernaum or Jerusalem were able to retain, for those who had heard them, their original power and inimitable accent; if his countenance could remain alive years later among those who had known him; and if, on the other hand, daily experience lived by witnesses, who remembered, and by the disciples, who joined them, attested to the extraordinary kinship between the words of yore and their truth today, between the face which one could not forget and the presence which one felt each day, very close and all-powerful—then perhaps it is not unlikely that the evangelists were able to preserve the original features of Jesus and his preaching as well as to make new developments spring from them without distorting his personality. If the same Jesus was accomplishing in his followers what he had promised before leaving them, it was legitimate to shed light on what he had said yesterday by means of what he was doing today. Perhaps he had not said everything, but at least they could be certain that everything which they were living today came from what he had said and done at that moment.

But what we are defining thus—a twofold fidelity: of memory in the witnesses and of presence in Jesus—borders on the miraculous, and how can we agree to embark upon a reading of the gospels if we first have to accept a postulate of this magnitude?

No, this is not a miracle, strictly speaking; it is an absolutely unique phenomenon, whose source, according to the witnesses themselves, is not man, but the power of the Holy Spirit, although the entire process takes place in the mind of man and results in human operations. That is why the evangelical tradition lends itself to both historical and critical study. It is not impossible to distinguish in the texts several superimposed or almagamated layers, corresponding to successive stages of composition; it is not forbidden to ask oneself whether a particular saying of Jesus' is a direct translation of the original Aramaic, an adaptation by a certain type of community, or even a creation of the evangelist as he wrote. Often, this is the only way to ascertain the meaning of texts, and we have no right to repudiate it.

Now, we believe that a critical reading of the gospels—sensitive to the diversity of materials which compose them, the multiple influences which governed the transmission of the texts, and the unique character of the Christian experience and of belief in the Risen One—remains capable of objectivity. We also believe that, through a composition as complex and sometimes as enigmatic as the gospels on the whole, we can yet reach the very consciousness of Jesus, seize it as a living consciousness: always the same, it is recognizable at whatever moment we espy it; and still it is alive, evolving, obedient to the rhythm of events. And this movement (which is that of existence itself) does not lie outside the texts, like something to be taken for granted; on the contrary, it appears right in the texts, in the unfolding of the narrative or, more exactly, in the development of the themes, the succession of styles. Thus, through a series of incontrovertible literary data, the gospels give us neither an informal memoir nor a carefully constructed chronicle of Jesus' life, but something far less deliberate and far more significant: the natural progression of human existence, the spontaneous expression of his consciousness.

Let us chart a series of indisputable facts, which stand out on first reading the texts and correspond, not to dates or localizable events in Jesus' life, but to the different stages of his existence and personality.

At first, Jesus still seems close to John the Baptist, somewhat like a replica of the great prophet. He frequents the same places: the Jordan (Mk. 1, 5.9; Jn. 1, 28; 3, 26) and the desert (Mk. 1, 4.12-13); he surrounds himself with disciples as does John (Jn. 3, 22; 4, 1); he baptizes in the manner of John (Jn. 3, 22-26; 4, 1-2); and several of his disciples come to him from the group organized by John (Jn. 1, 35.40).

In his Galilean period, we find another life style.[2] No longer baptizing, Jesus devotes himself to teaching; he travels from town to town and retires to the desert only to pray or rest (Mk. 1, 35.45; 6, 31); he is forever moving about (Mk. 1, 9.14.29.39; 3, 20; 5, 1.23. 38; 6, 1.53; 7, 31; 8, 10.22; 9, 33), always accompanied by his disciples (Mk. 1, 18.29.38; 2, 15.23; 3, 7; 6, 1.45) except when he sends them ahead to prepare his coming (Mk. 6, 7).

To this period there clearly seems to correspond a type of teaching, whose substance Matthew in particular distilled in the Sermon on the Mount (Mt. 6-7). There the announcement of the kingdom is not the expectation of an event which comes from outside, of an upheaval in the world, but a call to live a new experience: that of God the Father gathering his children together. This experience can be had as of today and is meant to last throughout one's life.

Jesus' new manner of living and teaching immediately draws opposition from the scribes and the Pharisees. Here is where the synoptic gospels situate a series of controversies (Mk. 2, 13-3, 6; Mt. 9, 1-17; 12, 1-14; Lk. 5, 12-6, 11) related to the message of the Sermon on the Mount: the old order is abolished, a new life has dawned, sins are forgiven, and Jesus' disciples celebrate the presence of the Bridegroom and the Messianic sabbath.[3]

The parables grouped here by Matthew (Ch. 13) and Mark (Ch. 4) have the same ring. The dominant theme is that of growth: the kingdom of God is already present, like a mysterious seed (Mk. 4, 3.26.31; Mt. 13, 24) buried in the earth (Mt. 13, 44). Though beset by obstacles, opposition and danger, it cannot fail to succeed and become something very great.

At this moment in Jesus' life, the future seems to be opening up before him—not a perfectly rosy and problemless future, for his adversaries dog his steps every day, and he encounters deep-rooted resistance; but as yet no drama looms on the horizon, so to speak, no event for which he must steel his soul. He has only to travel on, sowing the Good News everywhere and summoning Israel to conversion. That is how Mark (6, 7-13 = Lk. 9, 1-6) depicts the mission of the Twelve: directed to the immediate future, it is a short-term operation characterized especially by haste: they are not to lose any time or encumber themselves with superfluities, they are to stop over if received hospitably but to move on at once otherwise. To these features, which paint a coherent image of limited and localized missions with the Twelve always coming back to Jesus, Matthew links entirely different themes: announcements of separation and persecution (Mt. 10, 17-33) which entail the disappearance and absence of Jesus—the Church, in short. But at this point, the Church still exists only in embryo, the community is grouped around the Master, and although the Herodians and the Pharisees are already plotting to get rid of him (Mk. 3, 6), he himself, when he speaks of his end (Mk. 2, 20), does so without any note of urgency. The pagans are not ignored—indeed, after the conclusion of Isaiah (Is. 66, 18-24), their coming was expected on the last day; they may even have a better place than the Israelites then (Mt. 8, 5-13), but the center remains Israel, and that is where the mission is directed.

For the synoptics, Peter's confession at Caesarea marks a decisive turning point. This is the hour when, for the first time, Jesus announces to his own that he must suffer (Mk. 8, 31; Mt. 16, 21); the hour, too, when he draws them noticeably closer to himself and keeps at a distance from the crowd (Mk. 6, 45; 8, 27.29). John sets up an even clearer connection between the multiplication of the loaves, Jesus' break with the crowd (6, 14-15), the departure of the scandalized disciples (6, 65-71) and Peter's confession, which is placed in the synagogue at Capernaum. The unfolding of the facts matters little to us here; the important thing is that the same turning point is so heavily underscored in two traditions which lie very far apart.

From Caesarea on, mention of the Son of Man, which until then was occasional, becomes increasingly frequent. Before that, Jesus spoke essentially about a single subject: the kingdom of

God; now he does not abandon this theme, but that of the Son of Man assumes an ever greater place.

The Messianic entry into Jerusalem marks a new date and a change of atmosphere, in sharp contrast with the opening chapters. Once again we find the same literary context, the same ways of speaking and discussing, the parables, the controversies with the scribes or the Pharisees. But the questions have evolved and the perspectives have altered. Whereas the parables of Galilee counted on time and the expansive power of the Word and the kingdom, those of Jerusalem conjure up accounts to be rendered, the thief who comes in the night, the banquet-hall door about to close (Mt. 21, 33-22, 14; 24, 42-25, 46). Yesterday's disputes centered on the coming of the kingdom, which was there, while today's bring into question Jesus' own views, whether on the source of his authority (Mk. 11, 27-33), obedience to Caesar (12, 13-17), the resurrection (12, 18-27), the essence of faith (12, 28-34), or his very self (12, 35-37).

Among these parables and discussions, the synoptics intersperse a series of prophetic and apocalyptic teachings, whose chief object is to show the disciples what line of conduct to adopt when Jesus is no longer with them. What we have here—in a special literary form which is traditional when the Bible speaks of the future—is Jesus' farewell; and there are very numerous convergences between the "eschatological discourse" in Mark (Ch. 13) or the related passages in Matthew and Luke, and the "discourse after the Last Supper" in John. This time, Jesus is really thinking of the Church as such, of the community of disciples brought together by him and bearing his name, when it will no longer enjoy his visible presence. That will be the hour of the Spirit (Mk. 13, 11; Jn. 14, 26; 15, 27).

From these final days likewise, the gospels record a few very brief, very pithy and very mysterious sayings of Jesus in which his death is no longer merely announced as the event awaiting him at the end of the road, but is given a new dimension, associated with deeds in which existence assumes the form of rites and sacred gestures: a cup to drink (Mk. 10, 39), a baptism to undergo (Mk. 10, 40), a ransom to pay (Mk. 10, 45). These deeds are carried out in the great act of the Last Supper, where the partaking of the bread and the cup fulfill the Pasch and inaugurate the New Covenant, the forgiveness of sins in the kingdom of God (Mt. 26, 26-29).

Lastly, according to the gospels, it is in his passion that Jesus reveals his divine condition, his quality as Messiah and Son of God. Until then, only the Twelve had access to this mystery. Peter confessed it at Caesarea, and the voice from heaven confirmed it at the transfiguration. The discussions during these last days—considerably anticipated, no doubt, in John—already revolve around this theme of the Son (Mk. 12, 6.35-37). The high priest's point-blank question concerning Jesus' divine sonship draws from Jesus—something unique, according to the synoptics —a nuanced reply which nevertheless amounts to a categorical "yes" (Mt. 26, 63f and par.). For this blasphemous answer, he is sentenced to die. His death confirms the certitude of his adversaries that he cannot be the Son of God, since God has allowed him to perish (Mt. 27, 40.43), and elicits from the centurion on guard the first Christian profession of faith (Mk. 15, 39; Mt. 27, 54).

Such is the sequence which emerges from a rapid survey of the gospels. Must we conclude that this is how the story actually unfolded? To do so, we would have to prove that this sequence was not influenced in any way by the work of elaboration which took place throughout the whole period when these recollections were being handed down, and that the various steps in the sequence imposed themselves upon each successive author of this tradition because they represented indubitable, unassailable facts. This we cannot prove; on the contrary, at every stage along the road which we have followed we detect the hand of a writer, of an editor who has his own objectives and who underlines what interests him. The Sermon on the Mount is a synthetic composition: its several parts, though tied together in three chapters of Matthew's gospel, are scattered over the whole of Luke's. The turning point at Caesarea is a major piece of information from the synoptics; still, we would have difficulty proving that it precludes all approximation. In John's gospel, Jesus' decisive confession before the Sanhedrin is explicit from the time of the discussion in the Temple during the feast of the Dedication (Jn. 10, 30.36.38). It is unrealistic not to acknowledge the frequent intervention of conscious motives from the beginning to the end of the itinerary which we have traced.

Yet this situation should not dishearten us. It shows us that we cannot know Jesus or his way of acting except through the gospels, their authors and their intentions. But it also brings out an all-important fact: not only do these authors and their intentions give us a picture of Jesus which could not possibly be invented, a portrait which makes him present to us; but they take his existence, his experience and the evolution which he lives through and makes his followers live through likewise, and they outline all this in a manner so exact, so coherent and yet so natural in its movement that we would be grossly remiss to ignore it, for it is certainly worth examining from close and trying to understand from within. Above all, the road that the gospels point out to us, the progression they indicate, appears capable of resolving the fundamental question which faces us, a twofold and seemingly contradictory question: that the disciples' faith in Jesus comes to them from him and, therefore, that he knows from the start what he is; and still, that this faith actually emanates from them and can express the truth of the Son of God in human words.

The fact of the matter is that the itinerary sketched out in the gospels is that of a man who, from his first steps, seems to be led by an inspiration which comes from himself, as it were, and who nevertheless remains ready for anything; sufficiently sure of what he is and what he must do, to have no need of a program, to welcome each person and event, to remain himself constantly though always giving himself to anyone who comes to him; certain of the power that dwells in him, and not keeping any of it hidden for himself but living his whole existence under the eyes of others. And in this sense, he does not have to change, he does not have to abandon a point of view or a way of acting so that he may adopt another. He is always immediately himself. On the other hand, this is truly the itinerary of a human life, of a man who has appeared at this particular moment in history, sensitive to the spiritual currents of his day, situating his activity at the core of this world, implementing his program gradually, conscious of where he is going, but always open. There is, as has been written, a "gospel project" on the part of Jesus: "preparations, experiments, gropings, successes and failures." [4]

Finally, and this point is essential, we have here the itinerary of a revelation in the true sense of the word. It is striking to see how consistently the synoptic gospels adhere to the basic pattern: a period of preparation during which the disciples, as they come to know Jesus, enter gradually into his secret; a decisive moment when, at his instigation, they acknowledge who he is; and then a new stage designed to pave the way for the supreme revelation, that of his death and resurrection. Is this pattern the work of an evangelist—Mark, for instance—or of the earlier anonymous tradition? We would have difficulty determining whether this is an exact reproduction of the original facts, unconscious and spontaneous fidelity to an indisputable primary datum, or the result of reflective elaboration. In any case, it is certain that this pattern possessed such power that it imposed itself on the three synoptics, however different their perspectives. And it is likewise certain that this pattern—without premeditation, surely—happens to correspond astonishingly well to the conditions required so that we may give meaning to the revelation of God in Jesus Christ.

NOTES TO CHAPTER 2

1. See Xavier Léon-Dufour, *The Gospels and the Jesus of History*, pp. 80-84; and D. Mollat, "L'évangile selon saint Jean," in the French version of *The Jerusalem Bible* (Paris: Cerf, 1953), Introduction, pp. 41-44.
2. C. H. Dodd, *Historical Tradition in the Fourth Gospel* (New York: Cambridge University Press, 1965), pp. 292-293.
3. G. Minette de Tillesse, *Le secret messianique dans l'évangile de Marc*, p. 160.
4. Jean-Paul Audet, *The Gospel Project*, trans. by Edmond Bonin (New York: Paulist Press, 1969), p. 21.

3
Jesus and John the Baptist

Jesus inaugurated his mission by receiving the baptism of John. That is a primal fact (Acts 1, 22; 10, 37; 13, 24) which has always been inseparable from the announcing of Jesus Christ and which constitutes, for all the gospels, the starting point of his activity. For historians and exegetes of every school, it is also an incontestable fact, one of the points in his life concerning which there can be no doubt whatsoever. Jesus' disciples were too convinced of their Master's superiority even to dare imagine him bowing before John to receive his baptism. The fact had to be public and beyond all discussion for them to speak about it so freely, since their natural reaction was evidently the same as Matthew (3, 14) attributes to John: "It is I who need baptism from you, and yet you come to me!" From the gospels and the Acts of the Apostles, we see, moreover, that a certain rivalry between both groups of disciples, which was noticeable while Jesus and John were both alive (Jn. 3, 22-30; 4, 1-3), persisted for years in some cases after the resurrection of Jesus and the spread of the Christian faith (Acts 18, 25; 19, 3-5). It is rather interesting to note that when Paul went to establish the Church at Ephesus, he found some of John's disciples there. The Baptist's message could reach hearts even in pagandom.

Though we are sure this baptism took place, we have much greater difficulty knowing what it meant for Jesus and those who were present. The four gospels conceive of the episode as the solemn entry of Jesus initiating his activity, the presentation by God of the central character in the story which is beginning, a sort of portrait serving as frontispiece to their work. Now, this is the portrait of Christ to whom the faith of believers clings, the baptized

25

Son, the firstborn of all God's children who, through baptism, are adopted by the Father and given the Spirit. The whole of Christian experience has gone into the painting of this scene and overlaid it with its own riches; still, the result is not sheer fiction, for, from this very moment, Jesus was indeed what faith discovered him to be only much later. But what can it teach us about the nature of Jesus' experience at that moment, about the effect which this event had on the faith of his disciples? The only witness who steps forth to avouch what he saw and felt is John the Baptist, in the fourth gospel: "I did not know him myself, but he who sent me to baptize with water had said to me, 'The man on whom you see the Spirit come down and rest is the one who is going to baptize with the Holy Spirit.' Yes, I have seen and I am the witness that he is the Chosen One of God" (Jn. 1, 33-34). Although this solemn declaration assuredly deserves credence, it is so stylized, so lapidary that we should read it not so much for the impression of the moment as for the meaning of his testimony. This is the Baptist of the pointing finger as pictured in Christian art—the true John, no doubt, immobilized in this word and gesture which manifest his heart and his vocation.

There may, however, be some facts to glean from these very brief texts. Even though the figure of John had no analogue in the Judaism of his day, and even though his baptism differed profoundly from the various forms of baptism then practiced in several communities,[1] in particular at Qumran, the fact remains that the movement which led the crowds to the Baptist bespoke a deep-seated impulsion in the people, a need of purification, an appeal to the regenerative power of the Spirit promised by the prophets.[2] And if Jesus' first step was to go ask John to baptize him, that is doubtlessly because a spontaneous impulsion and an infallible lucidity were leading him directly to the place where the Spirit's presence was most active and the expectation of God was keenest. It was a gesture of humility, surely, but of a humility deeper and more genuine than we can commonly imagine, as we marvel that a man who knows he is sinless before God nevertheless comes to abase himself and give us an example, putting himself in a place which is not his.[3]

But if Jesus' humility is genuine and if it profoundly expresses what he is, that is because this place among these people really *is* his—since they are sinners and he has come to look for sinners, of course, but also since the circle around John the Baptist is the place where God is most active and his kingdom nearest. Already Jesus is fully solidary with sinners and bears their sins; but he cannot say so yet, because he has not yet totally lived this burden of sin. For now, he is going to associate with sinners where God is waiting for them and converting them; he is going to share their faith and their hope.

Did not associating with those who were receiving John's baptism mean making himself John's disciple? There is something repugnant about the idea of Jesus being a disciple of John's. Perhaps it should not frighten us. First of all, because it would hardly be natural to imagine Jesus appearing suddenly, asking John to baptize him, and then disappearing immediately. This would betray a very shortsighted notion of what a sacramental gesture can be: a sacrament has meaning only when linked to the Word of God, which is both its origin and its culmination. John speaks and baptizes; if Jesus receives his baptism, we can scarcely suppose that he has not listened to his teaching, mixed in with his hearers and comported himself like a disciple.

Moreover, the gospels seem to say so explicitly. All—except Luke, who may precisely be trying to avoid a distasteful expression—quote a statement of John's: "The one who follows me is more powerful than I am, and I am not fit to carry his sandals." [4] Perhaps "the one who follows me" should be interpreted to mean purely temporal succession: John came on the scene before Jesus. Yet C. H. Dodd has made two observations concerning this point. On the one hand, of the thirty-five examples in which the expression "to follow someone" appears in the New Testament with the Greek preposition *opisô* followed by the genitive, not one has a temporal sense; the phrase normally signifies "to follow as a disciple attached to his master." [5] On the other hand, the way John (1, 15.30) shows how he "who comes after" turns out to be "he who . . . ranks before" is really coherent only if "after" is understood in the same sense as "before"—that is, in the sense of a difference in rank. It is true, Dodd continues, that John finishes his sentence with a typically Christian affirmation: "because he existed before me," which posits the preexistence of the Word and cannot have been uttered by the Baptist. But the Johannine interpretation presupposes that the original statement, recorded by Matthew and Mark, gave "follow" the meaning of "adhere, like a disciple." [6]

Perhaps even the experience which Jesus lived at the moment of his baptism was not unrelated to the experiences of others who came to John to be baptized. While respecting the discretion of the gospels, we should not disregard the reflections of a Jewish historian who is particularly cognizant of the spiritual currents which animated Judaism at that time: "Having confessed their sins, [those who came for baptism] plunged their defiled bodies in the cleansing water of the river, awaiting the gift of the Holy Spirit who would now cleanse their souls from all the filth of sin. Could it be that none of them would have a special pneumatic-ecstatic experience in that hour when the Spirit of God touched them? . . . Echoing voices [coming from heaven] were not an uncommon phenomenon among the Jews of those days, and frequently these voices were heard to utter verses from scripture." [7] Indeed, it would be surprising if a movement as powerful as John's had not produced rather exceptional spiritual experiences; and it is altogether normal that, among men so deeply nourished by the biblical tradition, these experiences were based on words and images from scripture.

Although the gospels say little about the relationship between Jesus and John around the time of the baptism, they record several occasions on which Jesus spoke about John.[8] Always a trifle enigmatic, these indications are precious because they do not constitute explicit teachings but are rather like indirect confidences. Had Jesus mentioned John only to utilize his testimony and invoke his words, we might question the value of such self-interested argumentation. But Jesus' references to John are not arguments bolstering his own position: they are, first and foremost, reflections born of attentive observation. Jesus was visibly struck by this man, by his message, by his destiny. Of all the people whom Jesus met, John, as the gospels attest, unquestionably made the strongest impression on him. Now, as he watches John live, Jesus thinks of his own fate and defines his own role and personality. It is not John who teaches Jesus what he is, but Jesus, on the contrary, who delineates the person of John and assigns him his rightful place in the history of Israel and the plan of God:

"I tell you solemnly, of all the children born of women, a greater than John the Baptist has never been seen; yet the least in the kingdom of heaven is greater than he is" (Mt. 11, 11). This greatness is not something that Jesus decrees, as if he were reading a citation and proclaiming a laureate; it is inherent in John's very nature, and when Jesus draws attention to him, we know that Jesus himself is contemplating him with awe: "What did you go out into the wilderness to see? A reed swaying in the breeze? No? Then what did you go out to see? A man wearing fine clothes? Oh no, those who wear fine clothes are to be found in palaces. Then what did you go out for? To see a prophet? Yes, I tell you, and much more than a prophet" (Mt. 11, 7-9). In this description we see at one and the same time the historical figure of John, his singular garb and his opposition to King Herod and his court, as well as the figure of the prophets, their solitude and their courage before the mighty. A statement of this sort is certainly authentic, for it has meaning only insofar as it evokes the real story of John and stops at the mere evocation, without any concrete allusions such as we would find in a text which was inserted later as circumstances demanded. However profoundly he understands and admires John, Jesus knows that this is not exactly what he himself is meant to be; he knows that his mission and John's, though linked to the point of being parallel, are different: "John came, neither eating nor drinking . . . The Son of Man came, eating and drinking . . ." (Mt. 11, 18-19).

Besides contemplating John, Jesus hears his message and assents to it; but he does not adopt it as his own. Jesus does not speak like John: he has something else to say, though it does not rescind what John said. If the gospels have incorporated John's message into the picture they paint of Jesus, this continuity is not their own invention but surely goes back to Jesus himself. Each evangelist, furthermore, has his own way of indicating the relation between both messages. For Matthew, the moment John appears, he speaks like Jesus: "Repent, for the kingdom of heaven is close at hand" (Mt. 3, 2 = 4, 17); but this is a compositional procedure, for the other evangelists oppose John's "baptism of repentance" (Mk. 1, 4; Lk. 3, 3) to Jesus' proclamation of the kingdom. Contrary to Matthew, who stresses the closeness of both messages, Mark stresses the distance between them by say-

ing that, from the start of his preaching in Galilee, Jesus proclaims "the Good News from God" (Mk. 1, 14) and demands, as
of that moment, not only conversion but faith in the Good News
(1, 15). Now, the term *Good News* belongs to the Christian vocabulary and supposes that the object of this preaching is already
himself, his person and his coming.[9] For Mark, the Good News is
not so much the announcement of the event as the event itself.
But since John the Baptist's preaching already forms part of this
event and constitutes "the beginning of the Good News about
Jesus Christ" (Mk. 1, 1), Mark accentuates the distance between
John's message and that of Jesus, between the baptism of repentance and the coming of the kingdom, and at the same time the
link that unites them.

The gospels make this link explicit by recalling a solemn
page in Isaiah (40, 3) where a resounding voice cries out to Jerusalem that her God is coming and bringing her exiled sons back
to her. John the Baptist is the "voice [that] cries in the wilderness:
'Prepare a way for the Lord'" (Mt. 3, 3; Mk. 1, 3; Lk. 3, 4; Jn.
1, 23). Jesus is "the one who follows," the one who came "after"
John at first and then passed "before" him because he was
greater than John (Mt. 3, 1; Mk. 1, 7; Lk. 3, 16; Jn. 1, 27.30). If it
is difficult to determine, in formulas profoundly stamped by tradition, precisely what goes back to Jesus or to John, to the tradition derived from the Baptist or to that of the Christian communities and the gospels, it is far more important to observe the
acuity with which these expressions characterize John's message
and the consistency between this presentation of the Baptist and
his preaching.

John appears as the messenger, the envoy *par excellence,* the
harbinger, the evangelizer,[10] the herald sent ahead to announce
the coming of the long-awaited Prince. The way the gospels use
the text of Isaiah (40, 3) is significant. The Essenes at Qumran
knew this passage and applied it to themselves: the members of
the community "shall be separated from among the settlement of
the men of iniquity to go into the desert, to prepare there the way
of Him, as it is written, 'In the wilderness prepare the way of
[YHWH], in the Arabah they shall make straight a highway for
our God.' This means study of the Law [which] he commanded
by the hand of Moses, to act according to all that is revealed

from time to time, and according as the prophets revealed by the spirit of his holiness." [11] It is instructive to see the same text from Isaiah applied to John the Baptist and the Essenes of Qumran at just about the same time, to find the same importance attached to the desert, the same concern with penance and purification, the same cry to the Holy Spirit. One would be tempted to postulate a relationship between John the Baptist and the community of Qumran, except for the fact that the numerous and notable similarities between them enable us precisely to perceive the differences all the more clearly. The use made of the text from Isaiah furnishes a typical example of this. The men of Qumran retire to the desert in order to trace out a path for the Lord; they trace it out themselves through their own efforts, through their fidelity in studying the Law of Moses and keeping it, through their observance of their Rule, and in particular through the regular practice of ritual ablutions and purifications performed with the loyalty of a repentant heart.[12] No doubt they could not practice any of these works without the Spirit of God, for "to God belongs judgment and from his hand comes perfection of way . . . and apart from him it will not be made." [13] But from the moment they enter into the covenant, into the House of Holiness, they are there in order to "lay a foundation of truth for Israel, to make a community of an eternal covenant." [14] Qumran has broken off with the Temple, with a corrupt priesthood and rites emptied of meaning; and the movement which it represents constitutes in Judaism an admirable pursuit of authentic spirituality, an astonishing effort to adapt to the exigencies of the period while remaining faithful to the profound values of the Jewish faith. Qumran is a magnificent quest for perfection; but John the Baptist is something completely different: he is the prophet.

Because he is a prophet, what he says does not come from him, and what he does—as in the case of his predecessors, of Hosea and Isaiah, who gave their children symbolic names,[15] of Jeremiah, who smashed an earthenware jug and walked about wearing a yoke on his neck[16]—serves primarily as a sign, but a sign given by God. John is merely a voice, but this voice announces Jesus who is coming, and whoever believes in it is ready to welcome him. John's baptism boils down to a gesture which could be termed transitory and purely symbolic, it is conferred only once, it imposes no obligations, it does not give entry into some definite community—not even the "true Israel" [17]—or some new form of existence, it even seems to dispense with the effort of attention and sincerity required for the purifications at Qumran. Is it, therefore, less serious?

It is far more so, but in a wholly different way. It is serious the way the Christian sacraments will be: because of what it signifies and what it produces. John's baptism is not a gesture performed by man, not an act which would enable repentant sinners to express their need for purity and forgiveness visibly and forcefully. Come "from heaven" (Mk. 11, 30) and conferred by a prophet in God's name, it signifies, not the repentance of man, but the action of God. If anything on earth can convey some idea of this action, it is fire—the fire which devours corrupt cities and gathers families around the hearth, the fire which we cannot grasp in our hand but cannot do without, the fire which brings us death and life. Fire is likewise the Spirit: a presence which transforms those whom it inhabits, a flame which makes those whom it consumes live. Both from within and from without, around them and in their own life, the prophets have always been seized by fire. Flaming cities, charred crops, lamps extinguished or rekindled—this is their habitual horizon. Amos sees the four corners of the heavens catch fire one after another, over Damascus and Gaza, over Tyre and Edom, over Ammon and Moab, with Israel at the center of an immense conflagration (Amos 1, 4.7.10.12.14; 2, 2). Isaiah is consecrated a prophet when fire from the altar has purified his lips (Is. 6, 6-7). Jeremiah feels the word of Yahweh like "a fire burning in my heart" (Jer. 20, 9).

John the Baptist, too, lives the experience of fire, but he does so in a unique fashion. Before him, the prophets used to see fires break out over a city or a district, and sometimes over an entire country. It was always a definite country, even though vast as an empire. And the reason was always specific: a series of crimes, an intolerable situation, a sin whose stranglehold could not be broken. The prophets start from a concrete situation and announce a divine intervention provoked by it. Most often, the occasion is some crime which inadequate human justice is powerless to punish. Then a prophet rises up in the name of God to declare that God cannot brook injustice: *because* David made himself guilty toward Uriah of adultery and murder, he will see adultery and murder perpetrated among his own sons (2 Sam. 12, 9-12); *because* Achab had Naboth put to death like a criminal, his own corpse will be treated like a criminal's (1 Kings 21, 19); *because* God did everything for his vineyard and it yielded only sour grapes, he will let it be overgrown by the briar and the thorn (Is. 5, 4-6). But a prophet can proclaim salvation as well—not because of some logic or equivalence, but because of a gratuitous generosity: "because I am God, not man: I am the Holy One in your midst and have no wish to destroy" (Hos. 11, 9); because "there is no other god besides me, a God of integrity and a saviour . . . for I am God unrivalled" (Is. 45, 21-22). Whether threatening or promising, the prophet always addresses himself to an actual situation and announces a change to come, starting from the present moment. John the Baptist likewise uses the present moment to announce God's intervention. But this present moment is not the condition in which Israel finds itself actually; neither is it defined by a significant event, the Roman occupation or the unworthiness of the high priests. Not that John—a new Elijah—is incapable of taking Herod to task when confronted by a disorder which no one else dares criticize (Mk. 6, 18). Yet the originality of his message lies, not in such feats of courage, but in its absolutely radical character. The other prophets were sent at a precise moment to denounce such and such a sin, to herald a particular event or some special instance of salvation. John, instead, speaks to all sinners, whatever their rank or origin, simply because they are sinners and because God is coming to put an end to sin. Purely eschatological, the Baptist's preaching is not directed at Jerusalem or some category of leaders, but concerns each and every sinner. It announces neither war nor famine nor any event which can be foreseen or defined; rather, it announces one single event, as vast as the world—the whole earth ripe for harvest, the coming of the Spirit and of fire.

Because the judgment proclaimed by John is radical, and because it will overtake every sinner and the totality of sin, it calls into play at one sweep everything God is and everything he can do. The fire and the Spirit coming to baptize the world—this is, at one and the same time, all the tenderness and all the wrath of God, his intolerance of evil and his inexhaustible love, all the destruction foretold by the prophets and all their hopes fulfilled, all the works of sin overthrown and exterminated and the human heart completely renewed and transfigured. Between John's preaching and the "end of the world," there is room for only one event: the coming of him with whom the end of the world comes. John is more than a prophet (Mt. 11, 9); he is all the prophets in one. He does not announce an event of history; he announces the event which puts an end to history.

His activity is unique, too. A prophetic gesture analogous to those of Jeremiah or Ezekiel, it is already something more. John's baptism has something sacramental about it, and we can understand why the Christians were able to repeat his gesture to signify their own baptism. The sinners who approach John do not proceed to symbolic ablutions into which they put their heart and their sorrow for sin. They come to receive "John's baptism" (Mk. 11, 30; Acts 18, 25; 19, 3); they come "confess[ing] their sins" (Mk. 1, 5), else their presence would be sheer comedy; they enter into the water under the gaze and, doubtlessly, the hand of the prophet; and thus they penetrate into the prophetic zone, where the event which was foretold is already being realized. The characteristic gesture of every other prophet belonged solely to him, even when it concerned the whole nation; those who witnessed it might believe in its significance, but they remained on the outside. John's baptism does not demand less faith; on the contrary, by announcing an event which cannot be foreseen because it transcends all signs, it requires a far more total faith. But anyone who enters into this baptism through faith is introduced into the prophetic gesture, into the word and the action of God. This baptism is still only a baptism of water, only an image and a preparation; but the image is given by God, and the preparation is his work. Receiving this baptism is altogether different from preparing oneself adequately for an event which will sweep aside all one's preparations anyhow; it means already letting oneself be overtaken by this event in advance, surrendering to the flood tide which will submerge everything. This is no longer man's doing, but God's: the Spirit must come. From the moment John baptizes, the Spirit cannot fail to come; to receive this baptism is to be ready to receive him.

NOTES TO CHAPTER 3

1. See the treatment of this matter in George R. Beasley-Murray, *Baptism in the New Testament* (London, 1962), pp. 67-71; and, for more recent work, in H. Schürmann, *Das Lukasevangelium* in Herders theologischer Kommentar zum Neuen Testament, III, 1 (Freiburg-Basel-Wien, 1969), p. 154, n.b.; pp. 157-158. Both of these works focus on the similarities which would tend to over-emphasize the points of contact between John and the Essenes of Qumran, without sufficiently noting the differences.
2. See Rudolf Schnackenburg, *The Gospel According to St. John,* trans. by Kevin Smyth (New York: Herder and Herder, 1968), Vol. I, pp. 304-305.
3. Jesus' reply to John, "Leave it like this for the time being; it is fitting that we should, in this way, do all that righteousness demands" (Mt. 3, 15) has too definite a Matthean ring to let us hear Jesus' own voice. The problem has been taken up again recently by A. Feuillet, "La personnalité de Jésus entrevue à partir de sa soumission au rite de repentance du précurseur," *Revue Biblique,* 77 (1970), pp. 30-49. Although the word *solidarity,* which he uses to explain Jesus' course of conduct is somewhat anachronistic and anticipates a theology which would take shape only later, it seems to render with sufficient exactitude the constant movement which led Jesus to search for sinners, and the examples cited on p. 44 are enlightening. However, we may wonder whether, in an attempt to learn about Jesus' personality from this search, it is good methodology to base oneself on a line of conduct which certainly characterized him once he had fully begun his work, but which perhaps had not yet appeared at this date.
4. Mt. 3, 11. Jn. 1, 27 is almost identical; and Mk. 1, 7 is slightly different. The same formula appears in Jn. 1, 15 and 30.
5. The expression "to come after someone" is common in the Old Testament and in Judaism; it denotes not only chronological succession but also dependence and subordination, as in official retinues. See P. Bonnard, "L'Evangile selon saint Matthieu" in *Commentaire du Nouveau Testament* (Delachaux et Niestlé, 1961), Vol. I, p. 37.
6. C. H. Dodd, *Historical Tradition in the Fourth Gospel* (Cambridge, 1965), pp. 272-275. We find it difficult to subscribe to A. Feuillet's categorical denial: "Not a word in our gospels suggests a former disciple-master relationship between Christ and the Baptist." *Revue Biblique,* 77 (1970), *art. cit.,* p. 36. The author is correct when he writes (p. 37): "Everything we know about Jesus forbids us to think that he ever considered himself a sinner"; but why would Jesus have had to consider himself a sinner in order to go to John and listen to him? Must Jesus never have learned anything—he who "learnt to obey" (Heb. 5, 8)?
7. David Flusser, *Jesus,* trans. by Ronald Walls (New York: Herder and Herder, 1969), pp. 28-29.
8. Mt. 11, 7-19; 17, 13; 21, 25.32.
9. See G. Minette de Tillesse, *Le secret messianique dans l'évangile de Marc,* pp. 403-404. J. Delorme, "Aspects doctrinaux du second évangile," in *De Jésus aux évangiles,* Tradition et rédaction dans les évangiles synoptiques,

Donum natalicium J. Coppens, II (=*Ephemerides Theologicae Lovanienses,* 1967), pp. 79-84.

10. We should note the Greek words: *apostellô, aggelos, kèrussô, euaggelizo-mai;* Mk. 1, 2-4 and Lk. 3, 18.

11. *The Rule of Qumran,* VIII, 13-16; cf. IX, 19. This translation and those which follow are taken from *The Rule of Qumran and its Meaning* by A. R. C. Leaney (Philadelphia: The Westminster Press, 1966). The present quotation appears on page 209.

12. *Ibid.,* V, 13-14: "[The men of perversity] shall not enter the waters to approach the purity of the men of holiness, for men will not be purified except they turn from their wickedness." Leaney, p. 170. See III, 4-9: "He will not be made guiltless by atonement and he will not be purified in waters for purification; he shall not sanctify himself in seas or rivers nor will he be purified in all the waters of cleansing. Unclean, unclean shall he be all the days of his rejection of the precepts of God with its refusal to discipline himself in the community of his counsel. . . . In a spirit of uprightness and humility his sin will be atoned. In the subjection of his soul to all the ordinances of God his flesh will be purified in being sprinkled with waters for purification and by sanctification in waters of purity." Leaney, p. 137.

13. *Ibid.,* XI, 10-11. Leaney, p. 236.

14. *Ibid.,* V, 5-6. Leaney, p. 161.

15. Hos. 1, 1-8; Is. 7, 3; 8, 1-4.

16. Jer. 27-38.

17. H. Schürmann, *Das Lukasevangelium* (Freiburg, 1969), pp. 157-158.

4
The Baptism of Jesus

The baptism of Jesus was certainly a momentous date in his life and in the physiognomy which he gave to his activity. As we saw earlier, the occurrence is undisputed, and its importance is underlined more than once in the New Testament, in different traditions. Moreover, the description of this event constitutes a grandiose, solemn-toned and exceptionally significant page in the four gospels, a sort of frontispiece haloing with its mysterious glory the person whose story is about to be told. This portrait of the Son of God in direct communication with heaven, receiving the Spirit and hearing his Father's words, cannot date from the event itself and from Jesus' first contacts with his followers; in a completely different style, it corresponds to the features and language of the Christ presented in the fourth gospel. It is a Christian portrait, the work of a baptized believer who painted therein the archetype of the baptism conferred in the Church. Nowhere better than in this episode can we measure the distance between the initial event and the Christian description of it. Here, the distance is so great that sometimes one is almost tempted to leave the original fact aside and conclude that the early Christian tradition "was able to describe in theophanic and apocalyptic style the religious significance which this important event in the life of Jesus held for it." [1]

A considered opinion of this sort raises a difficult question: For whom was this event important—for Jesus himself, or for the bearers of the Christian tradition? Doubtlessly for both, we would reply. But the problem remains. If there is no connection between the reasons for this importance in the life of Jesus and in the Christian tradition, are we not dealing with an artificial coincidence? It would be as if the Christian tradition has said, "Since Jesus' baptism was an important date in his life, though we do not really know why, we shall fasten our presentation of him onto it."

Whether anxious to avoid this kind of solution, which more or less unconsciously troubles them; or fearful of blurring a page where Jesus' personality seems profoundly involved; or, on the contrary, drawn by the hope of recapturing a precious experience of Christ's at the beginning of his public life, many authors view Jesus' baptism as a decisive moment for him: the moment when he becomes aware of his own mission, of his role as Messiah, of his vocation as Servant, of his election as Son.[2]

All these attempts come up against an insurmountable objection. Unless one maintains that the words which Jesus heard were also heard by witnesses—something that even the Johannine tradition, according to which John the Baptist alone recognized the presence of the Spirit, does not say—one must postulate, at the origin of the gospel narrative, a confidential statement by Jesus. Now, although it seems obvious that Jesus must have trusted his followers with secrets we know nothing about, one fact is certain: when the evangelists report confidences, they present them as confidences. The gospels contain utterances by Jesus meant for his disciples alone—for example, the question he puts to them at Caesarea and follows with the announcement of his passion (Mk. 8, 27-34). Sometimes, but not often, they show Jesus sharing his thoughts with the group around him: "How hard it is for those who have riches to enter the kingdom of God!" (Mk. 10, 23). Very rarely, Jesus allows an overwhelming joy to break forth: "I bless you, Father, Lord of heaven and of earth, for hiding these things from the learned and the clever and revealing them to mere children" (Lk. 10, 21); or too burdensome a secret: "I have come to bring fire to the earth, and how I wish it were blazing already!" (Lk. 12, 49). During his last days as he says farewell, these confidences become more frequent and intense: "I have longed to eat this passover with you" (Lk. 22, 15) or "My soul is sorrowful to the point of death" (Mk. 14, 34). And the discourses after the Last Supper, even if their language and accent owes something to John's meditation, certainly convey the particular tone of those final hours. What the disciples had received as confidences, they transmitted as confidences, respecting the form of them but revealing to all men the secrets of a heart that was open to friendship with all. Now, the account of Jesus' baptism has nothing confidential about it, either in tone or in content: it never so much as mentions Jesus' inner experience or his reactions, and the only words reported are those of the voice from heaven. In short, nothing warrants our supposing that the episode goes back to a confidence imparted by Jesus at some later date.

The only event in Jesus' life which could serve as the origin of the divine words pronounced at his baptism would be the transfiguration, where the three privileged witnesses, Peter, James and John, are allowed to glimpse something of Christ's glory and hear God speak.[3] And there is a sort of confidence there. But if the endlessly repeated dictum that the transfiguration can only be the permutation of a resurrection account is one of the most debatable dogmas in exegesis;[4] and if it is perfectly reasonable to attribute this episode, so rich and so simple, not to the theology produced by the early Christian communities or to the psychology with which the disciples would be concerned, but to the person of the Word made flesh, at a crucial moment of his earthly existence;[5] the fact remains that the transfiguration narrative, modeled on the theophanies of the Old Testament, is the transcription, in a consecrated idiom, of an experience which included all this wealth from the beginning without having attained all this precision. The accounts of the baptism and the transfiguration are obviously interlinked, each composed with the other in mind, with fully premeditated intent, and with a very clear view of the similarities and dissimilarities between them. Neither one is presented as the direct echo of the experience lived by Jesus.

Must we, therefore, renounce all hope of finding, in the gospel narrative of the baptism, the record of the event lived by Jesus —except, obviously, for the certain and sufficiently eloquent fact that he insisted on receiving John's baptism? Must we be content to focus our eyes and ears, with attentive faith, on this solemn scene, more majestic in its simplicity than the Johannine prologue? If we do so, here is what we behold: God himself, on the point of sending this man into the world and before accompanying him on his mission by empowering him to act and speak in his name—God himself revealing to the believers who will follow this story the secret of this power and this life: the man he is sending is his beloved Son.

Such, it seems, is precisely what the gospels intend. The baptism is not a "narrative about Jesus," [6] but primarily a presentation of Jesus to Christian hearers, so that they may "learn who this Jesus, baptized by John and in this sense dependent on him, truly is." [7] But this presentation itself derives its value and importance neither from its sole content and the exactitude of the portrait it paints nor from the place it occupies, like the overture to an opera. There is a profound coincidence between the scene of the baptism and the moment in the Gospel where tradition places it, and no bright idea on the part of an author would suffice to explain such a masterstroke. The Jesus who shows forth at his baptism is assuredly the Christian Jesus, the Lord in whose name the Church baptizes and who dispenses the Spirit; but he is also a man, such as he was at this point in his life and experience.

The gospel scene combines, in a masterly yet simple architecture, many diverse elements from the Old Testament whose origin not only remains visible but is deliberately underscored. It recalls the vocation story of prophets like Isaiah, Jeremiah or Ezekiel, as well as the theophanies in which God used to speak to Moses or Elijah. It repeats the solemn pronouncements in the second book of Isaiah, when God presented to the world the Servant whom he had chosen in order to carry out his work, and whom he is giving to the world today. It presents Jesus in the situation of apocalyptic seers who behold the heavens opening up and hear God's voice. It shows him under the features of the Messiah receiving royal investiture. Now, not only do all these figures fuse into a single and unique personality—something which a miracle of art could explain and which sometimes occurs—but this personality also possesses a truth which belongs to Jesus alone, and a truth which corresponds with astonishing exactitude to the Jesus of that precise moment.

His baptism surely recalls the vocation of the prophets: it is the starting point of a new life, entirely consecrated to the work of God; in order to receive it, Jesus comes into contact with John and, through him, with the tradition of Israel's prophets; at the instant he receives it, the words he hears place him in the ranks of those to whom God confides his secrets. Henceforth, like Elijah, Jeremiah or John the Baptist, his life no longer belongs to him: he

is alone, so to speak, under the hand of God (cf. Jer. 15, 17), possessed by the message he carries. All these common traits serve
only to highlight the unique aspect of this "vocation." The word
which the prophets hear—or the Spirit who descends upon them
—transforms them, fashioning in them a new personality, a being
whom they do not know. Consequently, this word and this spirit
are something foreign to them, a force that imposes itself upon
them from without. Amos, for example, hears a roar (Amos 3, 8;
cf. 1, 2), and God takes him "from herding the flock" (7, 15); and
Isaiah, Jeremiah and Ezekiel feel God's hand seizing hold of them
(Is. 8, 11; Jer. 15, 17; 20, 7; Ez. 1, 3; 3, 14). And why does he take
possession of them thus? To make them act, so that they may go
out and proclaim his words and deeds. There is nothing of the
sort, however, at Jesus' baptism: the Spirit does not create a new
personality in him or send him out to perform a particular deed.[8]

If the circumstances of Jesus' baptism recall the vocation of
the prophets, the style used to describe his experience is more directly related to that of the apocalypses and tends to make of
Christ a seer, in the tradition of Ezekiel, Daniel and the heroes of
the apocryphal apocalypses—Baruch, Ezra, Enoch, and the like.
Over him the heavens open up (Ezek. 1, 1; Acts 7, 56; Rev.
4, 1; 19, 11); he sees *something like* a dove come down, just as
Ezekiel beheld "what seemed four animals" in the sky and above
them "what looked like fire . . . something that looked like the
glory of Yahweh" (Ezek. 1, 5.27-28), or just as the apostle John
would see in the sky, standing between the throne with its four
animals and the circle of the elders, "a Lamb that seemed to have
been sacrificed" (Rev. 5, 6). However, there are considerable differences between Jesus and the seers of the Old and the New Testament. Ezekiel, Daniel and John himself are admitted as spectators to contemplate from the outside a world to which they
remain strangers; awestricken, they are paralyzed with terror or
ecstasy; they witness scenes which they cannot understand until
an interpreter tells them the meaning (Dan. 7, 16; 8, 17; 9, 22;
Rev. 17, 7). Jesus, too, sees the heavens opening and sending
down something like a dove—the Spirit. Jesus is not in heaven
and does not communicate with heaven except in visions and in
words, but he is the very object of this word and this vision: the
dove, that symbol of God's favor regained after the Flood, having

left the ark and never returned again, now finally returns to bring Jesus the Father's joy and favor.[9] The heavens open up for him, not so that he may contemplate mysterious sights, but so that the Spirit may descend on him.[10] That is to say that in Jesus, the apocalypse—with its array of supraterrestrial images and succession of cosmic upheavals—is resolved into a simple image, an actual reality, a direct experience. Through the language of the apocalypses, Jesus here appears as their culmination: what the seers glimpsed becomes reality in him.

Jesus' baptism—the vocation of a unique figure, the vision of a seer who has transcended visions—climaxes in the divine utterance which closes the narrative: "You are my Son, the Beloved; my favor rests on you." [11] And these words teach us the ultimate meaning of the whole episode: it leads us from Jesus up to the Father. True, it manifests an interior reaction, but this reaction is not directly that of Jesus: it is the satisfaction and joy of the Father with regard to Jesus. *Rasahç rason,* the Hebrew behind the Greek *eudokein,* is not easy to translate.[12] *Joy* is too general and does not sufficiently emphasize the aspect of choice and volitional drive; *satisfaction* tends to be pejorative and suggests weakness and indulgence. The original Hebrew seems to come from court parlance and to denote the favor of the sovereign; cultual texts use it regularly to signify that God accepts the sacrifice offered to him; and the prophets disclose with what attention and passion God receives a sacrifice which is "proper" and worthy of him (Ps. 51, 19) and repulses the hypocritical offering which would attempt to buy him. So much so that, when in Isaiah (42) God presents to the nations "my servant whom I uphold, my chosen one in whom my soul delights," this accent of wonderstruck gratitude, this gaze filled with pride, teaches us perhaps more about God's personality than about his Servant's. What his Servant will be and what he will do still remains wrapped in a hazy dawn; but what shines forth from this hour is the certitude which God communicates to the world of having at last found, after so many disappointed efforts and hopes, a man capable of accomplishing the work planned since God chose Israel, his "servant." Even more than the tragic destiny which remains concealed until the last three songs (Is. 49, 4; 50, 6-9; 52, 13-53, 12), what gives this mysterious person his exceptional role and his unique character is the extraordinary assurance with which God presents him to the world. Whether he be king or prophet, whether he should or should not be called the Messiah, is not so important, after all. What is certain is that God finds delight in this person and voices his joy.

This characteristic tone of the songs of the Servant is precisely what rings out at Jesus' baptism and make the words from heaven a revelation of the Father. This revelation can take place only because Jesus is there, and it is addressed to him first of all. The change from "here is" in Isaiah (42, 1) to "you are" in Mark (1, 11) indicates that Jesus must at one and the same time discover who he is by reading Isaiah, and discover himself in the pages of Isaiah by listening to God speak to him. Only the Son can do this reading—the Son who became man and who sees his destiny taking shape as he peruses the scriptures, the only-begotten Son who penetrates the very heart of the scriptures because in his own heart he hears his Father's voice whispering them to him.

Of course, this revelation has no meaning except for a Christian and cannot be presented thus by anyone else. Still, it does not constitute an anachronism, precisely because it does not attempt to say what Jesus' baptism meant for him or what he experienced then, but merely states what he already was and what he began to teach us then.

At this instant begins the revelation of the Son of God to the world. But this revelation cannot be real, and Jesus cannot reveal himself from this moment on as God's Son, unless he already was that and already knew it. If Jesus has to learn that he is the Son of God, it is because he was not his Son before. A king's son who has been separated from his parents may learn, one fine day, that he is a king, and this discovery may change his life and provide someone like Shakespeare with the plot for a beautiful human drama; but the whole point of such a situation is precisely to show that, king or wretch, a man's worth comes from what he is, from his innermost being and his personality. If Jesus' personality consists in being the Son of God, he must be that from his birth, from the moment he exists; otherwise he will never be.

He has to be the Son of God and he has to know it, for no one on earth could tell him so. Suppose—and this is a pure hypothesis which, in any case, Luke's gospel would not uphold—suppose Mary had informed her Son of the circumstances of his conception. That is still not how Jesus can know that he is the Son of God. Mary herself cannot learn so except from him and from seeing him live. She can only meditate in this silence; for no human utterance, however subtle and precise, can convey this lived experience which is God. If Jesus is the Son of God and must someday say so, this experience has to inhabit him from the dawn of his existence, from the first awakening of his consciousness.

But it is not necessary—and is hardly probable—that this fundamental experience should from the beginning have taken the form of an intellectual certitude, of a clear concept. Even though a baby cannot yet speak and has not so much as opened his eyes, he is not an animal, but already a human consciousness, a will which is taking shape, a propulsion toward his fellowmen. So, too, with Jesus as an infant: his consciousness need not be more developed than that of any other newborn: enough if the force which carries him and the will which animates him are unswervingly directed toward God from this hour, enough if they receive from God the assurance of unparalleled attention and love.[13]

But this experience, which comes to him directly from the Father, is lived by Jesus in the consciousness of a child, a consciousness which grows and develops with what it receives from people and from outside. Jesus' development—the fundamental theme of Luke's infancy gospel (2, 40.42)—is not something superficial or marginal: it lies at the very heart of the way Jesus lives his experience as Son of God. The episode about his being found in the Temple among the doctors of the Law (Lk. 2, 41-50) is framed by two parallel observations: "The child grew to maturity, and he was filled with wisdom" (2, 40) and "Jesus increased in wisdom, in stature, and in favor with God and men" (2, 52). There is a connection, therefore, between this growth and the unexpected behavior of Jesus in leaving his parents. Luke may specify that Jesus was twelve years old at the time of this first pilgrimage because he remembers that that was the age when a Jewish child reached his "religious majority."[14] At any rate, he is anxious that the first statement of this child, who was so totally integrated into his parents' family life, should be a declaration that he belongs to the Father. And perhaps this incident sheds a little light on how Jesus' awareness of his sonship may have developed. It is by living close to his parents, by receiving from them what any child derives from the presence and attention of those who take care of him, that Jesus gradually and mysteriously discovers what has always inhabited him: the immediate presence and gaze of him whom he calls by a name which, doubtlessly, he first learned from his parents: "Abba, Father."

Although Luke says even less about Jesus' adolescence and early manhood, he tells us enough about them to make us ponder what Jesus is. Jesus spent these years growing, developing and working. Often described as hidden and seemingly empty years, they prove, on the contrary, that the simplest tasks are precious enough for the Son of God to spend thirty years at them—thirty years that were beneficial to all who profited from his work, thirty years that were indispensable to him and made him the man he was. To the human community where he lived, Jesus brought his work and his personal presence; from it, he received the traits which marked him. He did not lead two lives: first at Nazareth, hiding his secret—a sort of unnatural, double life; and then in the public eye, revealing himself freely. No, the prophet of Capernaum is the workman of Nazareth, and it is at Nazareth that he learned to speak, to think, to approach people. He spent thirty years becoming this man: had he manifested himself a few years earlier or later, he would not have been the same, his manner would have been different—more passionate, perhaps, or more ponderous—and his words would have had another ring. As it is, when he comes to John the Baptist, he is neither young nor old, nor even middle-aged: he is in the flowering of his strength and has just completed his apprenticeship as a man.

Without attempting to reconstruct what Jesus' baptism was, we can admire, in reading the gospel narrative, how well it falls into place in the itinerary of his life and sheds light upon it. Before presenting himself to Israel and proclaiming that with his arrival the prophecies are fulfilled (Lk. 4, 21) and the kingdom of God is at the door, ready to enter (Mk. 1, 15), Jesus must see the greatest of the prophets face to face, hear him announce the imminent coming of the day of the Lord, and discern in this voice and in this face the promise made by God and the expectation of his people. Throughout the gospels, it is clear that Jesus always rediscovered in the scriptures the law of his life and the person he was meant to be. We sense that he was always at ease in these scriptures, moving with unerring instinct to the very heart of them, spontaneously feeling at home there, and finding himself at every turn. But it is not without significance that this meeting between text and reader be supplemented by the living presence of John the Baptist. If Jesus comes to fulfill everything, it is understandable that he wanted first to meet him who had come to announce everything. In a sense, this succession is necessary and constitutes the thread of all the scriptures. For Israel to realize that its history was the work of God, miracles and unexampled prodigies were not enough; what was necessary, above all, was that these signs be preannounced, that a plan formed by God show through—a plot guided by his hand. Without prophetism and without the shared secrets of a divine will, there is no revelation; there may be manifestations which seem to be of heavenly origin, but no one can decode them. Thus, if Jesus is to appear as fulfilling God's promises, he must appear as sent by him who sent John. And we may ask whether John's presence did not affect the manner in which Jesus became conscious of his mission and of the way he would launch it.[15]

But, over and above John's action and his meeting with Jesus, the center of this episode is the presence and voice of the Father. God indicates that he himself is the origin of Jesus and of his mission. Jesus is not John's successor: he is the Son of God. He would not be a man like us unless he also, like us, had to accept the world and events, and interpret his mission through diverse encounters, the experiences of each day, and the riches of his religious and cultural heritage. But this deciphering is not a groping, this interpretation is not a search. It is immediate and unfailing discovery by him who always knows where he is going because he ceaselessly hears the Father's voice in his heart: "You are my Son, the Beloved."[16]

1. M. Sabre, "Le baptême de Jésus. Etude sur les origines littéraires du récit des évangiles synoptiques," in *De Jésus aux Evangiles, Tradition et rédaction dans les évangiles synoptiques*, p. 203. The author, however, immediately adds: "The history of the motives which we find in this account, however, is rooted in the life of Jesus, like the consciousness of being the eschatological figure of the Messiah." If the link with his baptism is tenuous in the final analysis, the link with his consciousness is well brought out, and this is certainly what counts most.
2. To mention only recent authors, Jean Guitton, *The Problem of Jesus*, trans. by A. Gordon Smith (New York: P. J. Kenedy and Sons, 1955), pp. 74-75; A. Misin, *Histoire de Jésus* (Paris: Seuil, 1961), pp. 136-138; J. Steinmann, *Vie de Jésus* (Paris: Club des Librairies de France, 1959), p. 31; D. Flusser, *Jesus*, p. 29; and O. Cullmann, *The Christology of the New Testament*, trans. by S. C. Guthrie and C. Hall (Philadelphia: The Westminster Press, 1959), p. 66.
3. See A. George, *La christologie de saint Luc. Notes d'étudiants* (mimeographed courses of the Faculty of Theology at Lyons, no date), p. 26.
4. H. Schürmann, *Das Lukasevangelium*, p. 565.
5. See A. M. Ramsey, *La gloire de Dieu et la Transfiguration du Christ* (Paris: Cerf, 1965 [Lectio Divina, 40]), p. 134; and X. Léon-Dufour, *Etudes d'Evangile* (Paris: Seuil, 1965), pp. 106-107.
6. A. Voegtle, "Réflexions exégétiques sur la psychologie de Jésus," in *Le message de Jésus et l'interprétation moderne* (Paris: Cerf, 1969 [Cogitatio Fidei, 37]), p. 110, n. 160. The entire fifth chapter of Voegtle's study, entitled "La conscience filiale de Jésus," centers on the exegesis of the gospel accounts of Christ's baptism and constitutes a model of textual analysis, rigorously scientific and authentically theological at the same time. It is hardly possible to be more thorough and more exact. The only way one might complete his work would be to reintegrate this scene into the momentum of the entire Gospel. Then, perhaps, new vistas would open up.
7. A. Voegtle, *op. cit.*, p. 110.
8. Some will object that there seems to be a direct link between the baptism and the temptation of Jesus. Does not the Spirit's first act consist in driving Jesus out into the wilderness to be tempted by Satan (Mk. 1, 12-13)? For the synoptics, especially Matthew and Mark, both scenes are closely connected: the Son's first victory is the one he wins over Satan. But this connection is expressed only by the juxtaposition of the two episodes, and that is the work of the evangelists. The baptismal narrative concludes with the words, "You are my Son, the Beloved; my favor rests on you." The scene is complete and does not imply any particular mission. E. Lohmeyer, *Das Evangelium des Markus* (Göttingen, 1959, 15th edition), pp. 26-27; A. Feuillet, "Le baptême de Jésus," in *Revue Biblique*, 71 (1964), p. 322; G. Minette de Tillesse, *Le secret messianique dans l'Evangile de Marc*, pp. 104-110.
9. A. Feuillet ("Le symbolisme de la Colombe dans les récits évangéliques du Baptême," in *Recherche de Science Religieuse*, 46 (1958), pp. 524-544) thinks that the dove symbolizes the people of God instead. This interpretation is in line with his constant concern, in his various studies on the baptism of Jesus, to emphasize the link between Jesus and the people of God, the na-

tion composed of the baptized. Though surely present when the narrative took shape, this link was only indirect at first: Jesus is the type of the baptized person, but everything takes place between God and Jesus. This perspective, moreover, seems much closer to the way Jesus began: the Church was still very far from being formed, and Jesus was only starting to become a figure among men and to define his relationships with them. Conversely, his situation with regard to the Father was fully defined from this very moment. Such appears to be the progression of the gospels and the unfolding of this existence.

10. Mark—intentionally, no doubt—writes *eis auton,* "in him." Matthew and Luke, following the practice of the LXX when describing the coming of the Spirit, write *ep'auton,* "on him." But the promise of Ezek. 37, 5.6.14 reads: "I shall put my spirit in you," *eis humas.* And Is. 63, 11, which Mark is perhaps deliberately alluding to, reads: "He who endowed him with his holy spirit," *en autois.* Cf. J. Buse, "The Marcan Account of the Baptism of Jesus and Isaiah LXIII," in *Journal of Theological Studies,* 7 (1956), pp. 74-75.

11. Mk. 1, 11. Mt. 3, 17 is slightly different: "This is my Son, the Beloved; my favor rests on him." The shift from the second to the third person doubtlessly results from a desire to adhere more closely to the text of Is. 42, 1: "Here is my servant whom I uphold, my chosen one in whom my soul delights." Luke 3, 22 contains two versions: one, better authenticated in the manuscript tradition, is identical with Mark 1, 11; the other, certified in the so-called "Western" tradition, is very ancient and proves to be a literal quotation from Ps. 2, 7: "You are my son, today I have become your father." Despite the antiquity of this tradition and despite the index of genuineness suggested by an "adoptionist" version offensive to Christian ears, it seems more likely that Luke's text is that of Mark. For Luke, this is a scene, not of royal enthronement, but of prophetic consecration by the Spirit. A scene of adoption and investiture would make no sense after the infancy gospels (Lk. 1, 34; 2, 49). Luke, therefore, does not give us any particular information as to the original meaning of the divine statement. See I. de la Potterie, "L'onction du Christ," in *Nouvelle Revue Théologique,* 80 (1958), pp. 225-252; H. Schürmann, *Das Lukasevangelium,* pp. 193-194.

12. See G. Schrenk, *Theologisches Wörterbuch zum Neun Testament,* II, pp. 736-740; W. Zimmerli, *Zeitschrift für die alttestamentliche Wissenchaft,* 51 (1933), p. 190; J. L'Hour, "Les interdits *to'eba* dans le Deutéronome," in *Revue Biblique,* 71 (1964), p. 483, n. 13.

13. After years of meditation on these mysteries, which he considered the very heart of Christianity, Maurice Blondel wrote: "The essential distinction and the effective gap which exists, in this life, between everyone's innermost personality and his actual consciousness of self, surely leave a great deal of room for all that is said or presumed about the 'development' of our Lord, a development which does not affect the fundamental certitude of his divine sonship . . . or of his universal and redemptive mission . . . but a genuine development . . . which leaves him *in fieri,* inadequate to himself in some way, subjected to the very real trial of obscurity, of effort . . . as long as he is in the state of servitude and passion." Quoted from *Au coeur de la crise moderniste. Lettres de Maurice Blondel,* edited by R. Marlé (Paris: Aubier, 1960), p. 245.

14. This is one of the principal themes developed by Robert Aron, *Jesus of Nazareth: The Hidden Years,* trans. by Frances Frenaye (New York: William Morrow and Co., Inc., 1962). See H. Strack-P. Billerbeck, *Kommentar zum Neuen Testament aus Talmud und Midrash* (München, 1924), Vol. II, p. 125; R. Laurentin, *Jésus au Temple, Mystère de Pâque et foi de Marie* (Paris: Gabalda, 1966), p. 146.
15. See U. Wilckens, "Das Offenbarungsverständhis in der Geschichte des Urchristentums," in *Offenbarung als Geschichte,* edited by W. Pannenberg, R. Rendtorff and R. Wilkens (Göttingen, 1961), p. 54, n. 31: "With regard to Jesus' unique claim to authority . . . we must suppose a particular and wholly contingent event, which should perhaps be sought in the context of the well attested fact that Jesus came from John the Baptist's circle. . . . Now, John the Baptist preached final conversion in view of imminent eschatological judgment; Jesus, for his part, repeated this call to conversion but, simultaneously and especially, began to guarantee eschatological *salvation.* . . . If, therefore, within general apocalypticism, John's eschatology is probably the direct historical condition of Jesus' eschatology, Jesus differs from him precisely in the immediacy with which he claims the right to *grant* eschatological *salvation.*" Quoted by H. Schürmann, "Le problème fondamental posé à l'herméneutique de la prédication de Jésus: Eschatologie et théologie dans leur rapport mutuel," in *Le message de Jésus et l'interprétation moderne* (Paris: Cerf, 1969 [Cogitatio Fidei, 37]), p. 142.
16. And he ceaselessly receives him with the Spirit. . . . The baptism is commonly interpreted as the Spirit's taking possession of Jesus. See I. de La Potterie, "L'Onction du Christ. Essai de théologie biblique," in *Nouvelle Revue Théologique,* 80 (1958), pp. 225-252. There is no conclusive proof that this interpretation is binding—not as regards Luke, in any case, although he, of the four evangelists, stresses the Spirit most. See J. Dupont, *Les Béatitudes* (Paris: Gabalda, 1969), Vol. II, pp. 133-134.

5
The Kingdom of God

"**A**fter John had been arrested, Jesus went into Galilee. There he proclaimed the Good News from God. 'The time has come,' he said, 'and the kingdom of God is close at hand. Repent, and believe the Good News'" (Mk. 1, 14). Even though the term "Good News" is anachronistic at that date, it very accurately says what Mark wants us to understand. This is the moment when for the first time the Gospel, the Good News, rings forth. Its point of departure is Galilee: Jesus leaves the Jordan and the region of sources; he abandons his earlier style of activity and preaching, which, no doubt, was more or less modeled on John's and was largely concerned with baptism by water; and he begins to travel through the towns of Galilee, speaking the novel language of the Good News and announcing the kingdom that is close at hand.

The evangelists establish a connection between his new manner and John's arrest, suggesting a reaction of prudence but offering us no specific information on what is, after all, a secondary point. Far more important is the fact that they invite us especially to compare this new message with that of the Baptist. His was already an announcement, whose basic theme came from *The Book of the Consolation of Israel,* at the beginning of "Second" Isaiah; it was the voice of the herald preceding the Lord who brings the captives back from Babylon to Jerusalem (Is. 40, 3; Mk. 1, 1). John the Baptist was making straight the paths of the Lord and preparing the people who came to him for their meeting with God, for that redoubtable and spellbinding event, so immeasurably greater than the most dramatic upheavals in human history. Beyond John's baptism, "he who comes" after him can bring only the Spirit and fire (Mt. 11, 11); beyond John's heralding, there can only come the long-awaited Event.

But he who comes now is also the bearer of a proclamation, as if there were still something to await beyond him. His proclamation, however, has an entirely different ring, and the expectation it produces has unfamiliar features. He talks about awaiting the kingdom of God, and this centuries-old theme in Israel[1] was still, in Jesus' day, one of the great images of Jewish hope.[2] From the Old Testament passages which expressed this hope, the gospel accounts of Jesus' early activities in Galilee evoke several verses in "Second" and "Third" Isaiah particularly. Is. 52, 7 greets the messenger "who brings good news . . . and tells Zion, 'Your God is king.' " Chapter 40, verse 9 is quite similar: "Go up on a high mountain, joyful messenger to Zion. Shout with a loud voice, joyful messenger to Jerusalem. . . . Say to the towns of Judah, 'Here is your God.' "[3] Very closely related likewise is the text Jesus commented on in the synagogue of Capernaum: "The spirit of the Lord Yahweh has been given to me. . . . He has sent me to bring good news to the poor, to bind up hearts that are broken . . ." (Is. 61, 1-2). It is interesting to note, in Is. 52, 7, the link established between the bearer of good news and the coming of the kingdom of God.[4]

All these texts concern the event announced in connection with John the Baptist: the return from exile, with God leading the caravan in person. They place the same character on stage—the herald who announces the arrival of the royal retinue. But the horizon is not the same, and the situation has changed. The messenger whose role John played was coming to prepare the way and map out a route; everyone was still marching through the desert, across a rugged landscape which had to be turned into a smooth and pleasant road.[5]

The texts applied to Jesus or quoted by him evoke Jerusalem and the final hours of waiting: the King is arriving, he will be there at any moment. No longer is the messenger sent on ahead, early enough to get the preparations under way; he himself forms part of the retinue and has stepped out of it in order to convene the people and give the signal for the solemn entry.

In Old Testament terminology, this messenger is the *evangelizer,* and his mission is to *evangelize,* to announce the coming of the glorious conqueror. The noun *evangel* (from the Greek *euaggelion*), though it already had a meaning in profane Greek, is practically a creation of the New Testament signifying the announcement of that unique event, Jesus Christ. But the verb was widely used in the Bible to denote the communicating of a piece of good news, a birth or a victory; and the triumphal message of "Second" Isaiah—the announcement of the kingdom of God—had set up the figure of this messenger entrusted with *evangelizing* Jerusalem by bringing it the good news.

Jesus therefore presents himself in Galilee as the *evangelizer,* this messenger of the kingdom of God. As a messenger, he could be taken merely for a second John the Baptist; but his message, although it concerns the same event, is very different. It is welcome news, tidings of joy and salvation. John did not banish joy, nor was his message one of condemnation, but he was still exterior to the event and unable to say what it would be. Like all the prophets, like his great predecessor Jeremiah, he was sent "to destroy and overthrow, to build and to plant" (Jer. 1, 10), to announce both calamity and salvation, to propose a choice and point out a road. Jesus, too, issues a challenge and proposes a choice: "Repent!" God cannot force his way into man's heart but must be acknowledged freely. John's motive, however, was in the future tense: "God will come, so be ready"; whereas Jesus' motive is in the present tense: "The kingdom of God is at the door, the unimaginable is here. You have only to open up and let it in." [6]

Letting it in would be easy if it had a consistency and a face, if one could give a descriptive definition of it and say exactly what the kingdom of God consists in. Jesus, however, does not do that: he tells his hearers to seek it, to wait for it, to welcome it, but always like something mysterious and disconcerting; he tells them what it is like—a seed, a field or a treasure, but these images are not descriptions that enable one to recognize it: they compare situations and suggest attitudes. To know what the kingdom is, at this time, one must look at Jesus and let oneself be caught up in his momentum.

In a sense, the kingdom is Jesus himself, and he knows it: he speaks of it as of a reality to which he alone has access and of which he alone can speak. Yet there is a distance between the kingdom and him—a temporal distance, for Jesus is already there, whereas the kingdom is still only at the door; and an interior distance, for Jesus speaks of it as of a reality distinct from himself. The action of the kingdom and his own action are not identical: Jesus speaks, he moves through the towns of Galilee, he heals the sick and eats with sinners, he performs visible deeds, he works and he plants. All the while, the seed thrown into the soil germinates and grows, and the harvest ripens. Thus, the kingdom would be the internal force of which Jesus' action is the external manifestation.[7] For the sower would not go out to scatter seed to the wind unless he were sure that, despite every obstacle, the grain he was exposing to so many risks would eventually yield a harvest. From the moment Jesus goes out, from the moment he starts giving of his doctrine and his life so prodigally despite such opposition, he does so because he brings with him a strength that can overcome all resistance—the power of the kingdom of God.

This explains "the secret of the kingdom of God" and its link with the parables (Mk. 4, 11). The mysterious nature of the kingdom results not only from its interiority, from its being a spiritual and invisible reality which can be expressed solely in images and metaphors; but even more from the fact that this reality has not yet come to light because it is still in the process of being born. Interestingly enough, Jesus, when speaking of the kingdom, uses two very different and yet convergent languages: that of geneses, of germinations and crops; and that of apocalypses, of secrets revealed, of hidden matters brought to light and mysteries unveiled (Mk. 4, 11.22; Mt. 11, 25). Although these processes seem quite dissimilar to us, for the evangelists they are much closer than we imagine: both effect a passing from darkness to daylight, and both require time. For us, it is the time of growth, of slow maturation; for the evangelists, it is rather more the time of mystery, of a reality which is concealed but already operative. The mystery of the kingdom for the gospels, and the mystery of Christ for St. Paul are of the same order: it is a coming, a delivering,[8] the visible apparition.

If the kingdom remains a mystery even when on the threshold, that is because it cannot be revealed except through Jesus' life and action. But this life is going on, and this action has just begun. From the very start, the power of the kingdom bursts forth in Jesus' deeds, in the force of his words, which rout unclean spirits and penetrate into hearts (Mk. 1, 27), and in his gift for healing the sick, reaching the unfortunate and transforming sinners. All these signs are indeed proof that "the kingdom of God has overtaken you" (Mt. 12, 28) and that there is nothing else to await. Yet it is still advancing and, to enter into it, one needs both the desperate pulsion of people who are starving to death[9] and the simple heart of a child (Mk. 10, 15). The kingdom is never a paradisal domain whose gates need merely be thrown open: it is always a discovery to be made, an adventure to embark upon.

The first to live this adventure is Jesus. For him, the kingdom is already there, since his deeds bear its stamp and his words can say what it is. But his words fall into parables, and his deeds are still only signs. Each of them is already the presence of the kingdom, but they are always like our deeds and always have to be repeated. Tirelessly Jesus can cure all the sick who come to him, yet endlessly he will find more to cure, and those who were cured today will fall sick again, and Lazarus will return to the grave. With every step Jesus takes, the kingdom of God comes with him; but he always has to press ahead, and the kingdom continues to come without his ever being able to say, "It is here."

From the day of his arrival in Galilee, Jesus' existence is the expressive figure of this kingdom which is always close but never here. Constantly on the move, he travels from town to town, generally accompanied by his disciples (Mk. 1, 14.29.39; 3,20; 5, 1.24; 6, 1.6.56; 7, 24.31; 8, 27; 9, 39), and we learn oftener where he has been than where he is going. He has "nowhere to lay his head" (Mt. 8, 20), no dwelling where he can feel at home;[10] his life is public, out in the open for all to see, within the reach of every request. He almost seems a vagabond, content to wander about Galilee as circumstances allow, with no definite purpose or program. Yet two or three statements recorded in the gospels show that he knows what he is doing. When he leaves Capernaum "in the morning, long before dawn," he does so in order to pray in a lonely place, but also to "go elsewhere, to the neighboring country towns, so that I can preach there too, because that is why I came" (Mk. 1, 35-38). If he accepts every invitation and eats with sinners (Mk. 2, 17), if he announces the kingdom, he does so in order "to bring the good news to the poor, to proclaim lib-

erty to captives and to the blind new sight" (Lk. 4, 18 = Is. 61, 1-2).
Wherever there are poor people, blind or sick ones, or sinners, he
has something to do.

Behind the seeming freedom and the improvisational manner
of this early period, there lies hidden a rigorous and permanent
exigency—that of the kingdom. Like the prophets, like John the
Baptist, Jesus obeys a mission, but in his own way. The prophets'
mission was like the horizon of their activity, the goal which held
fast their gaze and inspired their reactions, according to circumstances: Elijah and Hosea struggled to snatch Israelite religion
from the seductions of Baalism, Isaiah worked unceasingly to
maintain the kings' faith in Yahweh, Jeremiah was determined to
reform Jerusalem morally and religiously, and John the Baptist
lived in order to prepare his nation for the coming of the Lord.
They always reacted according to a particular event, aware of
what it announced and what it demanded; but their reaction was
always dictated by the mission with which they knew Another had
entrusted them. And most often, the event that triggered their activity was something from outside, a public fact.

Jesus, too, reacts to events—but events of a different order,
much more modest, much less striking: the same daily encounters
at every street corner, the jostling by the poor, the obsessive presence of the sick and crippled, and contact with sinners. There is
his mission. It does not direct him toward a future to be deci-
phered and announced but, instead, makes him react immediately
and respond with his whole being to the cry of all this wretchedness. Sometimes his answer may entail a miracle; but, for
Jesus, miracles are not a demonstration of his power or an argument in support of his message; they are, at one and the same
time, the spontaneous reaction of a vulnerable heart that cannot
leave anyone in his misery, and the sign of an unprecedented
event on earth—the coming of the kingdom, the revelation of
God.

To be sure, modern man is reluctant to admit the possibility
of miracles, and today's Christian often feels uncomfortable with
the miracles in the gospels. Nevertheless, his uneasiness should
not harden into denial, for that would be absolutely contrary to
the scientific method[11] and would unduly and arbitrarily limit the
possibilities of the material world itself.[12]

Above all, it is imperative to situate miracles correctly in Jesus' own thinking and activity. Wishing to minimize the role of miracles, some exegetes dwell on the spectacular aspect of many miracles in the gospels and on the tendency of the accounts to transform Jesus into a "divine personage" endowed with thaumaturgic powers meant to dazzle the crowds.[13] Indeed, the emphasis placed on wonderstruck witnesses, especially in Luke, may contribute to making the gospels read like a marvelous epiphany. But this glow, which seems a bit contrived, remains quite superficial and cannot mask the profound and very clear meaning of Jesus' miracles.

In the gospels as well as in the Old Testament, miracles are signs, but the value of these signs is not exactly the same. In the Old Testament, signs serve as proof: Moses demonstrates the authenticity of his mission by unleashing frightful plagues against Pharaoh and his subjects; Elijah establishes the nonexistence of the Baals by causing fire to fall from heaven upon the altar on Carmel; Isaiah urges King Ahaz to ask for such a sign "coming either from the depts of Sheol or from the heights above" (Is. 7, 11). When some of the scribes and Pharisees come asking Jesus for a sign (Mt. 12, 38; cf. 16, 1: "a sign from heaven"), they are thinking of this sort of phenomenon; and Jesus refuses, for, even if he showed them a sign, their faith would not increase. "If they will not listen either to Moses or to the prophets, they will not be convinced even if someone should rise from the dead" (Lk. 16, 31). On closer analysis, moreover, the demonstrative value of signs in the Old Testament derives, not from the stupendous character of a deed, but from the way the prophets tie up their person and their message with the sign they propose. If Pharaoh must acknowledge the hand of God in the plagues that beat down upon him, it is not so much because they are terrifying as because they set the divine seal on the daring and unprecedented maneuver of Moses the Hebrew. If the heavenly fire which descends upon the altar constitutes a proof of Yahweh's existence over against Baal's, that is because Elijah, in the name of the God of Israel, has come to Mount Carmel and risked his life there by single-handedly confronting Ahab and the four hundred and fifty prophets of Baal: "Let them know today that you are God in Israel, and that I am your servant, that I have done all these things at your command" (1 Kg. 18, 36). Signs from God do not simply manifest his might; they sanction the faith of his servants.

Jesus' miracles are at once very like and very unlike those of the prophets. In general, at least, his do not exhibit that tension which characterizes the purest miracles in the Old Testament, that suspense into which Moses or Elijah are plunged by their faith. If there is expectancy, it is not in Jesus but in those who come to him. In Jesus there is, at one and the same time, a deep-seated reserve which opposes him utterly to all wonder-workers, and an almost irrepressible force which, at the sight of suffering, elicits the saving gesture. None of his miracles is premeditated, planned in advance. The only one which entails a certain amount of staging and time for preparation—the multiplication of the loaves—is, like all the others, an answer to an immediate need: the hunger of the crowd gathered around him. And yet, though Jesus never goes about seeking an opportunity to perform miracles, he often seems incapable of resisting, to the point that he has to justify himself. But the reason is not an overflow of power which must be discharged; it is the wretchedness which he sees around him and cannot allow to go on any longer: "And this woman, a daughter of Abraham whom Satan has held bound these eighteen years—was it not right to untie her bonds on the Sabbath day?" (Lk. 13, 16). To which mere common sense could reply, "If she's been waiting eighteen years, couldn't she wait one more day?"

The surest indication that the miracles in the gospels are genuine is doubtlessly the originality and truth of the total physiognomy painted by these narratives. Still, many of the miracles do not rise above banality, and their stereotyped format must be rather foreign to the actual event. The astonishing thing is that, through this poverty, Jesus' personality and consciousness can appear with such coherence and consistence. Though he is not on the lookout for chances to perform a miracle, at least he does not avoid them. With his reputation, it is inevitable, as he travels about, that the sick should flock to him; and, seeing them and being so sensitive, he has no choice but to cure them. It is a vicious circle and illustrates the element of contrivance which the "Messianic secret" entails, at the very least in the rigid form that Mark's gospel gives to it.[14] But this way Jesus has of bringing out the sick and the miserable as he passes, and offering them life and joy, is the mission by which he defines himself. Announcing the Good News to the poor and preaching the Gospel to them is meaningless unless the blind truly see and the lame truly walk. If Jesus is not raving but telling the truth, he must demonstrate the efficacy of his words among the wretched whom he wants to reach and who will soon be able to tell whether he is just talking. Mark's gospel stresses that one and the same power gives Jesus' words the authoritativeness of a doctrine which compels recognition, and the might to drive out unclean spirts.[15] By wishing to eliminate miracles from Jesus' activity, one would eventually lose sight of the properly evangelical aspect of his existence: this daily contact, ceaselessly renewed, with every form of human misery. Because he is always sympathetic to the distressed, he finds them at every step; but because he can reach only those within the normal range of a man's activity and influence, and because miracles do not suffice to change the human heart, his miracles are never anything but signs, and the kingdom of God is still beyond, though already present in Jesus himself.

Proof that the kingdom is in him, is that Jesus saves and cures spontaneously, without listening to any other reaction but that of his heart, without being obliged to wait for God's "hour," without having recourse to any power but his own,[16] without running the risk, so to speak, which Moses or Elijah ran. Even with all these miracles, however, the kingdom still has not come, as proved by the fact that they reach only an infinitesimal group on the face of the earth and always have to be repeated; by the fact, too, that they do not transform men's hearts and that, out of ten lepers who were healed, only one knows enough to praise God (Lk. 17, 18). But these limitations and failures do not result solely from unforeseeably violent resistance; they result from the nature of things and from Jesus' very mission. His whole demeanor shows that the kingdom has not arrived for him either. His gestures are always only signs and intimations, parables of a reality which infinitely transcends them. And that is why, more than once, he explains them by further parables. When, on the sabbath day, he cures the man with a withered hand or the woman bent double for eighteen years, he is telling us that no one waits till the day after the sabbath to water his cattle; and therefore, if we have ears and can understand, he is also telling us that God is the one who unfetters and saves and that he has decided to make freedom and salvation known to the world.[17] Thus, when Jesus cures, he is simply himself with his power and his sensitivity; but, at the same time, he is conscious of being the bearer of a revelation, the witness to a secret which he alone knows: the kingdom that is coming is God's mercy.

NOTES TO CHAPTER 5

1. "The fundamental idea in the future hope [of Israel] is always *the kingly rule of Yahweh*, His victorious advent as King, and His reckoning with His enemies. Yahweh's victory is followed by the manifestation of His kingship." Sigmund Mowinckel, *He That Cometh*, trans. by G. W. Anderson (New York: Abingdon Press, 1954), p. 143.

2. See R. Schnackenberg, *God's Rule and Kingdom*, trans. by John Murray (New York: Herder and Herder, 1963), Part I, especially pp. 53-54.

3. The translation "messenger *to* Zion" and "messenger *to* Jerusalem" is made possible by cutting *mebassèrèt*, as E. Dhorme does in Ps. 68, 12 *(La Bible de la Pléiade)*, and reading *mebassèr èt*.

4. J. Dupont, *Les Béatitudes*, Vol. II, p. 100. A little further (p. 102), Dupont observes that the Targum of Is. 40, 9 replaces "Here is your God" by "the kingdom of God has manifested itself"—a pronounced new link between the kingdom and the proclamation.

5. The original text in Is. 40, 3 reads: "A voice cries, 'Prepare in the wilderness . . .' " The gospel text throws into relief the way in which John identified himself, as it were, with the desert: "A voice cries in the wilderness: 'Prepare . . .' " (Mk. 1, 3).

6. It is not easy to state with the utmost precision exactly what is meant by the expression "The kingdom of God is close at hand" (Mk. 1, 15 and par.). First of all, we face a linguistic difficulty. The text has a Greek perfect tense —that is, a present resulting from a past act: "has drawn near"; but *draw near* is a verb of motion, and this motion has not stopped: although a decisive fact has occurred and the drawing near has become proximity, the motion of drawing near has not ceased. Beyond this linguistic complexity, there is the mystery of God's presence and of his connection with man's response. One of the best studies on this subject is surely Rudolf Schnackenburg's *God's Rule and Kingdom*, especially pp. 140-142. See also J. Dupont, *Les Béatitudes*, pp. 108-111.

7. This is exactly the explanation of the parable of the sower. Quite possibly, this explanation, at least in the form which the gospels give to it, is a creation of the Christian community. After having long contested this position, Joachim Jeremias, in *The Parables of Jesus*, trans. by S. H. Hooke (New York: Charles Scribner's Sons, 1963), pp. 77-79, has espoused it categorically, pointing out how much of "Christian tradition" had entered into the vocabulary of this passage by the time of Mark's redaction (4, 13-20). See also G. Minette de Tillesse, *Le secret messianique dans l'évangile de Marc*, pp. 167-168. But in reality the explanation merely spells out what is already contained in the original parable (Mk. 4, 3-9), whose purpose is precisely to distinguish between the human gesture of the sower, as he does his work, and the mysterious power in the seed.

8. ". . . God made me responsible for delivering God's message to you, the message which was a mystery hidden for generations and centuries . . ." (Col. 1, 25-26). The word *delivering* is an addition to the Greek text, but it conveys the meaning exactly.

9. This is doubtlessly the meaning of the mysterious saying "The kingdom of heaven has been subjected to violence, and the violent are taking it by storm" (Mt. 11, 12). See R. Schnackenberg, *God's Rule and Kingdom*, pp. 129-132.

10. The phrase *in the house,* which is especially frequent in Mark, never designates a house of Jesus' own, but always one where he is being received as a guest. The only passage which would allow us to wonder is 2, 15; but Luke has carefully removed all ambiguity by modifying Mark's text: the house in question is Levi's (Lk. 5, 29). See J. Dupont, *Les Béatitudes,* Vol. II, pp. 224-225. In every other instance, the house mentioned is either Peter's at Capernaum (Mk. 1, 29 and probably 2, 1; 3, 20; 9, 33) or one at which he stops along the way (7, 24; 10, 10).

11. "A scientist is being too hasty if he brands as unthinkable the very hypothesis of such a physical occurrence (contrary to the well established rationality of the phenomena). Upon analysis, in fact, nothing can absolutely guarantee that established scientific doctrine, whatever it may be, allows us to rule out utterly any occurrence which is referable to its theses and which it would not fully govern. Between what happens *in nature* and may be competently judged by genuine science, and what *can happen absolutely speaking,* there is always for the human mind, an unbridgeable gap. . . . Indeed, we are all accustomed to ignoring this gap completely. . . . Perhaps miracles, or the accepted hypothesis of eventual miracles, are salutary instruments for rational thought, which should never presume on its constructs." D. Dubarle, "Réflexions sur le miracle," in *Approches d'une théologie de la science* (Paris: Cerf, 1967 [Cogitatio Fidei, 22]).

12. "If Jesus really healed sick people, he demonstrated thereby that he had a certain power over nature: the ability to re-inform, from within, that which was deteriorated. But we have no competence to declare peremptorily that this is impossible. For, ten billion years ago, with the same reasoning, we could just as well have said that the appearance of life was impossible; and, two or three billion years ago, contemplating the microorganisms which were the only form of life on earth, we could have said that the inventiveness of Mozart was absolutely impossible." Claude Tresmontant, *L'enseignement de Ieschoua de Nazereth* (Paris: Seuil, 1970), p. 35.

13. Witness, among many others, H. H. Koester's article entitled "One Jesus and Four Gospels," in *Harvard Theological Review,* 61 (1968), pp. 203-247.

14. G. Minette de Tillesse, *Le secret messianique dans l'évangile de Marc,* pp. 71-75.

15. J. Delorme, "Aspects doctrinaux du second-évangile," in *De Jésus aux évangiles—Tradition et rédaction dans les évangiles synoptiques (= Ephemerides Theologicae Lovaniensis,* 1967), pp. 85-86.

16. The fourth gospel, in Jesus' prayer at the tomb of Lazarus—"Father, I thank you for hearing my prayer" (11, 41)—strives to highlight John's fundamental theme: the constant union between Jesus and his Father; but, at the same time, it shows that this union is so perfect that Jesus retains all his spontaneity and freedom of movement.

17. True, it is not always easy to prove the connection between a particular miracle and a particular parable. To the cure of the man with a withered hand Matthew links the parable of the sheep that fell down a hole (Mt. 12, 11-12); yet Luke relates it to the healing of a dropsical man (Lk. 14, 4-5). Such

translocations are quite natural, and must have been frequent. Although it is very difficult—and not vitally important, anyhow—to determine the initial relation between miracle and parable, it is likely that several parables were occasioned by a miracle which had to be explained or justified.

6
Jesus and Sinners

Miracles are still only signs of the kingdom which is coming; the forgiveness of sins shows it to be closer yet; but between miracles and the forgiveness of sins, there exists a connection. When Jesus, seeing the faith of the paralytic who has been lowered in front of him through the roof, says, "Your sins are forgiven" (Mk. 2, 5), he is expressing the purpose of his mission and he understands that it has been accomplished in this man. If he then adds, "Get up, pick up your stretcher and walk" (2, 9) and if he performs this miracle to prove that he can forgive sins, he is telling us that the essential thing is the forgiveness of sins, but he is also showing that there is a connection between sin and physical evil. Not that the narrative tends to insinuate that this man's infirmity was due to his sins; but that one and the same divine will, of which Jesus is the witness and the bearer, has chosen both to cure and to forgive.

Still, Jesus does not cure and forgive in the same impulse or in the same manner. He does not come in order to cure and to perform miracles: it is the sick who come to him. But he himself actively goes to seek out sinners, those who have been branded such, the publicans and the prostitutes (Mk. 2, 15; Mt. 21, 31); he chooses one of the Twelve from among them; he lets himself be seen in their company; he allows a sinful woman to touch him for a long time (Lk. 7, 39); and he makes this scandalous conduct the object of his mission, the reason for his coming: "I did not come to call the virtuous, but sinners" (Mk. 2, 17); "Zacchaeus, come down. Hurry, because I must stay at your house today" (Lk. 19, 5). So conspicuous and exasperating is this way of acting that a group of men who have just caught a woman in adultery drag

her before Jesus in gleeful anticipation of killing two birds with
one stone by getting rid of an adulteress and forcing him to side
openly with or against the Law (Jn. 8, 5).

Though the scandal is very widespread (Lk. 19, 7), it disturbs
the scribes and the Pharisees most of all (Mk. 2, 16; Lk.
7, 39; 15, 2; Jn. 8, 3). And we must admit that Jesus' conduct is
unexampled. While in many ways, in his language and in his life
style, he is related to the prophets and follows in their footsteps,
on this point he parts company with them. The prophets did not,
of course, repulse sinners who acknowledged their guilt: Nathan
accepted David's repentance (2 Sam. 12, 13) as Elijah accepted
Ahab's (1 Kg. 22, 28-29). Jeremiah and Ezekiel lived in expectation of the day when the unfaithful Israelites would come back to
their God (Jer. 31, 19; Ez. 37, 31). But, even as their entire mission kept them tense with hope of this return, it also kept them at
a distance and in isolation. Their role was to defend outraged justice, to denounce unpunished crimes and egoistic schemes, to lay
bare the destructive ravages of sin. These men were hardly to be
seen with sinners.

John the Baptist, however, gathered sinners around himself.
They came in droves to receive his baptism and confess their sins
(Mk. 1, 6). Without hesitating, he received tax collectors—who,
in the eyes of the people, were the embodiment of iniquity—and
soldiers; and all he asked was that they do their work honestly
(Lk. 3, 12.14). This movement, which drew crowds of sinners, had
no precedent in the history of Israel and its prophets. But it was
the sinners who came to John and asked him what they should do
(Lk. 3, 10). In contrast, from the day Jesus left the Jordan and
the region of the sources to start covering Galilee, it was he who
went to find the sinners. The pattern was reversed.

In this reversal lies the whole of Christianity. Until Jesus
came, the religious impulse was always marked by man's need to
escape from his guilt, to find a way of overcoming the evil which
lives in him and making amends for the contagion which, despite
himself, he continually spreads around him. The dialogue Luke
records between John and the sinners who come to him is significant: the crowds, the tax collectors and the soldiers all have but
one question: "What must we do?" (Lk. 3, 10.12.14). This question is at the core of most religions, and the noblest.[1] There is

nothing blameworthy about it and nothing contemptible about those who ask it, for they are on the road which leads to Jesus. But Jesus' answer overturns all questions: instead of saying what one must do and where one must go, it asserts that God comes to forgive, and it offers proof of this: Jesus is now in the midst of sinners, eating and drinking with them.

Even so, we must admit that the gospels give very few particulars about the nature of his dealings with sinners. Certain as we are of the basic fact and its repercussions, we must refrain from fabricating all sorts of details as the fancy takes us. Two features of his activity, however, are indisputable and heavy with meaning. Though they seem contradictory, they actually afford us a precious insight into Jesus' personality. On the one hand, the force which carries Jesus toward sinners is absolutely spontaneous and immediate; on the other, it springs from his certitude that he is the chosen witness to God and divine pardon.

Jesus goes out to sinners spontaneously. This we sense from the bitterness with which he is accused of being "a friend of tax collectors and sinners" (Lk. 7, 34) and from the tone in which he is attacked: "Moses has ordered us in the Law to condemn women like this to death by stoning. What have you to say?" (Jn. 8, 5). We notice it likewise in his habit of mentioning "tax collectors and prostitutes" as illustrations (Mt. 21, 31; cf. Lk. 18, 10-13), and of seeking not just normal or even cordial relations with sinners but the ease and informality of mealtime in the intimacy of their homes. And we see it with astounding clarity at the dinner given by Simon the Pharisee (Lk. 7, 36-50). Simon does not seem ill-disposed; he merely concludes in his own heart that, if Jesus were the prophet everyone says, he would not let this woman approach him and put on such a performance. But it is precisely this scandalous behavior that Jesus is going to justify. Not only does he allow her to kiss and anoint his feet, not only does he defend her, but he publishes the secret she could not contain: she loves him with a great love, he knows it and is profoundly moved.

The astonishing thing is the miraculous purity of this meeting, but even more astonishing is the fact that Jesus makes a point of justifying it the way he does: by means of a parable, that of the creditor and his two insolvent debtors. How could a parable—an example taken from outside, a truth of common experience—explain the inmost secret of his heart, the impetus that drives him toward sinners and can elicit a response like this woman's?

Furthermore, this parable is not alone of its kind. Several parables in the gospels most likely originated in analogous circumstances. Immediately we recall the three which Luke grouped together: the lost sheep (Lk. 15, 4-7), the lost drachma (15, 6-10), and the prodigal son (15, 11-32). Luke himself states that the first of these was an answer to the complaints of the Pharisees and the scribes, who were shocked to see Jesus welcome sinners and eat with them (15, 1-3). All the same, the vague setting and the typically Lucan style of these three verses suggests that they are an introduction he composed rather than a scene he remembered distinctly.[2] The artificial character of this account, however, does not prevent it from furnishing an important clue. For, besides the parable about the two debtors, which is inseparable from the story of the sinful woman at Simon's house, we again find the same link between the welcoming of sinners and the justification parable in the episode concerning the dinner at Levi's: "It is not the healthy who need the doctor, but the sick."[3] Conversely, despite the artificiality of the way Luke has grouped and introduced the three lost-found parables, there is a good chance that each of them was spoken on a different occasion but that the basic situation was always the same: Jesus justifying his incredible conduct toward sinners. Without wishing to advance any hypothesis, one can easily imagine Jesus telling the story of the prodigal son when leaving Zacchaeus' house.

We must, therefore, explain the singularly close connection between Jesus' attitude in welcoming sinners and the parables through which he justifies himself. We must understand how so personal an attitude can be justified by a general principle: "It is not the healthy who need the doctor, but the sick." Now, the very paradox which surprises us happens to constitute one of the essential revelations of Jesus and one of the roads which give us access to the mystery of his being.

Jesus' parables, and particularly those where he justifies his attitude toward sinners, almost always possess this amazing characteristic of ringing profoundly true to the human ear and, at the same time, describing a mode of behavior which is quite exceptional in man. That is very noticeable in the trio of lost-found parables. The anxiety of the housewife who notices she has lost some money, her frantic search through bureau drawers, her breathless questions from neighbor to neighbor, and her squeals of delight when she finds it again—all these are genuinely human reactions, and the parable brings out admirably what a modern would call the absurdity of the human condition: that, for an instant's inattention because of a more urgent matter, we so stupidly lose what has cost us such pains. This anecdote is the very stuff of la Fontaine's fables and of existentialist meditations. But it is also a parable, and there the mystery begins: not only does God understand this woman's anxiety and agitation, and then her joy and her need to communicate it to everyone around her, but he truly feels all this himself, and Jesus is the one who tells us so.[4] The parable of the lost sheep is likewise based on a fundamental human reflex which springs neither from legitimate self-interest nor from generosity, but from the order of things, from the force that makes a man cling to his life and to what he does: "What man among you" would not do as much?[5] But this reflex is not necessarily always strong enough to overcome all our reasons for failing to undertake such an adventure. Already the parable itself unveils a different face from those we meet, a face so deeply human that we rarely find it in our midst. As for the father of the prodigal son, what earthly father could ever endure such an affront and yet remain free from all resentment and wounded pride, capable of enveloping the runaway in his joy to the point of winning him back completely?

All of this proves that, for Jesus, God is affined to the profoundest humanity. But it also proves that the most spontaneous impulses of his heart, his immediate reflexes, are at the same time the expression and the revelation of someone other than he and of an event to which he is the witness. In all his reactions, Jesus is entirely himself; never was any man freer, more independent of conventions and pressures. And yet, by an astounding paradox, his parables and his way of speaking about himself and defining himself in terms of a mission, an embassy or a road to follow, show that he is constantly inhabited by God's forgiveness, as if he were living a divine event and were entrusted with translating it among men. But translating it would not be enough. A translator transposes; but Jesus does not transpose, he does not reproduce a heavenly model; he himself, on earth, performs acts which belong to God alone: he remits sins (Mk. 2, 5-7). But he performs these acts only by virtue of a power and in the name of his mission. There is in him perfect harmony between the being and his function, between the person and the messenger—not the harmony of the messenger who gives himself completely to his mission and consecrates his life to it, like John the Baptist, the bridegroom's friend; but the immediate, original harmony of him who is himself only when he appears as having come from another, of him who does the deeds of God because he comes to tell us what God does.

What God does is to forgive. Proof that he forgives is the way Jesus welcomes sinners. Between what God does and what Jesus does, there is reciprocity. If Jesus forgives, it is because he knows what God expects of him, what God has resolved in his heart. The language he uses in forgiving denotes both a unique power and a power which he holds from God. "Your sins are forgiven" (Mk. 2, 5; Lk. 7, 48)—this passive, this Judaic way of designating God without naming him, clearly indicates that while Jesus performs the gesture and proclaims its effect, he is conscious of saying simply what God alone is capable of doing. In this, Jesus is the witness and, so to speak, the reflection of God's act. And still what Jesus does is his own work, and God himself could not do it. What would God's pardon signify for us if Jesus did not give us this image and this experience of it? It would be what we can dream of: a willingness to forget the past, a need for reconciliation, a proof of goodness and understanding, and an assurance of not going back on promises. What Jesus does is all that at once, but it is also something completely different: it is the long-pent-up explosion of a love which can express itself at last, the secret of a heart pouring itself out. Then man can finally stop wondering about his past, about the extent of his guilt and where it all stands. Then all the evil he has committed may well subsist, and its noxious effects still perdure; but once he has seen Jesus welcome sinners, he knows God's joy on finding his children again, he discovers that this joy is capable of submerging all the evil that men can commit, and he enters into this immensity, whose source he sees welling up in the meeting between Jesus and sinners.

NOTES TO CHAPTER 6

1. See Joseph Ratzinger, *Foi chrétienne hier et aujourd'hui* (Mame, 1970), p. 199: "Almost all religions gravitate around the problem of expiation. They spring from man's consciousness of guilt before God and constitute an attempt to put an end to this feeling of culpability . . . through expiatory works offered to him. The task of atonement . . . is central to the history of religions."

2. "Everything would indicate that Luke wrote this account himself, doubtlessly patterning it on the episode of the dinner at Levi's." J. Dupont, *Les Béatitudes*, p. 235.

3. Mk. 2, 17a. Short though it be, this sentence nevertheless contains a parable, for it implies an unexpressed parallel: "It is not the just who need me, but the sinners," and a still deeper presupposition: "I am for sinners what a doctor is for the sick—I am the Savior." Such is precisely the formula in verse 17b: "I did not come to call the virtuous, but sinners." A good many exegetes consider this verse a mere gloss of Christian origin. As J. Dupont has observed, there are valid reasons for hesitating to accept it: "Jesus does not tend to weaken a vivid image by tacking an explanation onto it" (*op. cit.,* pp. 226-227). In any event, this explanation is exactly what the preceding formula supposes, and it confirms the fact that the formula constitutes a parable. This is also J. Jeremias' interpretation in *The Parables of Jesus,* pp. 121, 124-125.

4. The expression "there is rejoicing among the angels of God" (Lk. 15, 10) is a rather cumbersome periphrasis, in the style of Jewish formulas meant to safeguard the divine transcendence; but its ultimate meaning is clear: if the angels witness this joy, they cannot see it other than in God. "There will be rejoicing in heaven" (15, 7) is likewise a way of designating God without naming him. In the parable of the prodigal son, no transposition is needed, for the father who acts and speaks thus can be none other than God.

5. Lk. 15, 4; cf. 13, 15; 14, 5. There is the same appeal to a universal reflex, although in a different context, in 11, 5-13; 14, 28; 17, 7.

7
The Sermon on the Mount

For Matthew as for Luke, the Sermon on the Mount stands out as an important moment in the gospel narrative. They do not put it exactly in the same place: Matthew situates it at the beginning of the Galilean period, and Luke a bit later, after a series of separate episodes which give us a concrete idea of Jesus' activity. But both attribute major significance to this discourse and present it in the habitual framework of this period: Jesus traveling about surrounded by a small group of disciples and performing numerous miracles, as the crowds press around him, bringing their sick.[1] The herald's tidings have therefore reached their mark, the message of the Good News has stirred hearts, and in the world something is starting to change around Jesus: where he passes, the cripple rise and sinners discover God's forgiveness. Yet this is not yet the long-awaited kingdom: suffering, death and evil are still at work in the world, and God has not yet torn open the heavens to let his face show through. But Jesus' actions prove that the power of God is with him, and his words show that he knows what God is in the process of doing. In him the kingdom becomes a concrete, present reality.

Besides announcing this presence to the crowds, Jesus gives it to his disciples so that they may live it. He already had disciples when he was living near the Jordan, like John the Baptist. But the synoptics heavily underline the relationship between Jesus' mission in Galilee and his choosing of the Twelve. Jesus' disciples come from Galilee, like him, but the nucleus of the group consists of fishermen from the lake. Henceforth, they will no longer leave their master; they remain with him (cf. Mk. 3, 14), and he carries on all his activity with them. When occasionally he sends them off by themselves for awhile, his purpose is to have them go to a nearby town and prepare his arrival by reproducing his manner of living and acting (Mk. 6, 7-13),[2] thus becoming, like him, the "evangelists" and heralds of the kingdom of God.[3]

If the disciples are to have a role in proclaiming the Good News, they must somehow share Jesus' experience. The Gospel Jesus announces—the kingdom that is on its way—is a reality of which he is the witness, bringing us the signs of it and, so to say, living its forward thrust in the world. Of these signs and this thrust, he is the origin and the source, the living demonstration. But if the kingdom is coming into the world, it must reach men and manifest its vital, transforming power. That is why Jesus takes on disciples: to repeat his teaching, but especially to live, like him, the experience of the kingdom which is coming, to be in the sight of men witnesses of what God can do. That is also why sinful women who have been forgiven rank among his disciples and why Mary the Magdalene is named alongside the Twelve (Lk. 8, 1-2). While less imposing than the testimony of miracles, that of the disciples is an infinitely more precious sign. Slow to believe, quick to distort, and heavy to carry, the disciples accompany Jesus: they are the first adumbration of the kingdom to come—a rough sketch as yet, but already animated by the rising yeast (Mt. 13, 33), the power of the Spirit.

It is to his disciples that Jesus addresses the Sermon on the Mount. Matthew notes this in his own way by placing them around Jesus as he is about to speak under circumstances that suggest an assembly (Mt. 5, 2); but Luke makes it even clearer by having the choice of the Twelve precede the Sermon (Lk. 6, 13-20). Both, moreover, call attention to the huge crowd, from all over the country, that had gathered around Jesus and his disciples (Mt. 5, 1; Lk. 6, 17). No doubt they want to show that although the teaching which Jesus is going to impart is meant for his disciples, there exists a bond between them and the crowd: they are present for the sake of the crowd, and what is said to them concerns all men (Mt. 5, 16). This is no secret doctrine, no special way reserved for an elite, no enterprise designed for a few hardy volunteers. It is an experience to be lived—but an experience proposed by Jesus, grounded on his word and his call. The presence of the disciples attests that this experience can be attempted by anyone who is willing to follow Jesus.

Both the setting and the redaction of the Sermon contain an element of construction. The word *sermon,* with all that it connotes of attentive audiences, ample expansion and formal rites, betrays the atmosphere of the Gospel and the style of these pages.[4] For this discourse is made up of short sayings on various subjects, sometimes constituting a whole, like the beatitudes, but never exhibiting true development. And its composition is certainly a literary creation, as evidenced in Matthew, who presents as a single block teachings which, in Luke, are found scattered throughout the narrative. Since it is unlikely that Luke knew such a well-constructed passage as Matthew 5-7 and then amused himself by fragmenting it, we may conclude that the Lucan version reflects a more primitive state than the Matthean. Even Luke, however, shows signs of rearrangement, the most obvious being the way he completes the beatitudes with a series of curses.[5] It is equally probable that he has rewritten the beatitudes in direct style, in the second person, though they were originally in the third, according to the usual rule of this genre.[6] Generally speaking, then, Luke is perhaps closer to the content of the initial discourse, whereas Matthew preserves the letter of the original formulas more strictly.

Nor are we forbidden to push criticism still further and ask whether—even in the condensed form found in Luke, and even reduced to the nucleus determinable by excising his elaborations —the discourse was not already a literary composition, a collection of sayings.[7] Though there is indeed unity of spirit, we cannot prove that there is unity of development.

Having stated these particulars and entered these reservations, we must now show to what point the discourse (in the simplest form to which we can restore it, beginning with the three beatitudes of the poor, the hungry and the afflicted, and grouping a series of sayings around a central theme: the new comportment Jesus proposes to his disciples by reason of their conditions as sons of God—brotherly generosity and forgiveness for their enemies) corresponds naturally to the conditions of his mission in Galilee. But we must also add that between this condensed form of the discourse—the initial "pre-Lucan" nucleus—and the vast composition laid out by Matthew, there is not only genuine continuity but profound coherence. In its Matthean version, the Sermon very probably constitutes "a proto-Christian catechism" [8] for the neophytes reached by the message of Christ and the preaching of the Church, a sort of program telling them what their life should be henceforth.[9] Yet this program cannot be described as a Christian work. It presupposes an event and draws consequences from it, but this event is not the birth of the Church, not the existence of Christian communities, of a faith and a cultus: it is simply the coming of the kingdom, and its horizon remains purely evangelical. For proof, there is the echo which it continues to elicit from so many men who are hardly interested in the Church but very sensitive to this unique message. It is noteworthy, too, that a radical critic like Bultmann draws very largely upon the Sermon on the Mount to define Jesus' teaching.[10]

These rather long preambles were necessary to allow us to approach the Sermon on the Mount without mental reservations and pass without scruples from Luke's text to Matthew's. Both of them place at the beginning of Jesus' activity a sort of manifesto outlining the life style to which he calls his disciples. Both open the discourse with a group of beatitudes and characterize a disciple's behavior in a series of contrasts with the generally accepted rules of life. Now, these two moments—beatitudes and life style —are in perfect accord with the twofold message Jesus delivered from the very start in Galilee: "The kingdom of God is close at hand" is the blessed news, and "Repent, be converted and change your way of living" is its immediate consequence. This twofold message, furthermore, had to develop some content: Jesus is no illuminist pursuing a fixed idea and obsessed by a slogan. It is natural that Matthew, by making the Sermon on the Mount (Mt. 5, 1) follow almost directly upon the Good News of the kingdom (4, 17.23), should give us to understand that the Sermon constitutes the development of the News. In Luke, the time span between the inaugural scene in the synagogue at Nazareth (Lk. 4, 18) and the opening words of the discourse (6, 20) is slightly longer, but it is likewise filled with joyous news of the kingdom (4, 43); and there exists a very close connection between Jesus' declaration at Nazareth, based on the oracle in Isaiah: "He has sent me to bring the good news to the poor, to proclaim liberty to captives . . . to proclaim the Lord's year of favor" (Lk. 4, 17-19 = Is. 61, 1-3, LXX), and the beatitudes: "How happy are you who are poor . . . you who are hungry now . . . you who weep now" (Lk. 6, 20-21).[11] Jesus' mission and the beatitudes are directly linked: happy now are those who suffer, because Jesus has been sent to them.

The beatitudes, therefore, do not attempt to formulate a general truth, nor do they reflect some brainstorm like "What was previously called misfortune will henceforth be called happiness!" In Jesus' mind, affliction and imprisonment, hunger and sorrow are still the various faces of human misery; and if he asserts that people stricken thus are happy, it is because he has come to deliver them. The originality of the Gospel does not consist in saying that black has suddenly become white, but in offering the distressed a new and happy solution to their problems. The beatitudes are a prophetic—or, more exactly, a Messianic—message, since he who proclaims them does so, not for some very near future, but for an immediate future to which he already belongs.

Yet the beatitudes are something more than a prophecy, more than the mere announcing of an event, even though that event be the Messiah himself. They include a call, they entail an attitude, they imply a transformation in man. Besides, their literary form relates them to the style of the wisdom writings in the Old Testament, where a beatitude is usually an invitation to follow a certain path and share the experience proposed by a teacher: "Happy the man who fears Yahweh" (Ps. 112, 1), who "finds his pleasure in the Law of Yahweh" (Ps. 1, 2), who leads a "blameless life" (Ps. 119, 1), "who cares for the poor" (Ps. 41, 2), who has found Wisdom (Pr. 8, 17) and "day after day watches at [her] gates" (Pr. 8, 34).[12] While these comparisons may not warrant our grouping the beatitudes along with exhortations,[13] they nevertheless enable us to hear, like an echo, a call to conscience and to conduct.

What is certain is that this conduct does not constitute a prerequisite or a condition. A "moralistic" interpretation, which would conceive of "spiritual" poverty or the inner thirst for justice as an indispensable state for anyone wishing to have access to the beatitudes, would be a fundamental misinterpretation, a radical misunderstanding of the Gospel—that gift of God to those who have nothing. But the Gospel brings with it a new kind of existence, a pattern for living, the equivalent—but in a very different style—of what the Old Testament called "the Law." We should not be surprised to find in Luke, starting with the simplest version of the Sermon, the sharply defined beatitudes-New Law sequence. At bottom, this is the framework of Israel's faith, the framework of the Covenant, the link established by God between his promises and his commandments: "You yourselves have seen what I did with the Egyptians. . . . From this you know that now if you obey my voice and hold fast to my covenant, you of all the nations shall be my very own" (Ex. 19, 4-5). The fundamental dyad Law-prophets seems clearly to have dictated the structure of the Sermon.

What we are discussing here is something entirely different from mere literary structure: just as the Law of Israel is not an arbitrary condition laid down for granting access to the promises, but is the means whereby the Chosen People may continue to live in the world the experience of their liberation and of the God who vouchsafed it to them,[14] so also the imperatives of the Sermon formulate the manner in which disciples of the Gospel should live among men the blessed experience they have just had—the discovery of the Father: "Love your enemies and do good, and lend without any hope of return . . . and you will be sons of the Most High. . . . Be compassionate as your Father is compassionate" (Lk. 6, 34-36). The New Law supposes the beatitudes, as the Law of Moses supposed the promise received by Abraham, as Christian justice consists in receiving God's gift in faith and making it fructify in life-giving works (Rom. 4, 1-18; Gal. 5, 22-25).

In its Lucan version, the Sermon expresses this bond between faith and works (to use Saint Paul's terminology) in simple form by the priority accorded to the beatitudes and by the character of consequences given to the commandments which follow them. But placing the Pauline doctrine of justification and the structure of the Sermon in Luke side by side, if we may legitimately do so, sheds light on the nature of the beatitudes.[15] They are certainly not an evaluation by Jesus of the people he has come to seek out, as if he were disclosing unsuspected values deep down within them. Actually, their happiness is not in them: it comes to them. Nevertheless, they are destined for this happiness: it derives from their condition and their existence; there is a relation between this happiness and what they are: they were created to discover it and taste it. To feel that I have been personally called thus by someone else to an experience which I cannot give myself—this is bliss, and this is faith. It has to be a personal effort, an experience that no one can have in my stead; yet this experience cannot spring from me, but must be given to me by someone else. The beatitudes do not just promise some marvelous gift or even offer it immediately. The gift is there, but the beatitudes are confirmed only if I accept it; the kingdom of God is at the door but cannot enter unless I open that door; I must believe these glad tidings (Mk. 1, 15) and welcome this joy into my heart. In keeping with the sapiential tradition, the beatitudes are a call, an invitation to follow a teacher and enter into his experience.

In Matthew's version of the Sermon, the relation between the beatitudes and the New Law is even closer than in Luke's. Both accounts present the same beatitudes-commandments sequence, with this important difference, however, that Matthew's stresses the commandments far more. But even his beatitudes display an original element. Not only does Matthew list eight beatitudes instead of four, but the four which he adds to Luke's are clearly different both in tone and content. Whereas the three basic beatitudes (concerning the poor, the hungry and the afflicted), while yet conveying a call and an impetus, have something passive about them and focus on situations, the four beatitudes proper to Matthew (concerning the meek, the merciful, the pure in heart and the peacemakers) aim more at comportment and action. The perspectives of the promise and those of the Law are interwoven here; it is less a matter of doing than of being—being meek, pure in heart, merciful and peacemaking. That is why Matthew's four new beatitudes can coalesce with the three initial ones and, together, form a genuine unity. On the one hand, Matthew has accentuated the interior and moral aspect in the first beatitudes: the poor are poor "in spirit," the famished hunger and thirst "for what is right," so that there is little difference between these poor and the meek,[16] between these starvelings and the pure in heart. On the other hand and in the opposite direction, by placing the meek, the pure, the merciful and the peacemakers in the ranks of the poor, the hungry and the afflicted, and calling them to experience evangelical joy, Matthew clearly broadens the original category of unfortunates and, at bottom, makes it include all who seek God in righteousness; but, at the same time, he maintains the two essential poles of the beatitudes: a joy made for the poor, a joy bestowed on them, not achieved by them. Even those who give, the peacemakers or the merciful, are promised a joy other than that of giving: that of discovering that they are sons of God (Mt. 5, 9)—or, more accurately, discovering that in giving they receive the gift of God. For, as Paul reminds the elders of Ephesus in the words of the Lord Jesus, "There is more happiness in giving than in receiving" (Acts 20, 35). And giving is one of the great refrains of the Sermon: "Do not refuse . . . give . . . do not ask . . . lend without any hope of return . . . give, and there will be gifts for you" (Lk. 6, 29-30.35.38). Yet giving may also be a means of dominating others and making oneself important. The pure joy of giving, the joy of uniting oneself with him who receives, can be known only by the poor, only by those who have experienced the beatitudes and discovered how God can give.

NOTES TO CHAPTER 7

1. One cannot help wondering why Mark does not mention the Sermon on the Mount. According to the classical theory of the two sources, the answer is obvious: the Sermon is a composite of maxims borrowed from a collection of *logia* with which Mark was not familiar. The explanation is simple, and this simplicity is the best argument for it. Some, however, find it too simple. L. Vaganay in "L'absence du sermon sur la montagne chez Marc," in *Revue Biblique,* 58 (1951), pp. 5-46, notes that Mark, in the third chapter of his gospel, follows the same direction as the two other synoptics, and then stops abruptly after listing the Twelve (3, 19-20), as if he had deliberately omitted the passage in his source which contained the Sermon. We cannot deny the hiatus which Vaganay points to between verses 19 and 20. Nevertheless, in order to be sure that Mark knew and deliberately omitted so important a passage, we would need very strong positive arguments. We can hardly invoke the missionary character of his gospel, since the beatitudes, which open the Sermon, definitely have the ring of a missionary proclamation (a ring which is muted in Matthew but clearer in Luke). The most probable explanation, therefore, is that Mark did not know the Sermon; but he connects with it when he states that, from the very beginning, Jesus "went all through Galilee, preaching in their synagogues and casting out devils" (1, 39). He does not separate the miracles from the preaching, and it is difficult to restrict this preaching to the parables, which proclaim the mystery of the coming of the kingdom but say almost nothing about the conduct of a disciple.

2. On the reality and consistency of the disciples' "pre-paschal apostolate," see X. Léon-Dufour, *The Gospels and the Jesus of History,* pp. 200-202; and H. Schürmann, "Die vorösterlichen Anfänge der Logientradition. Versuch eines formgeschichtlichen Zugangs zum Leben Jesu," in *Der historische Jesus und das kerygmatische Christus,* ed. by H. Ristow-K. Matthiae (Berlin, 1960), pp. 342-370; H. Schürmann, *Mt. 10, 5b-6 und die Vorgeschichte der synoptischen Evangelien* (Düsseldorf, 1968), pp. 137-149. See also Jean-Paul Audet, *The Gospel Project,* pp. 72-73.

3. The word *evangelizing* is found only in Luke (9, 6). The other gospels reserve for Jesus alone this mission as herald of the Good News (Mk. 1, 1.14.15; Mt. 4, 23; 9, 35), at least at this stage of his activity; but they describe the disciples' mission as being modeled on that of Jesus: Mt. 10, 1 (concerning the disciples) echoes 9, 35 (concerning Jesus).

4. See Jean-Paul Audet, *The Gospel Project,* pp. 47-48, 70-72.

5. Without ascribing to them any more certitude than does their author himself, we here adopt the conclusions of J. Dupont in *Les Béatitudes,* Vol. I, pp. 298-342. The only point which troubles us is the title given to this chapter: "Les malédictions" (p. 299). Neither the Hebrew *hoï* nor the Greek *ouai* nor the Latin *vae* is really a malediction calling down divine vengeance. In Hebrew, it is an interjection in the envoi of a lament, often of a funeral lament. On the other hand, if we reject *malédiction,* no French word is satisfactory. [The same holds true for the word *curse* used here by *The*

Jerusalem Bible.—Tr.]

6. J. Dupont, *Les Béatitudes*, Vol. I, pp. 272-289.
7. "We have, therefore, in the Sermon on the Mount, a composition of originally isolated sayings of Jesus. Sometimes, although by no means always, they consist of a single sentence. Each one of these sayings of Jesus, as we must envisage them, is the summary of something like a sermon by Jesus, or the essence of a piece of his teaching, that could have taken the form of question and answer and have lasted for a whole day, or it may have been the result of a dispute with his opponents. These isolated sayings were first gathered together in the form of an Aramaic Sermon on the Plain, out of which the Greek Sermon on the Plain in Luke and the Greek Sermon on the Mount in Matthew have in turn developed." J. Jeremias, *The Sermon on the Mount*, trans. by Norman Perrin (Philadelphia: Fortress Press, 1963), p. 17.
8. J. Jeremias, *op. cit.*, pp. 19-23.
9. Among recent commentators on the Sermon on the Mount, one of the best informed and most balanced is W. D. Davies, *The Setting of the Sermon on the Mount* (New York: Cambridge University Press, 1964). He believes that Matthew's synthesis might represent, at least in part, "the Christian answer" to Judaism as then defined by the rabbis who grouped together at Jamnia when the capture of Jerusalem by Titus' army in the year 70 could seem a deathblow to Judaism. "It was the desire and necessity to present a formulation of the way of the New Israel at a time when the rabbis were engaged in a parallel task for the Old Israel that provided the outside stimulus for the Evangelist to shape the S[ermon on the] M[ount]" (p. 315). This, the author specifies, is only a hypothesis. But it may explain the importance of the references to Jewish tradition in the Sermon as well as its proclamatory tone.
10. In *Jesus Christ and Mythology* Bultmann specifies that this name is a label but that it certainly has a meaning. Tradition, he says, calls Jesus the author of these thoughts, and he may very well be; but even if he were not, that would in no way change what has been handed down to us. Accordingly, Bultmann feels that he can describe the Sermon on the Mount as Jesus' teaching and speak of Jesus as its author. Such a view proves at least that the horizon of this teaching is Jesus' message, and not the life of the Christian in the Church.
11. J. Dupont, in *Les Béatitudes*, Vol. II, pp. 40-49, shows that around Is. 61, 1-3 there is evoked a constellation of analogous texts which always link the poor, the hungry and the afflicted. The first three beatitudes in Luke cannot be dissociated, nor can they be interpreted except together: the Good News is for all the wretched, whatever their problem.
12. A. George, "La 'forme' des béatitudes jusqu'à Jésus," in *Mélanges bibliques rédigés en l'honneur d'André Robert* (Paris: Gabalda, 1957), pp. 398-403.
13. M. Dibelius, *Die Formgeschichte des Evangeliums,* ed. by Bornkamm (Tübingen, 1959), p. 247. W. D. Davies, in *The Setting of the Sermon on the Mount*, pp. 369 and 382, surely has grounds to contest Dibelius' principle of classification, which is too exclusively formal. The beatitudes are a proclamation.
14. "You must not molest the stranger . . . for you lived as strangers in the land of Egypt" (Exod. 22, 20); "If [a poor man] cries to me, I will listen, for I am

full of pity" (Exod. 22, 26; cf. 3, 7); "Your scales and weights must be just . . .
I am Yahweh who brought you out of the land of Egypt" (Lev. 19, 36); "Be
consecrated to me, because I, Yahweh, am holy" (Lev. 20, 26).

15. The beatitudes in question, of course, are the three concerning the poor, the
hungry and the afflicted. The one about the persecuted belongs to another
category. It supposes the absence of Jesus and individual responsibility with
regard to the Gospel; consequently, it fits in later. See J. Dupont, *Les Béatitudes,* Vol. II, pp. 281-378.

16. It has been asked whether the beatitude concerning the meek could not be a
doubling of that concerning the poor. As a matter of fact, it repeats Ps.
37, 11, where the Hebrew text reads "poor" (*anawîm*). Rather than a doubling in the strict sense, due to flagging attention, it seems to be an explanation willed by the evangelist in order to illuminate the beatitude concerning
the poor and to complete in another way the addition "in spirit." See J.
Dupont, *Les Béatitudes,* Vol. I, pp. 251-257.

8
The New Law

Between the beatitudes and the commandments in the Sermon, then, there is a close link; Matthew highlights it by drawing up his list of beatitudes, but it also exists in Luke: those who experience the gift of God cannot let it lie fallow, those who have tasted his mercy cannot keep their hearts closed (Lk. 6, 36). The evangelical promise (which, more than a promise, is an invitation to enter) dictates—as a consequence and not a condition— an evangelical style, a law.

Matthew has heavily underlined this aspect of Jesus' teaching. Just as, in the infancy of Jesus, he describes the birth of a new Moses, so, on the hillside in Galilee, he presents the legislator of a new Sinai.[1] But he remains in control of his techniques and, with a sure hand, delimits the parallel he has established: "The strictly Mosaic traits in the figure of the Matthaean Christ . . . have been taken up into a deeper and higher context. He is not Moses come as Messiah, if we may so put it, so much as Messiah, Son of Man, Emmanuel, who has absorbed the Mosaic function. The Sermon on the Mount is therefore ambiguous: suggestive of the Law of a New Moses, it is also the authoritative word of the Lord, the Messiah; it is the Messianic Torah." [2]

Whether Mosaic or Messianic, it is clear at any rate that the Sermon in Matthew constitutes a careful synthesis and a literary composition, and supposes a certain distance from Jesus' preaching. The distance, however, may not be great, and a little attention may suffice to rediscover not only Jesus' words but the situation which gave rise to them and the meaning which they had in his life.

One of the most conspicuous devices in Matthew's version of

the Sermon is the repetition of the pattern "You have learned
how it was said . . . but I say this to you." It appears six times in
the discourse:

—You have learned how it was said to our ancestors: *You must
not kill . . .*
But I say this to you: anyone who is angry with his brother will
answer for it before the court (5, 21s).

—You have learned how it was said: *You must not commit adultery.*
But I say this to you: if a man looks at a woman lustfully, he
has already committed adultery with her in his heart (5, 27s).

—It has also been said: *Anyone who divorces his wife . . .*
But I say this to you: everyone who divorces his wife . . . makes
her an adulteress (5, 31s).

—You have learned how it was said to our ancestors: *You must
not break your oath . . .*
But I say this to you: do not swear at all (5, 33s).

—You have learned how it was said: *Eye for eye and tooth for
tooth.*
But I say this to you: offer the wicked man no resistance
(5, 38s).

—You have learned how it was said: *You must love your neighbor and hate your enemy.*
But I say this to you: love your enemies (5, 43s).

If we allowed ourselves simply to be carried along by the current of the discourse, we might easily take it for a replica of the
decalogue and think of it as a single outpouring. But we would
still have to explain the absence of the commandments concerning
theft, falsehood and the honor due to parents. What is more, two
of these pronouncements—the one about repudiation and the one
about love of neighbor—happen to have very close counterparts:
Mt. 5, 31s reappears in the same gospel (Mt. 19, 1-9 = Mk. 10, 1-

12); and Mt. 5, 43s is found, in a slightly different form, in Lk. 6, 27s. We must, therefore, admit that the sequence was constructed afterwards from isolated sayings. Who could conceive of Mark or Luke shattering such a beautiful ensemble? Perhaps it is in their gospels that we may hear these statements in their original setting.

Indeed, Mark and Luke seem to supply not only the isolated sayings but the situations from which they sprang. This is obvious in the case of the dictum on repudiation at least. In Mark, this verdict concludes a discussion begun by the Pharisees, who wished to test Jesus. And he is the one who counters their question with "What did Moses command you?" (Mk. 10, 3) and waits for their reply before stating his conclusion. In the parallel text in Matthew, the episode reads rather differently. There is a formal discussion, with assumptions and rebuttals; and in it we find the same contrast as in the Sermon: "Moses commanded . . . now I say to you . . ."—but this time on the lips of the outraged questioners (Mt. 19, 7.9). It is therefore probable that we may more than once trace this pattern back to some debate between Jesus and the scribes, those specialists in the Law. Again we find the same pattern and the same situation in the episode of the adulteress: "Moses has ordered us in the Law to condemn women like this to death by stoning. What have you to say?" (Jn. 8, 5).

We can surmise a fairly similar situation behind the commandment to love one's enemies. Here, the parallel text appears in Luke, and it is fairly different: the first part ("You have learned how it was said . . .") is missing, but the second contains a sort of equivalent: "But I say this to you who are listening . . ." (Lk. 6, 27). It may well be that these "listeners" are people who came to the synagogue to hear scripture readings, as in the episode at Nazareth (Lk. 4, 16-21).[3] The question "Who is my neighbor?" (Lk. 10, 29) certainly exercised the conscience of many Jews, and explicating the commandment "Love your neighbor" necessarily gave rise to controversies and interpretations. It is impossible to determine whether Jesus' precept "Love your enemies" (Lk. 6, 27.35) was first uttered in the peaceful liturgical atmosphere of a synagogue service or in the heat of a public dispute; but one thing is sure: it meant taking a position on a burning issue.[4]

But, although it is helpful to reinsert the teachings of the Sermon into a concrete setting and see them take rise in the pulsing world of Israel at that time, we would be mutilating them and disfiguring the Sermon if we reduced it to a summa of academic positions. Jesus is not a commentator on the Law, and the Sermon is not the synthesis of his solutions in Judaism's perennial debate over its scriptures and the meaning to be attributed to them. When situating Jesus on the hillside facing Moses and Sinai, Matthew puts him in the place he himself assumed throughout his life, and in the attitude which was his and which he alone could assume. Jesus lives permanently on the horizon of the scriptures: in everything—whether in his demeanor and his mission, or in defining man, his destiny, his relation to God, his duties and responsibilities—Jesus instinctively and constantly refers to the Bible of Israel, and especially to the books of the Law.

But his way of doing so is unique: at one and the same time totally faithful, pursuing the most rigorous logic all the way— "What God has united, man must not divide," and supremely free toward the letter of the Law, a letter shaped by circumstances—"because you were so unteachable." This certitude of penetrating to the very heart of the Law and of being able to say more and say it better bursts forth in the unthinkable and perfectly natural declaration "But I say this to you. . . ." Only a new Moses can speak like that, only an authority capable of matching the great founder. But this new Moses is not a replica of the first; nor does he bring a second Law, a more perfect model than the first. There is in Jesus, with regard to the Law, a complex mixture, consisting of immediate adherence to its authority, attentive understanding and absolute confidence in its value, but also of a certain distance and freedom—not the freedom of enfranchisement or emancipation, not a freedom achieved through force or based on principles, but the natural freedom of him who takes the Law with utter seriousness yet also knows what it cannot give. This freedom asserts itself in the expression "But I say this to you. . . ." Beyond Moses, Jesus does not establish a new Law, a superior system. He neither abolishes nor replaces; but he sets himself up, he goes to the very core and expands without limits. Instead of standing outside the Law, he relates his life and his message to it; but he himself is the last word of the Law, and his teaching is what gives the Law its ultimate consistency.

In a sense, Jesus goes further than the Law. He pushes its logic to the very end: "If a man looks at a woman lustfully, he has already committed adultery with her in his heart" and "Anyone who is angry with his brother will answer for it before the court." Yet Jesus is not driven by perfectionism, by the fear of never doing enough; his exigency comes from elsewhere. To be sure, he does not shrink from commanding and putting all his authority behind his words: "Leave your offering there . . . make peace with your adversary . . . throw away your eye . . . cut off your hand . . . offer the other cheek as well . . . give up your cloak . . . do not resist . . . love your enemies and pray for those who persecute you. . . ." This is definitely law, a law which goes very far. He himself, in fact, lays down as an essential principle the obligation of going further than the pagans. They can be gracious to one another (Mt. 5, 47); they pray—they even pray with persistence, "using many words" (6, 7). The question is: "What are you doing beyond that?" (cf. 5, 47). Throughout the Sermon there seems to be a continuous thread that characterizes the attitude of a disciple toward current behavior patterns, those of the Law, those of pagans,[5] and those of hypocrites. The relation is not the same, but there is always a comparison. One must go beyond the letter of the Law, do more than the pagans (Mt. 5, 47) and not do like the hypocrites (Mt. 6, 2.5.16). Jesus knows that situations differ, and he does not confuse them; but he always proceeds by contrast, proposing another mode of behavior. And one can understand how these echoes from the Sermon keep alive in many Christians the question which almost always remains unanswered: "What should we do not to be like the rest?"

Even allowing for images which no hearer took literally, it is quite true that the line of conduct Jesus proposes is unusual—giving up one's cloak, offering the other cheek when struck, tearing out one's eye and amputating one's hand. Obviously, his intention is to oblige one to make decisive choices and perform conspicuous deeds. The Sermon contains an undeniable radicalism which resists all attempts at watering it down. Several theories have been propounded to explain it: the logic rooted in the Jewish faith, with its uncompromising fidelity to God's will; a determination to bring "his hearers to the consciousness that they cannot, in their own strength, fulfill the demands of God," and, thus, to prepare them for grace; or the shadow of imminent catastrophe and the judgment of God.[6]

None of these solutions is satisfactory: the climate of the Sermon is neither the intransigence of a legal morality nor the ulterior motive behind impossible demands nor the panic of imminent judgment. To understand its radicalism, we must remember that it follows the beatitudes and the experience lived by the disciples. If Jesus demands so much, it is because "His teaching on discipleship is directed to men for whom the power of Satan has already been destroyed by the Good News, to men who already stand in the kingdom of God and radiate its nature. It is spoken to men who have already received forgiveness, who have found the pearl of great price, who have been invited to the wedding, who through their faith in Jesus belong to the new creation, to the new world of God." [7] All the same, this remarkably lucid explanation does not solve our problem entirely. It clearly shows, starting with the disciples, that the most radical demands of the Sermon have a meaning for anyone who follows in Jesus' footsteps; but it does not show quite so well what meaning those demands had for Jesus himself. At the risk of being rash, we think it possible to attempt at least a few steps in this direction.

The requirements of the Sermon are absolute and, in actual fact, limitless. Anyone who makes a rule of giving an hour of his time to those who request thirty minutes, and of depriving himself of necessities for those who beg from his superfluity, soon discovers that he no longer belongs to himself and is being devoured. But he chooses this, not in the name of some law or intangible prescript, but because he is inhabited by an exigency and would negate himself if he renounced it. Such is the absolute in the Sermon: not rigor and intransigence, not some observance to be maintained at any price, but a call which beckons ever further and becomes more and more identified with one's inmost personality. Eventually, the most imperious exigency is that of freedom.[8]

This blend of the most radical exigency and of total freedom is perceptible in the Sermon if we pay attention at all; but it can also be pinpointed and analyzed, since it appears very distinctly in the wording itself. One of the salient features of this wording is the series of formulas with *you* plural and formulas with *you* singular *(thou)*:

—*You* have heard that it was said to the men of old, Thou shalt not kill . . .
But I tell *you* that *any* man who is angry with his brother must answer for it before the court of justice . . .
If THOU art bringing THY gift, then, before the altar, and rememberest there that THY brother has some ground of complaint against THEE, leave THY gift lying there before the altar, and go home; be reconciled with THY brother first, and then come back to offer THY gift (Mt. 5, 21-24—Knox translation).

—*You* have heard that it was said, Thou shalt not commit adultery.
But I tell *you* that *he* who casts his eyes on a woman so as to lust after her has already committed adultery with her in his heart.
If THY right eye is the occasion of THY falling into sin, pluck it out and cast it away from THEE . . .
And if THY right hand is an occasion of falling, cut it off and cast it away from THEE; better to lose one of THY limbs than to have THY whole body cast into hell (5, 27-30—Knox).

—*You* have heard that it was said, An eye for an eye and a tooth for a tooth.
But I tell *you* that *you* should not offer resistance to injury;
if a man strikes THEE on THY right cheek, turn the other cheek also towards him;
if he is ready to go to law with THEE over THY coat, let him have it and THY cloak with it (5, 38-40—Knox).

—*You* have heard that it was said, Thou shalt love thy neighbor and hate thy enemy.
But I tell *you*, Love *your* enemies,
do good to those who hate *you*,
pray for those who persecute and insult *you*,
that so *you* may be true sons of *your* Father in heaven (5, 43-45

—Knox).

—Be sure *you* do not perform *your* acts of piety before men . . . if *you* do that, you have no title to a reward from *your* Father who is in heaven.
Thus, when THOU givest alms, do not sound a trumpet before THEE . . .
But when THOU givest alms, THOU shalt not so much as let THY left hand know what THY right hand is doing (6, 1-3—Knox).

—And when *you* pray, *you* are not to be like hypocrites . . .
But when THOU art praying, go into THY inner room and shut the door upon THYSELF (6, 5-6—Knox).

—Again, when *you* fast, do not show it by gloomy looks . . .
But do THOU, at THY times of fasting, anoint THY head and wash THY face . . . (6, 16-17—Knox).

We have here two slightly different sequences. The first one groups four assertions introduced by the contrast "You have heard that it was said . . . but I tell you." These assertions comprise three moments: the quoting of the Old Law with *thou*, in conformity with the letter of the biblical text and the style of decalogues; the formulation of Jesus' commandment with *you;* and a prescript with *thou*. The second sequence consists of three negative commandments with *you*, followed by three positive indications with *thou*. At first glance, perhaps, there may not be anything striking about this succession of *you*'s and *thou*'s. Indeed, a reader of the Bible is accustomed, from the laws of Israel or the discourses in Deuteronomy, to this alternation of *you*'s and *thou*'s, whose significance, while perhaps not negligible, is not immediately evident.[9] But here the alternance seems to be explained by the very movement of the thought. The principles with *you* have the force of general and absolute law; they possess the same character of universality as the principles which they correct or transcend—the fundamental articles of the Law of Israel.[10] Thus, Jesus' teaching comprises a certain number of articles which have binding power and which apply absolutely; they are addressed to "any man" (Mt. 5, 22.28) and admit of no exception. Unless one adopts them as rules of conduct, one cannot be a disciple and have God for a Father. We are now in the realm of faith: faith prescribes or forbids, it binds in all places and under all circumstances.

But these principles remain general and must be applied in concrete situations, which are always diverse. This is where the precepts with *thou* enter: they constitute examples, typical cases. Earlier, Israel's lawmakers distinguished between the fundamental "ten words," the decalogue, and the successive codes elaborated down through the centuries and in the course of history, in order to adapt the essential principles of the Law to the new conditions created by social, political and cultural evolution. In the Old Testament, this adaptation was the concern of the community and took the form of articles of law, provided with sanctions and incorporated in juridical collections and codes—the code of the covenant, the Deuteronomic code, the priestly code. In the Gospel, this adaptation is the responsibility of each disciple, of each conscience. No code can foresee every possible situation; and, what is more, no code can foresee concrete applications of the principles Jesus formulated: using no violence, not desiring a woman, offering no resistance to the wicked, loving one's enemies. This is up to the individual and his own conscience. It is to this conscience that the precepts with *thou* are addressed. They are still imperatives, not mere counsels; they carry the Master's authority and bind all who want to follow him. But they do not impose this or that particular action: they offer examples and leave the individual to find the equivalent in his own life. Of necessity, these examples possess singular value which depends on circumstances. We do not have an opportunity to bring offerings to the altar every day; but, every day and under many forms, we must banish everything that alienates us from our brothers. We are not called upon to accompany a churl down the road every day; but, every day, we must try to see the other person's point of view and prefer it to our own.

The transition from *you* to *thou* in the Sermon is equivalent to the transition from the Law to Wisdom in the experience of Israel. The Sermon is a law and, together with law, shares a universal, unconditional character, a tone of absolute authority; but,

90 THE CONSCIOUSNESS OF JESUS

together with wisdom, it shares the aspect of an experience that is
lived and communicated, a personal relationship between teacher
and disciple, an invitation to enter into a life style and reproduce
it, a need to justify precepts by means of motives and objectives
to be attained.[11] This combination of law and wisdom in the Sermon brings out in Jesus an absolutely original personality. By
adopting the tone of legislation, by evoking the figure of Moses
and imposing his own authority and the weight of his own self,
Jesus presents himself at least as God's personal representative,
the witness of his plan. But by appealing to his own experience
and inviting us to share it, by replacing words sprung from the
lightning flashes over Sinai with words born of his daily encounters and nurtured by the most ordinary happenings and most
common concerns, Jesus makes his law arise from his human
consciousness, from his own life, a life lived in the midst of men,
of their problems and feuds and ambitions and fears, a life indwelt by the gaze of his Father and the love of his brothers.

The Sermon's radicalism, then, does not result from the imminence of some extraordinary event which would overthrow the
regular norms. And yet it is true that the Sermon hangs on an
event—the coming of the kingdom. That is the basis for the beatitudes, the reason for sacrificing everything, be it an eye or a hand,
so as not to be left outside (Mt. 5, 29-30); that is what turns the
most fabulous treasures to ashes (6, 19-21) and must take priority
over all interests (6, 33). But the paradox is that this imminent
and decisive event cannot be dated and is not connected with any
contemporary occurrence—so much so that the Sermon seems to
escape contingency altogether and remains as literally true today
as in the time of Jesus. What is amazing is the fact that it supposes a stupendous event, as vast as the universe, a drastic upheaval in living, and yet that it has so completely eliminated all
apocalyptic images and all overtones of catastrophe, and that it
unfolds against the familiar horizons of daily life, amid the low-
liest household concerns, in the marketplace, the neighborhood
and attitudes toward others. It is the humdrum life of a village or
a block, the life of every day, the life of all time. Where, in this
dreary round of monotonous obligations and unchanging humanity, could a fulgurous event possibly take place? The day after a
most cruel loss or horrendous calamity, we must start eating and

drinking again. Part of the Sermon's impact consists in always bringing us back to these elementary truths.

Between the announcement of the supreme event, the coming of God's kingdom, and the description of evangelical life, that of a disciple of Jesus and a child of the Father, there seems to yawn an unbridgeable gap, so that we must choose one or the other of these two perspectives. Some think that the Sermon itself has not chosen, and they take this incoherence as a sign of its composite origin, consisting of various layers from diverse milieus and irreconcilable traditions. This contrast between Jesus' eschatological preaching and his ethical preaching remains one of the fundamental questions of contemporary exegesis,[12] and each author, according to his tendency, strives to answer it. With Heinz Schürmann, we believe that the solution lies in the person and in the coming of Jesus. Because Jesus is God's Son and knows it, he can say what the Father expects from man, his child; because Jesus has come into the world to bring the reality of this paternal presence and the radical transformation of man, he announces the coming of the kingdom as the supreme and decisive event in human history.[13]

Jesus announces the coming of the kingdom, and he reveals the Father. These two incontrovertible facts seem simple. In reality, they are complex and raise several problems. First of all, questions of fact: although the announcement of the kingdom is immediately associated with the start of Jesus' preaching in Galilee (Mk. 1, 14), it is impossible to say when and how he began speaking about the Father. According to Luke (2, 49), the twelve-year-old Jesus already uses the word *Father* to tell his parents why he let them leave Jerusalem without him. And we saw above that, in one way or another, this filial consciousness is indispensable so that Jesus may in truth be the Son of God.[14] But the word *Father* does not appear in Jesus' preaching before the Sermon on the Mount (Mt. 5, 16; Lk. 6, 36) and, when we consider the element of literary composition in the Sermon, this fact can give us pause to think. Thinking becomes all the more necessary when we notice that perhaps Jesus did not pronounce the name *Father* as frequently as our recollections of the gospels would lead us to believe. God is called Father one hundred and eighteen times in John, forty-five times in Matthew, seventeen times in Luke, and

only four times in Mark.[15] Since all these instances, except the
two in the Johannine prologue (Jn. 1, 14.18), are drawn from
Jesus' own words, since Mark's gospel contains proportionately
fewer quotations from Jesus than the three others do, and John's
contains noticeably more, we cannot take these figures at face
value; nevertheless, they are sufficiently telling and lead us to
conclude that Matthew and John had a tendency to generalize
this expression of Christ's. But they did not create it; and here
Mark's testimony is crucial, since the four texts in his gospel correspond to four typical uses of the word *Father* and to four decisive statements by Jesus. In Mk. 11, 25, Jesus, speaking to his
disciples, calls God "your Father": "And when you stand in
prayer, forgive whatever you have against anybody, so that your
Father in heaven may forgive your failings too." [16] This is exactly
the Sermon, on a capital point. In Mk. 8, 38, Jesus conjures up
"the Son of Man" coming "in the glory of his Father" on the last
day: "But as for that day or hour, nobody knows it, neither the
angels of heaven, nor the Son; no one but the Father" (Mk.
13, 32). This way of speaking about the Son in the third person,
as of a unique figure with no possible *vis-à-vis* except the Father,
this way of portraying them as fulfilling two different roles in one
common enterprise, is typically Johannine language; but it is also
the language of Jesus' thanksgiving in Matthew and Luke: "No
one knows the Son except the Father, just as no one knows the
Father except the Son and those to whom the Son chooses to
reveal him" (Mt. 11, 27 = Lk. 10, 21). Mark is already familiar
with this language, and that is a good sign of authenticity. No less
precious is the fourth statement: "Abba (Father)! Everything is
possible for you. Take this cup away from me" (Mk. 14, 36). This
is the prayer of the Son in Gethsemane. The most instinctive and
most personal of prayers, it is addressed to the Father.

    Therefore, even if the repetition of *Father* in the Sermon
results largely from a procedural device, it is not artificial but
harks back to the language of Jesus himself. Moreover, the name
does not appear haphazardly, like a meaningless term triggered
by some unconscious mechanism.[17] To limit ourselves to the Sermon in Matthew, we find the examples instructive:

—Your light must shine in the sight of men, so that, seeing your good works, they may give the praise to your Father in heaven (5, 16).

—Love your enemies. . . . In this way you will be the sons of your Father in heaven, for he causes his sun to rise on bad men as well as good, and his rain to fall on honest and dishonest men alike (5, 45).

—You must therefore be perfect just as your heavenly Father is perfect (5, 48).

—But when you give alms, your left hand must not know what your right is doing; your almsgiving must be secret, and your Father who sees all that is done in secret will reward you (6, 3-4).

—But when you pray, go to your private room and, when you have shut your door, pray to your Father who is in that secret place, and your Father who sees all that is done in secret will reward you (6, 6).

—In your prayers do not babble as the pagans do, for they think that by using many words they will make themselves heard. Do not be like them; your Father knows what you need before you ask him (6, 7-8).

—Our Father in heaven, may your name be held holy (6, 9).

—If you forgive others their failings, your heavenly Father will forgive you yours; but if you do not forgive others, your Father will not forgive your failings either (6, 14-15).

—When you fast, put oil on your head and wash your face, so that no one will know you are fasting except your Father who sees all that is done in secret; and your Father who sees all that is done in secret will reward you (6, 17-18).

—Look at the birds in the sky. They do not sow or reap or gather into barns; yet your heavenly Father feeds them (6, 26).

—It is the pagans who set their hearts on all these things. Your heavenly Father knows you need them all (6, 32).

—If you, then, who are evil, know how to give your children what is good, how much more will your Father in heaven give good things to those who ask him (7, 11).

—It is not those who say to me, "Lord, Lord," who will enter the kingdom of heaven, but the person who does the will of my Father in heaven (7, 21).

Let us notice the words which characterize the Father and his activity: the Father gives (6, 4.6.18; 7, 11) and forgives (6, 14.15), he sends rain, sunshine, food and everything man and animals need (5, 45; 6, 8.32), he knows their wants and attends to them even before they are felt (6, 8.32), he sees all that is done in secret and rewards generosity (6, 4.6.18), he waits for his will to be done (7, 21) and for his name to be held holy (6, 9) and praised among men (5, 16). These traits delineate a face—one which rather differs from the notion of "father" commonly held today. On many levels, the image of fatherhood strikes the modern mind as ambiguous and debatable: too many unsuccessful efforts leave dubious memories of the father, and even his successful ones are never definitive. Psychological analysis has emphasized the key role the father plays in the evolution of infantile consciousness but has also pointed out the danger of impasses and deviations, with the result that "many of our contemporaries would like to see the world of fatherhood transformed into a world of brotherhood." [18]

Without attempting to sort out fruitful intuitions and morbid resentment from these reservations and downright condemnations of fatherhood, we can at least see that the evangelical image of the Father is quite different from what modern analysts are investigating. Not that it represents an ideal image, however, so lofty and so pure that it could not be questioned. For Jesus, the heavenly Father is "perfect" (5, 48), not evil like man (7, 11). But this perfection is not the sum total of all virtues; it consists in extending the same welcome to the just and the unjust, to those who stay close and those who are strangers, to friends and enemies. Jesus does not paint the portrait of some captivating father endowed with every charm, free from any weakness and beyond all criticism. He does much more: he transposes the concept of "father," so to speak, tearing it away from the past to project it into the future and, in the process, liberating man from a view of fatherhood which tended to identify with inexorable destiny and arbitrary omnipotence.[19] To be sure, the Father in the Sermon on the Mount is, in Old Testament language, the creator of heaven and earth, the God of origins, he who makes the sun shine and the rain fall, who feeds the birds of the air and clothes the flowers of the fields. But Jesus makes very special use of that self-evident fact. From out of this creative omnipotence, he stresses God's extraordinary attentiveness, his interest in everything that lives—a solicitude quite unlike that of a landowner surveying his domains or of a businessman checking the implementation of his program. This God, who is all eyes and ears, bends over his work to see what it will produce, what will come out of it. Though it cannot do anything without him, he places all his hope in it. Above all else, he is interested in man's actions. They possess a worth which man himself cannot imagine, and that is what gives them their inestimable significance. The noblest deeds, generosity, detachment and the quest for God, reach their full value only when man stops trying to evaluate them and offers them to a better appraiser than he.

This God has plans and waits for them to be executed. But his plans are not stipulations to carry out; they are works to build, and the examples Jesus mentions are designed to stimulate our imagination: "Give, forgive, love. How? That is up to you. Look at your neighbor, your enemies or an outsider, and do something." This is what God awaits and what he recompenses, not by a sumptuous equivalent, but by his gaze, helping us discover the incomparable worth of our deeds and the joy he takes in them. God's gaze upon his children, as the Sermon describes it, is akin to that with which he envelops Jesus at his baptism: "You are my Son, the Beloved; my favor rests on you" (Mk. 1, 11). The father portrayed in the Sermon is not the figure who so often provokes rebellion today, the representative of destiny, of things as they are, of the world we have not chosen, of the past which persists and weighs heavy. If he produces children, it is not that he may prolong himself but that they may exist and be themselves. This Father is wholly taken up with what they are going to do, with the state in which he will find them again and receive them, with the import of their lives and the secret of their deeds. Only he can understand and appreciate them; only he can gather up all this trouble which no one suspects and fathom the mystery of their heart.[20] This Father creates in order to have free wills before him, in order to encounter hearts, to make sons exist.

This transformation is not merely a personal episode in the history of an individual conscience; it is an event properly so called in the history of the world, for it is real only if it touches the life of others, too. For Jesus, discovering that God is our Father and wanting to make our neighbor a brother are two inseparable things. The paternal gaze resting upon me, the attention which gives meaning to my life, the divine gesture beckoning and creating me is intended to rouse everyone around me. I cannot keep it for myself alone, I cannot even recognize it if I reserve it for a limited group, I cannot adhere to it without also changing my view of men: "Give, and there will be gifts for you . . . forgive as God forgives you . . . love as God treats you . . . be merciful in order to be sons of the Most High." The golden rule itself—that summary of the entire Old Testament: "Always treat others as you would like them to treat you" (Mt. 7, 12)—takes on its full meaning only within the Sermon, which reveals the love of God the Father.[21] Short of that, it could be just a selfish scheme or a lovely Utopia.

The proof that the Sermon is really directed toward an event, toward a transformation of this world manifested in positive acts, toward an event which is real and possible today, an event which nevertheless remains abeyant and uncompleted until the end of history when the whole of creation will be new—the proof, we repeat, is the place which forgiveness of one's enemies occupies therein. This is the decisive criterion, the sign which distinguishes God's children. But this commandment has no meaning except in a real world where evil is active and violence holds sway. It does not aspire to change such a universe into an idyllic haven where gentleness would disarm force; rather, it demands something more realistic and more mysterious: treating our enemy like a brother even though he remains an enemy and we suffer his attacks, and even though we should perhaps resist him. Forgiving means accepting our enemy as he is and desiring that, such as he is, he should exist. It means accepting the fact that he does the good we judge him incapable of and would rather not acknowledge in him. It means accepting the fact that the secret of his life escapes us and waiting for God to give us access to it. It is an act of faith identical with the one through which we place the secret of our own existence in God's hands. Now, such an act has meaning only if I can truly hope to reach my brother, and this hope supposes the decisive event which will put an end to evil. That event is already here from the moment I can forgive; it is a reality in Jesus, who proposes it and lives it; it remains a promise and is accessible only in faith and hope.

To create a freedom is necessarily to call it and demand an answer from it. That is why the Sermon is the announcement of an event, an invitation to live an experience; that is why it is both an eschatological proclamation announcing the new world of the kingdom, and an "ontological" revelation describing God's behavior. For this revelation is not a datum of mere experience: the God who makes his sun shine on good men and bad alike also seems to let them perish indifferently in the same catastrophe. Neither is it the fruit of more profound reflection and greater insight, or the object of a mysterious illumination reserved to privileged beings. We do not discover that this God is a Father until the instant we hear his call and agree to surrender to him, to believe in his solicitude and live under his eyes, and, at the same time, to change our outlook and our behavior toward others. But no one can effect this transformation within himself, even though it cannot occur unless he accepts it and yields to it. And because it involves the whole man and everything he does, because it operates at all levels of existence, because it directly concerns the whole of humanity and because it gives life a radically new meaning, this transformation already creates a new world and possesses an eschatological reality. To call God "Father," in the sense in which Jesus bids us do so, is not to give him a title designating his action or symbolizing his face; it is to hear a call and surrender to it; it is to renounce being our own judges and evaluating our own conduct, to renounce what St. Paul terms justification through works, so that we may cleave to God in faith.[22]

Perhaps then we understand how the Sermon can make un-limited demands without ever lapsing into intransigence or perfectionism, and how it can at one and the same time transcend the norms of pagans and just men and invoke the most human and spontaneous reflexes. It demands everything, in demanding that we believe in God who can transform life and bring a new man to birth in the bosom of our universe. Jesus' warning to Nicodemus, "Unless a man is born from above, he cannot see the kingdom of God" (Jn. 3, 3), surely holds out a different experience from that of the Sermon, but it refers to the same reality and the same event. This reality has consistence, this event possesses verisimilitude only because of Jesus and his presence. Without him, the Sermon is a mere compendium, at once sublime and naïve, an impressive but unfinished and discouraging endeavor. But with him, the beatitudes are accomplished, the New Law is a feasible experience, and the figure of the Father becomes the secret of human existence.

Notes to Chapter 8

1. W. D. Davies, in *The Setting of the Sermon on the Mount,* pp. 25-108, points out the parallels purposely underlined by Matthew, but also shows that the evangelist operates with many nuances and is far removed from a simplistic Moses-New Moses scheme. The relation between Christians and Jesus is completely different from that between Moses and the Israelites. The relation between the Gospel and the Law is not that of a new economy to an outdated system.
2. W. D. Davies, *op. cit.,* p. 93.
3. O. J. F. Seitz, "Love your Enemies," in *New Testament Studies,* 16 (1969), pp. 39-54.
4. Matthew's text "You have learned how it was said: You must love your neighbor and hate your enemy" comes as a shock, since there is not a single text in the Bible which urges hatred of one's enemies. This addition may very likely echo the commentaries which could then be heard on the precept in Leviticus: "You must love your neighbor." *The Rule of Qumran* enjoins its followers to "love all the sons of light . . . and hate all the sons of darkness" (I, 9-10), to "curse all the men of the lot of Belial" (II, 4-5) and nurture "eternal hatred for the men of destruction" (IX, 21-22). This does not mean, however, that the Essenes of Qumran lived in an atmosphere of hatred, but that their thinking was dominated by a rigorous dualism, a strict division into good and evil. A few lines after the promise of "eternal hatred," we read: "I will return to no man evil recompense but for good will I pursue my fellow, for with God is judgment over all that lives and it is he that shall pay to a man his recompense" (X, 17-18). These translations are from A.R.C. Leaney, *op. cit.,* pp. 117, 124, 229 and 234. And *The Testaments of the Twelve Patriarchs,* which seems to represent a semi-Essene milieu, has succeeded in overcoming the imperative of hatred: "The good man has no darkness in his looks, for he has compassion upon all, even upon sinners when they plot evil against him" (The *Testament of Benjamin,* 4, 2-3). See D. Flusser, *Jesus,* pp. 78-83.
5. Here Luke writes "sinners" (6, 32-34). He means the people placed in this category: the tax collectors and the prostitutes, for example.
6. Cf. J. Jeremias, *The Sermon on the Mount,* pp. 1-12.
7. J. Jeremias, *op. cit.,* p. 32.
8. We cannot help recalling a passage from Péguy here: "It is the rigid moral systems that may contain niches for dust, for microbes, for mildewing. And it is the flexible ones, on the contrary, which require a heart that is perpetually renewed, a heart that is perpetually pure. . . . Just as it is the flexible methods, the flexible systems of logic which require a mind that is perpetually renewed, a mind that is perpetually pure. It is the flexible moral systems, and not the rigid ones, which exert the most implacably hard constraints, the only ones which are always present. . . . That is why the best of men is not he who acts according to apparent rules. It is he who stays in his place, works, suffers and remains silent." Charles Péguy, *Note sur M. Bergson et la philosophie bergsonienne* in *Oeuvres en Prose, 1909-1914* (Paris:

Bibliothèque de la Pléiade, 1957), pp. 1291-1292.

9. It is in Deuteronomy that the succession of *thou*'s and *you*'s appears most frequently. Exegetes do not agree on the meaning of it. According to N. Lohfink, *Das Hauptgebot, Eine Untersuchung literarischer Einleitungsfragen zu Dtn. 5-11* (Rome: Analecta Biblica, 1963), p. 247, it is an oratorical device meant to arouse attention and used in other works of this sort outside Israel. According to H. Cazelles, "Passages in the Singular Within Discourses in the Plural of Dt. 1-4," in *Catholic Biblical Quarterly,* 29 (1967), pp. 206-219, it is a vestige of different sources; on this view, the passages with *thou* would derive from historical evocation and would be anterior to Deuteronomy, while those with *you* would belong to the paraenetic language proper to Deuteronomy. In any case, it seems to us that the sequences in the Sermon on the Mount obey a rhythm which is much more interior and much closer to the content.

10. These are formulated with *thou*: they bind each and every Israelite, who is answerable for himself.

11. It is an ancient feature of Israelitic laws that justifications be appended to them. Whether historical in content or humanitarian in inspiration, they testify to the profound link between law and the memory of God's deeds and the experience of his "humanity," as well as to his love for man and his need to make himself understood by him. See B. Gemser, "Motive Clauses in Old Testament Law," in *Vetus Testamentum, Supplementum I,* Copenhagen Congress Volume (Leiden, 1953), pp. 63-66.

12. H. Schürmann, "Le problème fondamental posé à l'herméneutique de la prédication de Jésus. Eschatologie et théologie dans leur rapport mutuel," in *Le message de Jésus et l'interprétation moderne* (Paris: Cerf, 1969 [Cogitatio Fidei, 37]), pp. 115-149.

13. H. Schürmann, *art. cit.,* p. 146.

14. See Chapter 4.

15. The statistics are slightly different in Vincent Taylor, *The Person of Christ in New Testament Teaching* (New York: St. Martin's Press, 1958).

16. Verse 27 is missing in the best manuscripts and doubtlessly comes from a reminiscence of Mt. 6, 15: "But if you do not forgive others, your Father will not forgive your failings either."

17. When speaking about his Father to the disciples, Jesus generally calls him "your Father." J. Jeremias, *Abba, Studien zur neutestamentliche Theologie und Zeitgeschichte* (Göttingen, 1966), pp. 45-46.

18. A. De Waehlens, "La paternité et le complexe d'Oedipe en psychanalyse," in *l'Analyse du langage théologique: Le nom de Dieu* (Paris: Aubier, 1969), p. 247. The author continues: "To tell the truth, many of the proponents of this new order do not exactly realize what this radical mutation might entail, since they do not fully understand the basic and ultimate meaning of what they are contesting."

19. "Far from being easy, as it would be in a reversion to archaism, the act of addressing God as father is rare, difficult and audacious, because it is prophetic, directed toward culmination more than origin. It looks, not behind in the direction of a great ancestor, but ahead in the direction of a new intimacy patterned on the knowledge of sons." Paul Ricoeur, "La paternité: du fantasme au symbole," in *Le conflit des interprétations. Essais d'herméneutique* (Paris: Seuil, 1960), p. 480.

20. "With the phrase 'your Father who sees all that is done in secret,' the New Testament revelation reaches an absolute summit. It reunites human comprehension and divine judgment, confident proximity and the strictest inaccessibility." W. Marchel, *Dieu Père dans le Nouveau Testament* (Paris: Cerf, 1966 [Lire la Bible, 7]), p. 87.

21. See O. du Roy, *La réciprocité, Essai de morale fondamentale* (Paris: Epi), pp. 48-49.

22. In well-weighed and doubtlessly more precise terms, A. Vergote seems to us to express the exact signification of God "the Father" in the Gospel: "God's paternal name is not, properly speaking, a symbol. . . . Symbols spring from the intertwining of mind and things, from their indissociable presence. . . . When calling God 'Father,' in the strong sense of the word, man expresses a precise meaning, which no longer refers to a secondary one. That is because the term does not derive from signific thought, but from recognizant speech. In addressing themselves to God by this name, believers consent to the real act through which he takes up his fatherhood in their regard. Thus the name *Father* can only echo the name which God gives himself at the very moment when he effectuates and manifests his fatherhood. The historical inscription of this act in the signifiant *father* certainly implies the qualities which the paternal symbol can signify. But the act itself is an event which constitutes fatherhood in the truest sense. . . . The fatherhood of God was symbolic only in the period before the advent of Fatherhood." A. Vergote, "Le nom du Père et l'écart de la topographie symbolique," in *L'analyse du langage théologique: Le nom de Dieu* (Paris: Aubier, 1969), pp. 263-264.

9
The Profession of Faith
at Caesarea

The Sermon on the Mount—the substance of Jesus' teaching and the rule of life for his disciples—is a call to faith. When Jesus seeks out the sick and the sinful, he does so to stir up their faith (Mt. 8, 10; 9, 2.22.29; 15, 28; Mk. 5, 34; Lk. 7, 50); when he invites men to follow him, he appeals to their faith. The life which he opens up to those who meet and welcome him, he also proposes to anyone who is willing to hear him. To try living the Sermon, to cling to the beatitudes, to believe in the Father and, under his gaze, make oneself a brother to all—this is to follow Jesus and become his disciple, even if one cannot accompany him on the roads of Galilee. Through everything he says and does, Jesus elicits, awakens, animates and nourishes faith.

Is this faith addressed to God or to Jesus? The synoptics record only one instance when Jesus speaks of "these little ones who have faith in me" (Mt. 18, 6; the parallel text of Mk. 9, 42 says only "these little ones who have faith"). On the other hand, neither does he talk about believing in God. Most often, he speaks of those who believe or who have faith. If we attempt to specify the object of this faith, the one which seems to correspond most exactly to the texts as a whole would no doubt be the Good News. Indeed, "Believe the Good News" is the very program of Jesus' early preaching in Galilee (Mk. 1, 14). To believe the Good News is to believe in the event which Jesus has come to announce —the kingdom of God; it is to believe that God is in the process of performing a decisive act, that something unique is happening in the world—something of which Jesus is both witness and agent; it is to believe that this event can reach us and transform our life. God, Jesus, and the event itself are not identical: each has a particular form and role; but they are inseparable. As a result, we could, in most cases, round out the verb *believe* with any of the phrases *in God, in Jesus,* or *that such and such a thing is happening,* and the meaning would be the same. Nevertheless, the phrase which generally presents itself most spontaneously is *in Jesus.* John only spells out what the synoptics' regular mode of expression assumes: for them, to believe is, above all, to believe in Jesus. But to believe in Jesus is not to discover a personage who, by himself, would compel faith; on the contrary, it is to discover the unique bond which links him to God and the kingdom that is coming; it is to recognize in him God's envoy, the agent entrusted with his work, and the witness of this event.

Now, to recognize in Jesus this unique link with God and the coming of the kingdom, is to proclaim him the Messiah. The Messianic profession of faith is man's response to Jesus' proclamation of the Good News of the kingdom. Such is the Christian perspective—the one which, with various nuances, inspires all the evangelists and the writers of the New Testament. For them, "Jesus is the Christ" is an affirmation of faith, which proclaims that in Jesus God accomplishes his work and rescues men's existence by introducing them into his kingdom.

Determining how the title *Messiah* came to be an expression of faith among the disciples is another matter. For, to Jesus' contemporaries, the word itself could conjure up all sorts of images.[1] The Messiah always represents a central figure in Jewish expectation and plays an essential role in the founding of the kingdom of Israel; but, as it happens, this role is stamped with the quality of that expectation and can include every possible level, from the purest to the most ambiguous. As the personification of Israel's hope, the Messiah takes on the diverse faces of this hope. In Jesus, the Christians proclaimed that this hope had been fulfilled in a way no one could have imagined, by a Messiah who shared the very grandeur of God: "God has made this Jesus whom you crucified both Lord and Christ" (Acts 2, 36). In Jesus, the expectation of the Messiah becomes faith, adherence to Jesus Christ.[2] Here is the basic fact, the object of the Church's earliest belief and initial preaching.

The decisive moment for that faith was the resurrection. The gospels spring from that faith and were written to give testimony to it. They make no attempt to retrace the road which the disciples traveled in order to pass from Messianic hope, as they had cherished it before meeting their Master, to the faith of Easter, to the discovery of the risen Messiah. Still they are the account of this discovery, they recall the genesis of this faith, and they hint that this genesis was a fierce combat between a genuine faith being born and a persistent attachment to the hopes of their people and their own dreams. In this adventure, Peter's profession of faith marks a decisive moment, both for Peter and the Twelve, who proclaim the Messiah, and for Jesus also, who starts speaking about his passion and declaring that his disciples must follow him on the road he walks.

The turning point of Caesarea is very heavily underscored by the synoptics, especially Mark, who makes it a real hinge in the development of his account. This is the hour when the "Messianic secret" imposed by Jesus on the witnesses of his power begins to lift: it ceases to be necessary the moment he speaks openly of his passion.[3] Perhaps this turning point is more accentuated in the gospels than it was in actual fact. A historian has to delimit periods and characterize them, and he can hardly do so except by simplifying the facts. If, beneath the evangelists' composition and intentions, we look for reminiscences that are less fully worked-out, it seems that we can come up with two fairly solid facts. On the one hand, a literary datum: a series of statements and episodes extending from the first multiplication of the loaves to the profession of faith at Caesarea (Mk. 6, 31-8, 26; Mt. 14, 13-16, 2), and having as its theme the revelation of the person of Jesus amid opposition, and the grounding of the disciples in faith.[4] On the other hand, a historical recollection, perceptible in John but totally veiled in the synoptics: Jesus' vigorous repudiation of any attempt made to exploit his success with the crowds for purposes of political Messianism.[5] Though the texts are too allusive and incidental to warrant definite conclusions, the turning point of Caesarea fits naturally into the course of events Jesus initiated. Caesarea supposes an aloofness from the crowds of Galilee, a very sharp distinction between "the people" and "the Twelve" (Mk. 8, 27), a climate of incomprehension and antagonism,[6] a difficult hour for the disciples. This is precisely when, according to Jn. 6, 60, "many of his followers," finding his language intolerable, broke with him. There is a striking parallelism between the "profession of faith at Caesarea" according to the synoptics (Mt. 16, 13-16; Mk. 8, 27-29; Lk. 9, 18-20), and the "profession of faith at Capernaum" according to John (Jn. 6, 68-69). Both are professions of faith in the person of Jesus, uttered by Peter in the name of the Twelve, at a moment when their Master stands forsaken.

Though the profession of faith at Caesarea seems to fall into place smoothly in the development of Jesus' mission, it assumes its full importance only in the very deliberate and suggestive framework Mark provides for it. His composition is so powerful and so coherent that it commands attention on its own merits, with no need of historical verisimilitude and conventions. Granted that there is something artificial and schematic about it; still, it is too original and too expressive of Jesus' personality not to reflect his own experience.

Peter's words at Caesarea are not just an ordinary proclamation or outburst of faith. They are his reply to a question Jesus asks concerning his own identity: "Who am I?" Now, this is a startling question, not at all normal. We do not ask even the most unusual of people who they are but, rather, question them about their motives and the reason for their behavior. The most provocative prophets, like Elijah or Amos or Jeremiah, never had to answer the question "Who are you?" They had to explain why they were speaking and who had sent them, but their personal identity raised no problem. Neither should Jesus' identity have done so: anyone in Nazareth could say, "This is the carpenter, surely, the son of Mary, the brother of James and Joset and Jude and Simon" (Mk. 6, 3).

Knowing who Jesus is, however, is a crucial question for Mark. It constitutes almost a leitmotif in his account of the Galilean period. Sometimes it appears as the question posed by eyewitnesses to some stupefying deed: "Who can this be? Even the wind and the sea obey him" (Mk. 4, 41); and sometimes as the answer given in spite of themselves and in spite of Jesus, as it were, by the unclean spirits whom he drives out of their victims (Mk. 1, 24.34; 3, 11; 5, 7); or as the idea which haunts Herod after his crime: "It is John whose head I cut off; he has risen from the dead" (Mk. 6, 16). The fact is that Jesus' deeds strike us not only because they are extraordinary but especially, perhaps, because they are exclusively his. Not dictated or inspired by someone else, they come from him, from his words and his authority, so that we pass spontaneously from the question "What does this mean?" (1, 27) to the question "Who can this be?" (4, 41).

To this question Jesus offers no answer, and he imposes silence on those who know or think they know the answer, for what could "Jesus is the Son of God" mean on the lips of an unclean spirit? But Jesus himself, even though he never reveals his identity by saying openly who he is, has a singular way of referring to himself as a personage, familiar and yet mysterious, one despite his several roles: he is "the Physician" come to heal the sick and call sinners (2, 17); he is "the Bridegroom" surrounded by his attendants, who must never think of fasting while he is still with them (2, 19); he is "the Son of Man [who] is master even of the sabbath" (2, 28) and "has authority on earth to forgive sins" (2, 10). There is a remarkable unity in all these examples: Jesus is always justifying a deed which has given scandal. In these cases, as we have seen, he often invokes in his defense the spontaneous behavior of a man in danger of losing something precious, or even the profoundly human and at the same time unimaginable reflex of God, of the Father. There enters a new element here, one which more closely concerns the personality of Jesus and the role he is playing. It is more than a mere parable: he is not "like a physician" or "like a bridegroom," he *is* the Physician and the Bridegroom. He is playing a role, but that role belongs to him alone, and, in the language of the theater, he is appearing "as himself." He is not just entirely absorbed in his mission, like an inventor in his research, or totally identified with his persona, as a great actor can be. In playing his role and acting out his part, he causes his own nature to show forth. That is why he is not the ideal physician or the unparalleled bridegroom, but simply the Physician and the Bridegroom; and there is only one, come into the world to accomplish that act which man performs but once, just as there is only one source of living water, one single Father, one Shepherd.

This language is peculiar to Jesus. If we were dealing merely with titles to be attributed to him, we might wonder whether the mention of them is not the outgrowth of a Christian practice, as when the gospels call him Lord. But this way of identifying himself with a personage while still keeping at a distance, as if he were not that personage yet; this way of designating himself through a figure, as if it were going to be absorbed by his own face—this cannot be a later invention. Of course, this mode of expression will be imitated, more or less skillfully—and John's gospel affords the most beautiful example of this—but Jesus is the one who created it.[7] Nevertheless, it is obvious that the progression of the narrative in Mark follows a definite plan: this interplay between those who know Jesus' identity but must not reveal it, those who do not know and puzzle over it, and him who knows but discusses it only enigmatically—such exchanges around a central issue suppose a strong conceptual framework.[8] The summit of this architecture is the profession of faith at Caesarea.[9] There, Jesus himself asks the question: "Who do you say I am?" (8, 29).

The episode itself raises several literary problems. The most glaring is the difference between Mark's and Luke's versions, where Jesus immediately imposes silence on Peter without replying directly to his profession of faith, and Matthew's version, where Jesus replies with the great promise: "Simon, son of Jonah, you are a happy man! . . . You are Peter and on this rock I will build my Church" (Mt. 16, 17-18). Like the majority of exegetes, we find it more likely that Mark's account was the first and that Matthew, with this model and with equally solid facts, then proceeded to write his own. The force of his construction and the vigor of his contrasts—between the people's views and those of the disciples, between "You are the Christ" and "You are Peter," between "flesh and blood" and "my Father in heaven," between "God's ways" and man's, between Peter as rock and Peter as Satan—these give the episode overwhelming and yet perfectly natural power. But Matthew is capable of achieving such power and naturalness, and we cannot believe that Mark and Luke, had they been familiar with his version, could have destroyed so beautiful an edifice.

If we can see the compositional process in Mark, where Peter's profession of faith stands at the summit of a carefully prepared ascent, and if we find further construction in Matthew, who crowns his edifice with a superb dome—the promise to Peter,

then what is left us of Jesus and his consciousness in this episode
at Caesarea? Perhaps the trace of a peripeteia in his career, or evidence of the place his disciples occupied in his life—especially
Peter? These are precious data, but very vague. Must we, to be
honest, content ourselves with these modest but sure results?

Yet it seems we can go further, not in the unfolding and
reconstructing of the facts, but in the substance and the meaning
of this story. Through a schematic design, at once simplified and
enlarged, the episode at Caesarea is too right, too profound and
too marvelously exact to be only a beautiful monument. This is a
piece of architecture where individual styles can be detected, but
where they continue to express an original drive, an authentic experience.

The first characteristic of this experience is that it comes
from Jesus himself. He it is who, without preamble and without
being led thereto by the drift of the discussion, poses the question,
the double question: "Who do people say I am? . . . And you,
who do you say I am?" An astonishing question, indeed: first of
all, because no one would dream of using it except in a game or a
very dramatic situation and, especially, because no one would
phrase it this way, making a distinction between "the crowd" and
"you." Would Jesus be something other than what he is for all
who know him: Jesus of Nazareth, a carpenter, the son of Joseph
the carpenter? And if Jesus knows that the real question before
him is not "Who has sent you, and what are you doing?" but,
rather, "Who are you?" this is undoubtedly a sign that he is conscious of being something other than a messenger—or more exactly that, for him, being a messenger and being what he is coincide.
But then how can he expect an answer from a man, however perceptive? This is a datum so unique that he alone can experience
and communicate it. No one else can know it unless Jesus first
imparts it to him. Aware of this difficulty, no doubt, several authors, while recognizing a genuine revelation of Jesus here, think
that the question does not come from him but is a device introduced by the evangelist.[10]

But it is the paradox which is logical, and the apparent in-
consistency is coherent. Precisely because Jesus coincides totally
with his mission, and because his mission corresponds totally to
what man can expect from God, it is normal—even necessary—

that the question should come from him and that the answer should come from man. He alone can ask the question, and ask it in this astonishing form, focusing on his own identity—not just because he wants to display his initiative, to prove that he ceaselessly guides those he has taken under his care, and that he knows where he is leading them and at what moment he can have them make this personal gesture, but because this very question is a way of revealing himself, of saying who he is. The prophets do not pose any such question, nor do they yet have to, since we know what they are: Amos is a shepherd in Tekoa and cultivates sycamores (Am. 1, 1; 7, 14); Hosea is the son of Beeri and is married to Diblaim's daughter Gomer, who has borne him three children (Hos. 1, 1.3); Isaiah, the son of Amoz (Is. 1, 1), lives in Jerusalem with his wife and children; Jeremiah comes from a priestly family at Anathoth, in the territory of Benjamin (Jer. 1, 1), where he has cousins and owns fields (32, 8-9). The prophets do not have to say who they are, but they have to answer the question put to them: "Why do you live this way and speak in this tone?" Hence they recount the story of their vocation and explain why they have adopted this life style and this tone: they remain what they are, but a hand has seized hold of them (Is. 8, 11; Jer. 15, 17), a word resounds and boils up in their heart (Jer. 15, 16; 20, 9), someone else inhabits them, and their mission consists in giving testimony to that Other whom they are not, but whose Word they must speak. Little does it matter what they are, for they are only signs (Is. 8, 18) and voices (Is. 40, 3.6).

In Jesus' case, however, it is crucial to know what he is, and he compels those who see him live to ask themselves this question. The intellectual and religious leaders of the time try their best to define him according to their categories and demand to see his credentials in order to discuss or verify them: "What authority have you for acting like this?" (Mk. 11, 28); "We know that you are a teacher who comes from God" (Jn. 3, 2). But the answer to such questions is not forthcoming. To Jesus, the only question which matters concerns what he is, and it allows of a single answer—a *yes* or a *no*. Whether he himself poses it explicitly, as at Caesarea, or whether he obliges others to pose it, as he does by his whole manner of being, makes no great difference after all. Even if it were really a device introduced by the evangelist, the question he causes Jesus to ask would still be the very one his person poses to whoever sees him: "Who am I?"

Strictly speaking, the question "Who am I for you?" has meaning, among men, when asked under certain circumstances. It has meaning for two persons who love one another and discover what they are in each other's mind and heart. It has meaning for someone who assumes a responsibility toward others and needs to have it acknowledged. When educators are mistaken for soup vendors, when priests are treated like civil servants, when employees become a mere social security number, they must, in order to compel recognition, ask the question, "Who am I for you?" The *who*, here, refers to the role being played, to the personage and the service he provides. In Jesus' case, "Who am I for you?" is equivalent to "Who am I in reality?" but this does not prove that he expects unusual penetration from his followers. It proves that he is entirely what he is for them. In him, being and function co-incide totally—not that he disappears behind his function or is absorbed by it, and not that he lets himself be swallowed up by his being and his function or engulfed by their needs. To be the Messiah is to exist solely for all men, so as to be Jesus—he who saves (Mt. 1, 21) all men by introducing them into the momentum of the gift which is his being.

But who has any inkling of this gift? Who can answer this question? If Jesus is the only one who can ask it, is he not also the only one who can answer it? So, then, what have we here—a pedagogical trick, perhaps, impressive theatricals, a way of dictating the answer while making it seem spontaneous? All artifice would be unworthy and repugnant. There is only one possible solution: the answer must be real, possess genuine meaning for the one who formulates it, express an authentic experience, be able to spring from a human heart and a human intelligence—and, at the same time, spring from the question itself and reply to its interrogation. A purely schoolish answer, the repetition of a formula that has been carefully memorized, would create a fatal equivocation. Jesus' pedagogical gifts are dazzling; he has no equal for illuminating a question, finding words that hit home and shaping axioms that engrave themselves in one's memory. But such gifts would be redoubtable here: they could make the answer a mere echo of the question. That is why Jesus' question contains no hints, no leads; it obliges men to stand squarely before this mysterious personage, to find the answer by looking at him alone, and to put their whole self into that answer.[11]

These conditions seem unrealizable and contradictory. Nevertheless, they are fulfilled at Caesarea with astounding exactitude. It is not impossible that Peter's answer comes to him both from himself and from Jesus' question—on one condition, however: that this answer mean adherence through faith. Now, this is precisely what Jesus calls it. Peter's profession of faith in Jesus the Messiah can be a true affirmation and say what Jesus really is; but it can be a human affirmation and have meaning for Peter only if it is found and spoken in faith.

If Jesus is the Messiah, in the sense glimpsed by Jewish hope and affirmed by Christian faith, that means nothing less than this paradoxical and unexampled fact—or, more exactly, this twofold fact: that he is not entrusted with a mission but is identical with his mission, and that, by his very being and not only his deeds, he is the one who expresses and fulfills the hopes of man. If, in Jesus, man can recognize himself and recognize not so much his own dreams—for even the noblest are not unalloyed—but God's plan for him; and if, in Jesus, he can rediscover the countenance which God expects of humanity, then he can hail Jesus as the Messiah, the Savior of mankind. This is a human step, one which man can take: discerning in Jesus a likeness of humanity found to be willed by God and produced by God. The assertion "Jesus is the Messiah" can have meaning for man, if at least we admit that God can make himself recognizable to man.

Is that what Peter recognizes in Jesus? It seems unlikely. After all, how would Peter know what humanity is longing for? And yet he does know it and can express it, because of his hope and the Jews' expectation of the Messiah. His profession of faith is a profession of Jewish faith: the Messiah is the personage given by God to his people Israel. In Jesus' day, this expectation assumed widely divergent forms, since the outline of the Messiah had no predetermined features and could be that of a royal prince leading his people, a priest restoring the true religion, or a prophet establishing justice.[12] To those who expected everything from national liberation, a prestigious commander like Simeon Ben Koseba, who kept the Roman legions at bay and restored the independence of Jerusalem (132-134), could look like the Messiah. But even the most nationalistic Jews did not separate their hope from the destiny of the entire world. Their Messiah was to reign over all men; Israel was meant to be the center of all nations.

When Peter recognizes the Messiah in Jesus, he is not renouncing his hope as a Jew but giving this hope the face he sees before him. Under the features of Jesus—features that have become familiar, but no less disconcerting, from living with him constantly—Peter discovers, at Caesarea, the one whom his people await, the one who will alter the destiny of the nations. The Messiah whom Peter acknowledges is Jesus as he sees him: this astonishing person who carries a marvelous power within but scarcely draws on it, who goes through life with total assurance but keeps running into hostility and rejection, who makes one feel perfectly secure in his presence and yet can disappear and leave one alone at the most critical moment; this Jesus who is always waiting for the kingdom of God but speaks about it as if he already dwelt there, who is completely sure of God and yet asks nothing of him, who has a unique knowledge of man but seems incapable of acting upon him. That is not the Messiah Peter would ever have dreamed of; still, it is the one he acknowledges. And, in acknowledging Jesus as he is, Peter discovers a new face of God's. For if such is the Messiah whom God gives to man, and if this Messiah is there only to testify concerning God, it must be that God himself is not what Peter imagined either. By accepting Jesus as he is, Peter substitutes for his own image of God the image the Messiah proposes to him; he surrenders to the Messiah in faith.

So that Peter's answer may truly be a profession of faith, Jesus proceeds in two stages, asking first "Who do people say I am?" and then "Who do you say I am?" There are two ways of understanding Jesus, then: one which remains on the surface, and one which penetrates to the reality. The true answer is not the one that says more, but the one that says something other. For people on the outside, Jesus is an extraordinary person, one of the prophets come back on earth—Elijah or Jeremiah or John the Baptist. But he has no personality of his own; he is defined purely in terms of his miracles and arouses only stupefaction or the enthusiasm of dazzled or dumbfounded spectators. When Peter acknowledges the Messiah, however, he says something completely different: he affirms that Jesus is sent directly by God to his people; he attains the real personality of Jesus, his relation to God, which differs from anything the prophets knew, and his mission in the world, which vitally concerns all the children of Israel and, through them, the whole of humanity. If Jesus is the Messiah, one must go to him; and if this Messiah sets out on some path, one must follow him.

Such, it would seem, is the meaning of Peter's profession of faith as recorded in the most ancient version, which we take to be Mark's. It is an authentic profession of faith—in which case the texts raise a problem, for Jesus makes no explicit reply to Peter's statement but immediately enjoins silence and proceeds to announce his passion (Mk. 8, 30-31). These "strict orders" and abrupt change of subject are sometimes taken to mean that Peter's answer was erroneous and that Jesus rejected it.[13] But this reading is indefensible. To take the text as it stands, Jesus deliberately maintains silence, avoids pronouncing himself by a *yes* or a *no,* and imposes a similar silence upon the disciples.[14] And, in Mark's perspective, this double silence, far from signifying error and the repudiation of it, indicates truth—a capital truth, but one which must remain hidden, lest it be disfigured by the very people who first discovered it, until the Messiah has revealed his true face and the Son of Man has accomplished his destiny.[15]

Elicited by Jesus and accepted by Jesus, Peter's profession of faith, formulated by a man and expressing his experience as a man, contains an affirmation which has meaning for Peter and which Jesus can accept as true. Man is therefore capable of saying what Jesus is, of receiving and expressing the revelation of God in Jesus Christ. According to Bultmann, this "objectivist" claim is the hallmark of the mythologizing process, the idolatrous temptation of sinful man, who dreams of laying hands on God by defining him and by fitting him into human categories.[16] Bultmann's observations are penetrating and touch upon a central point: indeed, it seems impossible for man to remain in his creaturely condition listening to God's challenge and, at the same time, to define, according to his own views, the God who is challenging him—unless God does what is impossible for man, poses the question himself and then helps man answer it; unless,

furthermore, this answer is not a mere definition designed to sat-
isfy the intellect but, in saying what Jesus is, proves to be a commitment to him. That, according to the gospels, is what happened
at Caesarea Philippi.

Modern man, deafened by so many trumpeted revelations,
appreciates such discretion. In the words of a contemporary phi-
losopher formed by the Bible, "The power of transcendent truth
resides in its humility. This truth manifests itself as if it did not
dare speak its name; it does not step forth to assume its place in
the world with which it would merge immediately, as if it did not
come from beyond. One may even ask, when reading Kierke-
gaard, whether the revelation which discloses its origin is not contrary to the essence of transcendent truth, which would thereby
once again affirm its authority, powerless against the world. One
may ask whether the true God can ever lay aside his incognito,
whether the truth which has spoken itself should not immediately
appear as unspoken, in order to escape the sobriety and objectivity of historians, philologists and sociologists who will dress it
up in all the names of history and reduce its voice of deepest
silence to an echo of the noises arising from the battlefields and
the marketplaces or to a configuration built out of meaningless
elements. One may ask whether the first word of revelation must
not come from man, as in the ancient Jewish liturgical prayer
where the believer gives thanks, not for what he receives, but for
the very fact of giving thanks." [17]

Peter's profession of faith at Caesarea fulfills these requirements to a tittle. It is immediately followed by orders that the disciples should remain silent, lest it be interpreted and distorted at
will by the crowd—or by the disciples themselves, who can live it
by imitating Jesus but cannot yet expound it. It is born in Peter's
mind and language; the first word comes from man, but man is
not the one who conceives it: "Simon, son of Jonah, you are a
happy man! Because it was not flesh and blood that revealed this
to you but my Father in heaven" (Mt. 16, 17). Jesus' reply is so
well-timed that it can hardly be disjoined from the preceding
question, and this is the strongest argument in favor of Matthew's
version of the episode.[18] Without being able to solve a difficult
problem, let us only remark that Jesus is not necessarily speaking
of a sudden illumination. On the contrary, he deems it necessary

to unveil the Father's work to Peter precisely because it remains unconscious.

To be sure, this work is primarily interior and lies beyond our ken; some light is thrown on it, however, by Mark's mode of development with its series of declarations concerning the person of Jesus. The cry of the unclean spirits—"You are the Holy One of God" (Mk. 1, 24); "You are the Son of God" (3, 11; 5, 7)—says something true, and already this truth comes from God, torn from the evil spirits by a force they cannot withstand. The people's answers (8, 28) and Herod's (6, 16) are but wild theories concocted to explain strange facts. Peter's answer is the fruit of an authentic experience, of prolonged intimacy with Jesus, of the difficult and slow but real and profound penetration of his word into the heart of this disciple. When he declares, "You are the Christ," Peter defines Jesus correctly and objectively, in terms of his relationship to God who sends him and to the people whom he comes to save; he gives Jesus his rightful place and role in the work of God and the faith of Israel. And yet, this "objective" definition has nothing in common with the idolatrous myth Bultmann feared, since Peter, in his association with Jesus, has truly lived what it says. This profession of faith is not a proclamation in the third person, but an answer in the second; it is, so to speak, a declaration, in the sense in which love declares itself. "You are the Messiah" means "I have listened to you speak and watched you live. As I see it, you are God's witness and the kingdom's. That is why I follow you: you lead me to God."

Matthew's version of the episode at Caesarea ends with Jesus' promise to build his Church on Peter. Coming at this point in the narrative, the assertion is a trifle anachronistic. This is the first time Jesus mentions what the Church will be, but he talks as if Peter and the Twelve knew what it was all about, as if it were already a familiar reality. The juxtaposition of Peter's profession of faith and Jesus' promise may result from Matthean architecture, and the promise may in fact have come considerably later, when the prospect of Jesus' absence drew nearer.[19] But Matthew's construction is striking not only because of its forcefulness and balance but because of a profound logic. Mentioning the Church after Peter's profession of faith is by no means extraneous to the subject; for his definition of who Jesus is, is a decisive moment in the birth of the Church. Caesarea demonstrates that Jesus cannot reveal himself except by making men say what he is for them. There is no revelation without men to receive it and formulate it. This is tantamount to saying that there is no Christ without a Church. Even before having to receive Christ's teaching in order to transmit and implement it, the Church is present from the moment there is question of recognizing him and saying who he is. Revelation is not consigned to the Church, but is born of God in the Church. From the moment Jesus cannot say what he is except by having his disciples say it, from the moment he cannot be revealed except through the words of believers, the Church is already present in Caesarea. She already speaks and already holds all her authority from Jesus, from the confirmation he accords Peter: "Simon, son of Jonah, you are a happy man . . ." Such was the Church at the very beginning, and such she remains through the centuries. Her authority does not consist in forcing on weak minds certitudes which are too lofty for them; it consists in shedding the light of an authentic expression on the experience of faith lived personally by each Christian, and giving it the assurance of a certitude made to be universal. The Church cannot impose her faith; she watches it come to birth in her children, she teaches them to recognize it, to express it and live it. That is what mothers do.

NOTES TO CHAPTER 9

1. O. Cullmann, *Christology of the New Testament*, pp. 113-117.
2. R. Schnackenburg, *God's Rule and Kingdom*, p. 259; see also V. Taylor, *The Person of Christ in New Testament Teaching*.
3. G. Minette de Tillesse, *Le secret messianique dans l'évangile de Marc*, pp. 291 and 309. For the first gospel, see P. Bonnard, *L'évangile selon saint Matthieu* (Neuchâtel, 1963), p. 241.
4. L. Cerfaux, "La section des pains," in *Recueil Lucien Cerfaux* (Gembloux, 1954), Vol. I, pp. 480-481.
5. C. H. Dodd, *Historical Tradition in the Fourth Gospel* (New York: Cambridge University Press, 1963), pp. 216-217.
6. For example, the Pharisees' demand for "a sign from heaven" (Mk. 8, 11-13)—a text which should perhaps be put alongside Jn. 6, 30.
7. Since it seems impossible to attribute Jesus' saying about the bridegroom to a Christian invention, especially since no Jewish tradition linked the Messiah and the Bridegroom, one may be inclined to relativize the import of this saying and the consciousness it implies in Jesus, viewing it as a mere apothegm, more or less profane in nature: no one fasts at a wedding reception. J. Jeremias, *Theologisches Wörterbuch zum Alten Testament*, Vol. IV, p. 1906, subscribes to this solution on the grounds that if Jesus were called the Bridegroom, he would have proclaimed himself the Messiah—a thing he never did before his passion. *Idem, The Parables of Jesus*, pp. 51-52. It seems incontestable to us that Jesus did not proclaim himself the Messiah before his passion; but in order that he might claim the title then, the question had to be asked earlier and, in a way, asked by him. This could not be a sudden and unprepared step. In evoking the Bridegroom indirectly thus, Jesus remains true to his habitual style, a style too delicate to have been fabricated afterwards.
8. "All these questions reported and orchestrated by Mark create the climate of the first part and orient it all toward Peter's discovery. . . . All these questions are the prelude and variations on an ostinato theme, always the same, which recurs dozens of times throughout the first eight chapters and is finally formulated by Jesus himself in the question that brings Peter suddenly face to face with the facts." G. Minette de Tillesse, *Le secret messianique dans l'évangile de Marc*, p. 304.
9. O. Cullmann, *Peter—Disciple, Apostle, Martyr*, trans. by Floyd V. Filson (Philadelphia: The Westminster Press, 1953), pp. 170-184. P. Benoît, "Saint Pierre d'après O. Cullmann," in *Exégèse et Théologie* (Paris: Cerf, 1961), Vol. II, pp. 294-295. A. Voegtle, "Messiasbekenntnis und Petrusverheissung, Zur Komposition Mt. 16, 13-23 Par.," in *Biblische Zeitschrift*, N. F., I (1957), pp. 252-272; II (1958), pp. 85-103.
10. E. Haenchen, "Die Komposition von Mk VIII, 27-IX, 1 und Par.," in *Novum Testamentum* 6 (1963), p. 86; see G. Minette de Tillesse, *Le secret messianique dans l'évangile de Marc*, pp. 299 and 314.
11. Already, in the language of his day, J. A. Moehler wrote, "When Christ presented himself in Judea, he did not say, 'I am the Son of God,' for he

would not have impressed anyone. He waited until his disciples, living with him and accepting his own life, were able to understand the great realities, until sublime sentiments had awakened in them, sentiments whose normal culmination was the cry, 'You are the Son of the living God.' " J. A. Moehler, *L'unité dans l'Eglise* (Paris: Cerf, 1938 [Unam Sanctam, 2]), p. 221.

12. O. Cullmann, *The Christology of the New Testament,* pp. 111-117; H. Cazelles, *Naissance de l'Eglise, secte juive rejetée?* (Paris: Cerf [Lire la Bible, 16]), pp. 64-66.

13. J. Héring, *Le Royaume de Dieu et sa venue* (Neuchâtel: Delachaux et Niestlé, 2nd ed., 1959), pp. 122-127; A. Voegtle, "Messiasbekenntnis und Petrusverheissung. Zur Komposition Mt. 16, 13-23 Par.," in *Biblische Zeitschrift,* N. F., I (1957), p. 255.

14. O. Cullmann, *The Christology of the New Testament,* p. 120. Later, on p. 281, Cullmann is inclined to return to the preceding interpretation: "I should even say that . . . Mark 8.27 ff . . . has to do, not with a confession of Peter, but on the contrary with a reprimand of Peter because of his false understanding of the Messiah." We find that Cullmann is straining the text: forbidding someone—even vehemently—to speak is altogether different from reprimanding for a misstatement.

15. "From Mark's point of view, there is nothing equivocal about the title *Christ,* since it expresses the content of the Gospel (1, 1; see also 9, 41). Far from implying disagreement, the silence imposed on the disciples suggests instead that one is touching upon the mystery of the person of Jesus, as with the titles *Holy One* or *Son of God* (1, 24s. 34; 3, 11-12)." J. Delorme, "Aspects doctrinaux du second évangile," in *De Jésus aux évangiles, Tradition et Rédaction dans les évangiles synoptiques* (= *Ephemerides Theologicae Lovanienses,* 1967), p. 92.

16. R. Bultmann, *Jesus Christ and Mythology,* p. 83.

17. E. Levinas, "Un Dieu homme?" in *Qui est Jésus Christ?* (Paris: Desclée de Brouwer, 1968), p. 189.

18. See R. Bultmann, *History of the Synoptic Tradition,* trans. by John Marsh (New York: Harper and Row, Publishers, 1963), p. 258. For Bultmann, this episode is a creation of the Church, akin to the Christian professions of faith.

19. O. Cullmann, *Peter—Disciple, Apostle, Martyr,* pp. 170-184.

10
The Son of Man

After Peter's profession of faith at Caesarea, Jesus' teaching takes on a different cast and includes a new element: the passion he must undergo. It is not only an announcement, the prediction of an ineluctable event; it is a teaching, the explanation of a necessity, of a law from God. The first three evangelists strongly accentuate this decisive turning point (Mt. 16, 21; Mk. 8, 31; Lk. 9, 22). Mark and Luke relate this necessity to the person of the Son of Man: "The Son of Man is destined to suffer grievously, to be rejected . . . and to be put to death . . ." (Lk. 9, 22; Mk. 8, 31). It is a fact that mention of the Son of Man, which was relatively rare before Caesarea, becomes much more frequent as the interlinked perspectives of the coming passion and of the world's destiny after Jesus' departure come into sharper focus.[1] In the gospels, "Son of Man" is not simply another name given to Jesus; it is the figure of an existence, of a mission and a destiny. The fact that this name recurs much oftener after Caesarea and in Jesus' final days signifies that, as his hour approaches, the secret of his existence and the mystery of his person are revealed ever more fully. When Jesus announced the Good News in Galilee, he was primarily the messenger of the kingdom and the witness of its coming, and he seemed to efface himself behind God's initiative; after Caesarea, he continues to speak of the kingdom but associates it more and more with the figure of the Son of Man, with his own personage. In the Sermon on the Mount, Jesus discusses the kingdom which is coming, witnesses to it and lives it from within; but it subsists as something afar. When he speaks of the Son of Man, he speaks both of the kingdom and of the person who inaugurates it. If he is the Son of Man, he is the one through whom the kingdom comes.

Nevertheless, to gain some understanding of Jesus' thought, we must pause awhile over his statements concerning the Son of Man. Accustomed as we are to reading the gospels and picking out our facile patterns, we think of Jesus' statements as little more than a habitual way he had of speaking about himself. On reflection, his language should perhaps astonish us, but there are so many astonishing things in Jesus that we no longer notice them.

The gospels' use of the expression *Son of Man* supposes a tradition. In the Aramaic spoken by Jesus, it could mean simply *man,* but this purely general sense is incompatible with the gospel texts as a whole, where it designates a particular personage. Now, three Jewish works relatively close to Jesus' day refer to someone called "the Son of Man": these are three apocalypses—that of Daniel, that of the Ethiopic book of Enoch (the parables in Ch. 37-71), and that of the fourth book of Ezra (Ch. 13). The gospels certainly utilize the passage from Daniel[2] and very probably the parables of Enoch.[3] Consequently, the term *Son of Man* in the gospels evokes a personage who is already familiar, at least in certain Jewish circles, a distinctive physiognomy. This personage belongs to the world of apocalypses, appears in visions and plays a role in the judgment of the world.

Apocalypses easily baffle us. With their incoherent images and obscure symbols, their enciphered calculations constantly belied, and their anxious awaiting of events that are always imminent but never materialize, they conjure up a world that seems to smack of decadence. The prophets evinced another kind of realism, a sobriety born of faith, which did not seek to scrutinize the future and explore God's secrets: "I wait for Yahweh who hides his face from the House of Jacob; in him I hope" (Is. 8, 17). They saw no need to kindle their imagination and scour the heavens, since God does his work and produces his signs here on earth: "I and the children whom Yahweh has given me are signs and portents in Israel" (8, 18).

It is true that the apocalyptic style has a baroque flavor about it which easily lends itself to graceless imitations; and the efflorescence of this literature, in Christ's day, is not necessarily an index of creative vigor. Yet apocalypses play an indispensable part in the development of Israel's faith and in the expectation of its Messiah.

What characterizes apocalypses is the fact that they are the work of "seers." Heaven opens up, and visions unfold before their eyes. These celestial visions have their counterparts on earth in the history of the nations. In general, they describe something yet to come, but continuous with what has already passed. Both moments are seen in a vision. Daniel "in a night-vision" (Dan. 2, 19) comprehends the meaning of the composite statue in Nebuchadnezzar's dream: it signifies the four kingdoms under which the Jewish people lived after losing their independence—those of Babylon, of the Medes, of the Persians, and of Alexander and his successors, a colossus of iron with clay feet (2, 43). In another vision (7, 1-9), that of the four sea monsters, he reads the same historical events, which lead up to the period when the author of the book is writing—namely, to the persecution under Antiochus Epiphanes. Then comes the properly prophetic announcement, the vision of that future which God is preparing for his persecuted saints. When these empires have followed one another beneath the dust, "the God of heaven will set up a kingdom which shall never be destroyed, and this kingdom will not pass into the hands of another race" (2, 44). When the sea monsters whose cruel reign encroached upon land are either destroyed or rendered powerless, Daniel sees, "coming on the clouds of heaven," a human form, that of the Son of Man. While the beasts devour one another to conquer the realm of earth, the Son of Man is led before God, the Ancient of Days, who confers on him "sovereignty, glory and kingship over all peoples, nations and languages . . . an eternal sovereignty which shall never pass away, nor will his empire ever be destroyed" (7, 13-14). This is the kingdom into which harassed believers are to enter, the "saints of the Most High" (7, 22.25).

From these visions, which gave rise to the Jewish representations of the Son of Man and upon which, under varying symbols, all Jewish or Christian apocalypses basically draw, we should retain two features that go hand in hand. Firstly, apocalypses are not descriptions of the future, but symbolic visions. Despite their copious imagery, apocalypses are as discreet about the future as are the most sober prophets—even more so. Strong in the word which sends them forth and sure that God's plans will be realized, the prophets can point out the coincidence between the future which their lucidity foresees and the purpose which God has revealed to them. Thus Isaiah announces the fall of Damascus and Samaria (Is. 7, 8-9), and Jeremiah the destruction of the Temple (Jer. 7, 14). Daniel, on the other hand, gives absolutely no details about the date or the future of the kingdom he announces. The vision he beholds in the heavens is but a symbol and warrants no inferences concerning events to come. Attempting to make an apocalypse throw light on future developments is demanding from it exactly what it refuses to give. What the visionary sees is not the terrestrial unfolding of history, but its substance, its reality. That is why the heavens open up before his eyes and the true history of the world appears to him, as God sees it and makes it.

Secondly, this history is one of kingdoms and empires, a universal history. That is a constant theme in all apocalypses and an essential difference between them and prophecies. The prophecies —particularly those about the Messiah: Nathan's prophecy to David, and Isaiah's concerning the Child who is to be born—announce a kingdom without end (2 Sam. 7, 16; Is. 9, 6). But this kingdom is that of Israel and of its dynasty. The other nations are called to recognize this kingdom and, undoubtedly, to benefit from it in peace; but, for the prophets, they have no history of their own: they are simply integrated, at the last moment, into the fulfillment of the promises. The exile and the growth of world-wide empires taught Israel that God's purpose is more complex than the naïve dreams of a people isolated within their boundaries. It cuts through the history of empires and takes on the dimensions of the world. This is no longer the kingdom of Israel, but the kingdom of God. Empires have to fulfill their destiny, a mixture of greatness and cruelty; they have to expand and devour one another, crumble and disappear. God judges them and carries on his work, revealing it to the seer: "Thrones were set in place and one of great age took his seat" (Dan. 7, 9; the same sudden change appears in 2, 44: "In the time of these kings, the God of heaven will set up a kingdom which shall never be destroyed").

At first, the Son of Man is but another character in these apocalyptic visions and is far from being present everywhere. One among many, he does not, strictly speaking, constitute the hope of Israel in the same right as the Messiah. What the people of God is awaiting is the kingdom of the saints, the dawning of a transfigured world. When Daniel presents the figure of the Son of Man, he sees in it first the symbol of this kingdom, which differs so completely from the empires represented by the four monsters. Everything in his vision is symbolic; but the features with which he endowed the Son of Man apparently possessed a power of suggestion and a fittingness capable of expressing the most profound and genuine hope[4]—so much so that the figure of the Son of Man could later be detached from its original framework and incorporated into other frameworks and visions, like the parables of Enoch or the apocalypse of Ezra; and that finally, when Jesus appeared, this title could suffice to designate the personage associated with the coming of God's kingdom. However, judging from the fluidity of the Son of Man's features in the gospels, it would seem that this figure, while yet remaining strongly stamped by its apocalyptic origins, was susceptible of very diverse interpretations.

From our reading of the gospels, we may think *Son of Man* was a fairly common way for Jesus to designate himself when, for some reason or other, he did not use the first person. On closer examination, however, questions arise. Indeed, they multiply so fast that some exegetes doubt whether Jesus ever called himself the Son of Man, but believe instead that this title was given to him later in Christian communities where eschatological expectation ran high and where Jesus was principally he who would come from heaven in the likeness of the Son of Man.[5]

Far from shedding light on the gospels, these solutions strike us as leading to impasses. In our opinion, on the contrary, the term *Son of Man,* as Jesus used it in referring to his work, corresponds perfectly to his situation and his comportment. But before illustrating this point, we must present the data of the problem and, first of all, survey the texts in question.

TABLE I (p. 125) lists the thirty-four different passages where, in one synoptic or another, the expression *Son of Man* appears. The order followed is that of Matthew's gospel—not because his is the source of the two others or deserves more credence, but because it furnishes most examples and because its order coincides largely with Mark's and Luke's. (The question of order, we must add, is secondary in this discussion.) When possible, the translation presented is usually from Matthew; otherwise, it is from Mark.

TABLE II (p. 126) includes several options. It attempts to group the various texts (indicated by their number from Table I and left in that same order), first according to a division which is easy enough to check and is generally adopted, and then according to more precise affinities. Headings B and C are self-explanatory, for there is unquestionably one series of very closely related texts announcing the sufferings of the Son of Man, and another, more important, announcing his coming in heaven. Category A is noticeably less well defined; it comprises no series, properly speaking, and consists mainly of what does not fit into the other two categories. As to column D, we have placed there only those texts which are clearly the work of a writer, whether the evangelist or someone else; those where *Son of Man* merely substitutes for the pronoun *I* (text 11) or echoes a phraseology in which the originality and the intrinsic value of the authentic expression have practically disappeared (texts 9, 10 and 16). The list is certainly incomplete, and there is a strong probability that Matthew, who added *Son of Man* in 13, 37; 13, 41 and 16, 13, also added it elsewhere. Likewise, the passion texts (34, 35, 36, 37) may have been composed according to the pattern of Christ's announcements (12, 18, 22), and even these announcements may have become stereotyped. As a result, a rather rigorous examination, even when free from all bias, can considerably diminish the number of texts which, in their original form, contained the term *Son of Man*.

However rigorous such an examination may be, it affects nothing essential. Enough authentic texts subsist to assure us that Jesus called himself the Son of Man more than once, and that this expression was sufficiently characteristic of his manner to be generalized without scruples. But there are more virulent critics.

To begin with, they point out that the expression *Son of Man,* in Aramaic, can have the very general meaning of "an individual belonging to the human race"—that is, "the man," "a man," "someone." [6] It cannot designate a particular individual and become a personal title except in reference to a consecrated tradition or a well-known text. Now, the sayings in category A ("earthly existence") seem devoid of any such references. They will therefore be interpreted as meaning "the man in front of

Table I

THE SYNOPTIC TEXTS CONCERNING THE SON OF MAN (SM)

	Mt.	Mk.	Lk.	
1	8, 20		4, 58	Foxes have holes . . . but the SM has nowhere to lay his head.
2	9, 6	2, 10	5, 24	The SM has authority on earth to forgive sins. . . .
3	10, 23			You will not have gone the round of the towns of Israel before the SM comes.
4	(10, 32)		12, 8	If anyone openly declares himself for me in the presence of men, the SM will declare himself for him . . .
5	11, 19		7, 34	John came . . . The SM came, eating and drinking . . .
6	12, 8	2, 28	6, 5	The SM is master of the sabbath.
7	12, 38		12, 10	Anyone who says a word against the SM will be forgiven; but . . . against the Holy Spirit and he will not be forgiven . . .
8	12, 40		11, 30	As Jonah was . . . so will the SM be in the heart of the earth for three days and three nights.
9	13, 37			The sower of the good seed is the SM.
10	13, 41			The SM will send his angels and they will gather out of his kingdom all things that provoke offenses . . .
11	16, 13			Who do people say the SM is?
12		8, 31	9, 22	The SM is destined to suffer grievously, to be rejected . . .
13	16, 27			The SM is going to come in the glory of his Father . . . and . . . he will reward . . .
14		8, 38	9, 26	If anyone . . . is ashamed of me . . . the SM will also be ashamed of him . . .
15	16, 28			There are some . . . here who will not taste death before they see the SM coming with his kingdom.
16	17, 9	9, 9		Tell no one about the vision until the SM has risen from the dead.
17	17, 12	9, 12		Elijah has come already and they did not recognize him . . . and the SM will suffer similarly . . .
18	17, 22	9, 31	9, 44	The SM is going to be handed over into the power of men . . .
19			17, 22	A time will come when you will long to see one of the days of the SM . . .
20			18, 8	When the SM comes, will he find any faith on earth?
21	19, 28			When . . . the SM sits on his throne . . . you will yourselves sit . . .
22	20, 18	10, 33	18, 31	We are going up to Jerusalem, and the SM is about to be handed over . . .
23	10, 28	10, 45		The SM came not to be served but to serve, and to give his life . . .
24			19, 10	The SM has come to seek out and save what was lost.
25	24, 27			The coming of the SM will be like lightning striking in the east . . .
26	24, 30			Then the sign of the SM will appear in heaven . . .
27	24, 30	13, 26	21, 27	They will see the SM coming on the clouds of heaven with great power . . .
28			21, 36	Stay awake, praying . . . for the strength . . . to stand with confidence before the SM.
29	24, 37		17, 26	As it was in Noah's day, so will it be when the SM comes.
30	24, 39		17, 30	They suspected nothing till the Flood came . . . It will be like this when the SM comes.
31	24, 44		17, 40	Stand ready because the SM is coming at an hour you do not expect.
32	25, 31			When the SM comes in his glory . . . he will take his seat on his throne . . .
33	26, 2			It will be Passover . . . and the SM will be handed over to be crucified.
34	26, 24	14, 21	22, 22	The SM is going to his fate, as the scriptures say he will . . .
35	26, 24	14, 21		But alas for that man by whom the SM is betrayed.
36	26, 45	14, 41		The hour has come when the SM is to be betrayed . . .
37			22, 48	Judas, are you betraying the SM with a kiss?
38	26, 64	14, 62	22, 69	You will see the SM seated at the right hand of the Power . . .

Table II
CLASSIFICATION OF THE SNYOPTIC TEXTS CONCERNING THE SON OF MAN

A: earthly existence　　　　B: imminent suffering　　　　C: heavenly kingdom　　　　D: redactional texts

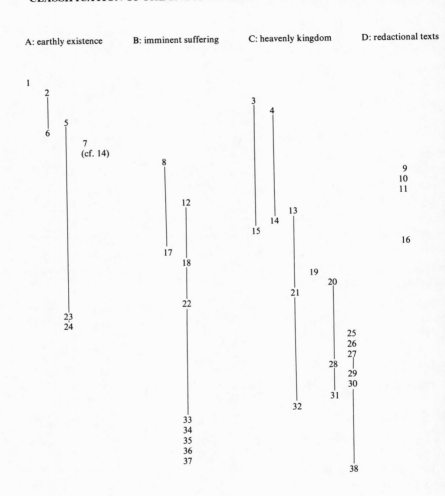

you," "the man whom I am." And text 1, for example, retains all its meaning even when translated simply as "Foxes have holes and the birds of the air have nests, but the man [to whom you are speaking] has nowhere to lay his head." It is altogether natural for Jesus to contrast the living habits of animals with the life he himself leads, since his humanity places him well above them. Similarly, text 5 seems to lose none of its force if read thus: "John came, neither eating nor drinking, and they say, 'He is possessed.' A man came [I myself], eating and drinking, and they say, 'Look, a glutton and a drunkard.' " Generalizing such observations, these exegetes suggest construing texts 2 and 6 as broad statements: Jesus' deeds mark the dawning of a new era in which man ceases to be the slave of the sabbath and becomes its master, and in which the power of forgiving sins is handed over to men.

As regards the texts in category B, concerning the passion of Jesus, it is said that they repeat one another and, in any case, must stem from a single original. It is further stated that the details they supply cannot have been garnered until later, after the event, and that Jesus cannot have spoken these words as they now stand. Lastly, some critics find it strange that these texts, spotlighting the Son of Man as they do, comprise no apocalyptic image and no allusion to the eschatological perspectives commonly associated with this figure. This is taken as proof that they are artificial and subsequent creations.

In general, the texts in category C inspire a little more confidence, since they are in harmony with apocalyptic currents and express a form of Israel's expectation which it is normal to find in Jesus. Moreover, they retain their Jewish character: in them, the Son of Man exhibits the traits of an apocalyptic personage, not those of Jesus as seen in categories A and B, which were formulated in a Christian milieu.[7] The only problem is that for several exegetes—Bultmann, for example—this distance, which is a good sign of authenticity, becomes proof that Jesus himself, though he ardently awaited the Son of Man, never dreamed of identifying himself with him. Jesus' mission was to announce the coming of the Son of Man, the appearance of this personage who was new to the world—not his own return under the traits of the Son of Man.[8]

These observations are rather disheartening.[9] Still, in our opinion, they do not strike at anything essential. There is no denying, however, that they raise issues which must be taken into consideration and that it is often advisable, when studying a text concerning the Son of Man, to ask whether the evangelist or his source has not, consciously or unconsciously, generalized a habitual way of speaking. Though we cannot undertake such a task or prove the authenticity of each text here, we think it possible to demonstrate the presence of a unique and coherent thought pattern in the three categories and the three types of formulas, and feel justified in attributing this pattern and this coherence to Jesus himself.

The first hint of coherence in the use of the expression *Son of Man* comes from the fact that it is constantly associated with an action, either performed or undergone. Never is it used to say what Jesus is, but always to say what he does or will do and what he will suffer: the Son of Man has power (texts 2, 6, 27; cf. 32, 38) but also experiences powerlessness (1, 17), he has come (5, 17, 23, 24) and will come (3, 13, 20, 25, 27, 29, 30, 31, 32; cf. 38), he will be delivered up (12, 18, 23, 35, 36, 37) and will sit in glory (21, 25, 38), he will be seen (15, 19, 26, 27, 38), he has his days (19, 29) and his hour (31, 36), he is rejected (12) and will reject in turn (14). The question, therefore, is not whether Jesus is the Son of Man and whether this title is due him, but rather why his deeds are presented as the deeds of the Son of Man. The situation is altogether different with regard to the Messiah. *Messiah* is a title, the name of the personage whom God gives to his people; and the question raised by Jesus' presence is knowing whether or not he is the Messiah. That is what his adversaries ask him: "How much longer are you going to keep us in suspense? If you are the Christ, tell us plainly" (Jn. 10, 24). It is what the high priest asks him: "Are you the Christ?" (Mk. 14, 61). And Jesus replies at one and the same time with a *yes* that requires explaining and with a prediction about the coming of the Son of Man (Mk. 14, 62). The two modes of speech do not harmonize: *Son of Man* is a title only to designate a precise role in a definite activity.

This activity is eschatological: the Son of Man's deeds are those of the mysterious personage who will appear the day God intervenes to judge the world, put an end to evil and establish justice. Almost all the words and phrases associated with the Son of

Man and quoted above belong to the idiom of eschatology: "might," "coming," "day," "hour," "sitting in glory," "appearing before the nations gathered together." An exception is the series of announcements concerning the passion, where the vocabulary is unusual: Jesus must be "delivered up," he must "suffer." This very unusual style—in Bultmann's mind, for instance—is a sure sign that those announcements are a later creation of the Christian community.[10]

Nevertheless, we may ask ourselves whether the distance between the apocalyptic sayings and the announcements of the passion is as great as it seems; or, more exactly, whether this distance, far from denoting initial independence, might not on the contrary translate a conscious and deliberate disjunction. For everything takes place as if there were a paradoxical but strict correspondence between the apocalyptic sayings about the kingdom in heaven and the prophetic announcements of the passion on earth. By a sort of symmetry, the deeds which the Son of Man performs on earth are the reverse of those written in heaven. He has his hour on earth as well as in heaven, but on earth it comes when he is handed over to his enemies (text 36), whereas in heaven it is when he appears on the clouds as a judge (26, 27, 38: "from this time onward"—Mt. 26, 64); on earth he is reviled (7), spurned (12) and betrayed (18, 22, 26, 35, 36, 37), but in heaven he acknowledges his own (4) or rejects those who have rejected him (14). All these deeds are not simultaneous: they are separated in time and seem independent; but in point of fact, they complement one another. With his genius for synthesis, John in his gospel presents the supreme instance of this correspondence between both levels by making them coincide in time and in space, on the cross. The crucified Jesus exposed to the rabble's gaze is the Son of Man exalted in his glory (Jn. 3, 14; 12, 34; 13, 31).[11]

Does not the word *symmetry* immediately suggest artifice? After all, nature does not proceed by symmetry. But the symmetry between both categories here is not literal: it resides in the facts, not in the words. Above all, it is natural because it springs from the situation itself. As we remarked earlier, apocalyptic visions are never more than symbols of terrestrial happenings. Daniel's vision of the Son of Man is followed by its interpretation on the level of history (Dan. 7, 17-27), as is customary in apocalypses. Jesus' case is analogous but special. Without being a seer strictly speaking—though on occasion he, too, sees "the heavens torn apart" (Mk. 1, 10)—he frequently depicts the manifestation of the Son of Man on the last day, in the style proper to apocalypses. But, unlike ordinary seers, he does not have to go into ecstasy in order to behold these celestial secrets. He speaks of them simply, as of familiar realities; and this simplicity may sometimes deceive us and make us forget that he remains at the level of the vision and of literary expression.

What is absolutely unique in Jesus' case is the interpretation on the terrestrial level. In apocalypses, the earthly happenings symbolized in visions are regularly announced afterward in prophetic interpretations relating to the course of history. In the gospels, the interpretation is equally prophetic and looks ahead to the future—but to Jesus' own future, which he announces as the deciphering of the apocalypse of the Son of Man. Jesus is not a seer who, from outside, contemplates the unfolding of some alien and wondrous existence. In the celestial images of the Son of Man, he contemplates the law wherein is written the destiny which he is actually living on earth.

From this comes the apparently surprising but absolutely natural disjunction between the Jesus who speaks and the Son of Man about whom he speaks. Never does Jesus explicitly state that he is the Son of Man, and from this some conclude too hastily that he is awaiting someone other than himself. Indeed, one of his sayings, if taken literally, seems to imply as much: "If anyone in this adulterous and sinful generation is ashamed of me and of my words, the Son of Man will also be ashamed of him when he comes in the glory of his Father with the holy angels" (Mk. 8, 38).[12] And it is strictly true that, at the moment at which he is speaking, Jesus is not the Son of Man who is to come on the clouds of heaven. Before this vision is realized, and in order that it may be realized, Jesus has to accomplish on earth the task which God has assigned to him. But this does not mean that Jesus and the Son of Man are two distinct persons; it means that the heavenly vision of the Son of Man cannot become a reality unless Jesus first lives his human life on earth.[13]

It is therefore not surprising—but, on the contrary, absolutely logical, if we may say so—that the sayings about the Son of

Man should fall into two such sharply differentiated groups. One concerns the actual destiny of Jesus on earth and establishes strict identity between him and the Son of Man. These sayings deal exclusively with him, with what he must do and undergo, with the most profound law of his life. Unless he is rejected, betrayed and put to death, he is not the Son of Man, and the heavenly vision will no longer mean anything. Category C, therefore, is again Jesus—but in the new world which he cannot yet speak about except as another world and through images. But whereas in A the whole emphasis is on Jesus himself and his destiny, in B the dominant perspective is that of revelation: now the role of the Son of Man consists in appearing, and the scene is broadened to the dimensions of the world and the assembled nations which see him loom up in heaven.[14]

If the coherence between the apocalyptic series relating to the parousia of the Son of Man and the prophetic series announcing his passion is really solid, we can surely go a step further and ask ourselves whether category A—the sayings about the Son of Man's actual situation—would not likewise fit naturally into this aggregate. Here again it is impossible for us to make a critical examination of all these texts; neither can we rule out instances of later products of the gospel tradition or the possibility that *Son of Man* could sometimes be translated simply as "this man" or "man" in general. But here, too, if we look at the overall picture, we cannot fail to see significant convergences.

First of all, in the two sayings about the forgiveness of sins and the sabbath (texts 2 and 6), there appears the theme of *power*. Not only does this word belong to the vocabulary which, in category C, describes the coming of the Son of Man (27), as well as to the theme of the Son of Man in his capacity as sovereign Judge; but it also seems that in deliberately associating the power bestowed on the Son of Man and his presence on earth, Jesus gives us to understand that Daniel's vision has already begun to be realized.[15] In addition, there is the very striking parallelism between the situations described in texts 7 and 14. Paradoxically, their dénouement is entirely different: in 7, "a word against the Son of Man" will be forgiven at the hour of judgment; whereas in 14, denying him calls down rejection. But in either case, the presence of the same Son of Man and of his mysterious destiny decides the fate of those who meet him, so that each of these sayings belongs in both categories A and C. Lastly, we notice the same way of presenting the Son of Man, who has come eating and drinking in contrast to John the Baptist (text 5), and has come to serve in contrast to all those who take advantage of their office in order to be served.[16]

Of course, these affinities can be attributed to anterior associations already established around the themes of the Son of Man; in fact, there is no doubt but that such associations did come into play. Must we, for all that, rule out the possibility that they may have been at work in Jesus himself? The question arises because this process, which is inherent and largely automatic in all language, happens at the same time to correspond with astonishing exactitude to the figure of Jesus as it emerges from the gospels and as we have been able to delineate it so far.

An essential trait of Jesus' is that, at one and the same time, he is spontaneously himself in all his deeds and is inhabited by a mysterious presence, of which he is at once and from different viewpoints the herald, the servant, the witness and the confidant. . . . Sometimes this presence is the kingdom, sometimes the Father's forgiveness, and sometimes his gaze or his voice. Jesus' whole mission springs from this impetus, not as from an external force to which he would have to submit, but as from the fount which makes him live. In a sense, there is no distance between him and this source, and he can say *I* because his activity really comes from him: "The Spirit of the Lord has been given to me" (Lk. 4, 18), "Of course I want to! Be cured!" (Mt. 8, 3), "I will make you fishers of men" (Mt. 4, 19), "I did not come to call the virtuous, but sinners" (Mt. 9, 13), "It is not peace I have come to bring, but a sword" (Mt. 10, 34). More than once, however, in similar situations and in the same vein, Jesus speaks of himself in the third person, in the shape of someone else. The most frequent instance of this is the figure of the Son of Man, and it has particularly excited the ardor of the critics; but it is not the only one—a fact which seems to exemplify a fairly common feature of Jesus' speech. At times, he is the prophet despised in his own country (Mt. 13, 57); at other times, he is the bridegroom come for the wedding feast and surrounded by his friends (Mt. 9, 15); or again, he is "greater than Jonah" and "greater than Solomon" (Mt.

12, 41-42). There is not always strict identification, but sometimes only comparison. But he does have this habit of presenting himself in relation to some personage and situating himself spontaneously in the framework of a few major figures in Israelite tradition. If the identification seems perfect in the case of the Son of Man, that is because Jesus apparently found this figure to be the clearest expression of his mission and his existence. A celestial figure, it plainly reveals its origin; an apocalyptic figure, it becomes real only by being fulfilled on earth; a figure derived from a prophet and outlined by God, it expresses a destiny imparted from on high; an empty figure, it is designed to contain an existence; an eschatological figure, it announces the transformation of the world and the kingdom of God.

On the surface, the figure of the Son of Man and the announcement of the kingdom seem totally independent. Neither the early preaching of the Good News nor the Sermon on the Mount nor the parables ever mention the Son of Man. Yet these three moments certainly contain the essence of Jesus' teaching. Accordingly, some wonder whether the theme of the Son of Man is not foreign to this teaching, something introduced later[17] in communities which expected Jesus to return soon. Quite the contrary: the themes of the kingdom and of the Son of Man, far from excluding one another, are interwoven. This is true from the very start, in Daniel, where the Son of Man comes to destroy the earthly kingdom symbolized by the four monsters and inaugurate the kingdom of the saints of the Most High (Dan. 7, 17-27); it is also true in the gospels, where the images of the kingdom—especially in the parables—consciously evoke Daniel's perspectives.[18]

Though valid, such answers are incomplete. The only real answer to critics like Vielhauer is to acknowledge the soundness of his analyses but delimit their application exactly. It is true that, when Jesus first begins speaking in Galilee, he seems as yet only the herald and evangelist of the kingdom. The Sermon on the Mount appears to reflect a moment during which he effaces himself behind the kingdom which he is announcing and the experience to which he is inviting his hearers. On closer examination, however, he is already inseparable from his call. This experience is his own, and we enter into it only by following him. As for the kingdom which he announces, he is the witness to it, the only one who knows it from inside. He presents no credentials to corroborate what he says: for those who are willing to listen, his teaching is sufficient proof. But, as soon as he performs deeds and becomes a person of figure in the world, when he forgives sins (text 2), places himself above the sabbath (6) and involves people in a life centered around him (1), then he certainly has to give a meaning to these unusual actions. Just as the actions of farmers or carpenters, of doctors of the Law or prophets are dictated by their respective trades, professions and callings, so too do Jesus' actions require an explanation—all the more so since they are startling and commit him entirely. Of ourselves and our activity we all form a certain concept which expresses both what we are and what we dream of doing, and it is natural for us to refer to this self-image when performing actions which commit us. Similarly, Jesus justifies his unique behavior by appealing to a unique figure in the tradition of his people—the Son of Man.

Thus we can understand why he speaks sometimes about the kingdom and sometimes about the Son of Man, and why he speaks about them in a different way and on themes which rarely converge. About the kingdom, he speaks as a witness: it is a reality which already inhabits him and offers itself to anyone who welcomes it; about the Son of Man, he speaks as a seer: this is the personage he must incarnate through his activity. About the kingdom, he speaks for others, to show them that it is coming to them and is made for them; about the Son of Man he cannot speak except by acting and for the purpose of explaining what he is doing. The kingdom is the object of preaching and teaching; the Son of Man is first of all a theme for explanation and personal justification.

Still, these two themes are not so far apart. The kingdom and the Son of Man are both coming, both have a celestial origin and a terrestrial fulfillment, and both gather all of mankind around themselves. These linguistic affinities evince a profound kinship. Between the kingdom and Jesus there is, at one and the same time, coincidence and distance; so, too, between Jesus and the Son of Man. Jesus is not the kingdom, nor even yet the one who inaugurates it: he must await it in faith and patience; still, he already knows it from experience and is inhabited by this reality to which he bears witness. Likewise with the Son of Man: he is what Jesus will be when the kingdom comes; and just as Jesus' whole undertaking consists in the coming of the kingdom, so his whole life consists in being the Son of Man.

To strip Jesus of the consciousness that he is the Son of Man, and reduce him to his mission of announcing the kingdom, would be to deprive him of half his existence. If Jesus merely spoke about the kingdom, he would just be one more prophet, exterior to the kingdom on which he discourses. For the evangelists as well as for the first believers, the coming of the kingdom and Jesus' activity are correlative. If this is the truth, if it expresses the disciples' fundamental experience, and if this experience was real, it has to have rested on that of Jesus himself: when speaking about the kingdom, Jesus has to have known and said that its coming depended on him, his life and his death. That is exactly what happens when he speaks about the Son of Man. But his way of speaking about him manifests both his certitude and the limits of what he knows. In calling himself the Son of Man, he indicates that he knows his mission and that it coincides with the coming of the kingdom; he proclaims this coming as an event he is absolutely sure of; and, in the words of John's gospel (8, 14; 13, 3), he knows where he is going. But he sees this event "in heaven" and through apocalyptic figures; he does not see its realization on earth and cannot map out its future history. He knows simply that his own history, his life at every moment, is the Son of Man's, and that all his deeds delineate this mysterious figure.

The mystery of this figure, the mystery of the Son of Man, consists in being both given to Jesus from on high, like a law imposed on him and a destiny he must accomplish, and at the same time lived from within, arising from his deepmost self. The Son of Man is indeed Jesus himself, totally free in his choices, ever spontaneous in his reactions, independent of all influences and pressures from men or from the devil, and yet always conscious of obeying, of keeping his eyes on the blueprint of his life and learning its meaning from someone else. Thus the paradox of the sayings about the Son of Man is explained by the mystery which constitutes the ground of Jesus' personality. This double registration, this correspondence between heaven and earth, which keeps the themes distinct and yet makes them converge, is Jesus himself.

He does not have a two-storey consciousness, nor is he a being divided between two worlds, but someone who is entirely himself in everything he does and entirely oriented by the personage he must live—the Son of Man.

Notes to Chapter 10

1. Table I, on page 125, lists the synoptic texts which contain the expression *Son of Man* (SM). The order followed is that of Matthew, who provides the largest number of texts. Remembering the artificial character of his groupings, we see that texts 3 and 4, from the "mission discourse" (Ch. 10), are misplaced in the progression of the gospel and belong rather with the eschatological texts of Ch. 24. As for texts 9 and 10, from the "sermon of parables" (Ch. 13), it is quite likely that he himself inserted the words *Son of Man;* for when Jesus speaks of the Son of Man, he does not merely designate a personage but describes a destiny. Thus, out of the ten texts antedating Caesarea, at least four are not in the right place, and six at the most offer a quotation from Jesus mentioning the Son of Man.
2. Texts 27 and 38 refer to Dan. 7, 13-14.
3. E. Sjöberg, *Der Menschensohn im äthiopischen Henochbuch* (Lund, 1946), pp. 63-66. See G. Minette de Tillesse, *Le secret messianique dans l'évangile de Marc,* pp. 383-385; C. Colpe, *Theologisches Wörterbuch zum Neuen Testament,* VIII, pp. 425-428.
4. A. Feuillet has admirably brought out the richness of this figure in "Le Fils de l'homme en Daniel et la tradition biblique," in *Revue Biblique,* 60 (1953), pp. 170-202 and 321-346. However, awed by the grandeur of the personage thus disclosed, Feuillet has perhaps been led to project him unaltered into reality, like a direct prophetic announcement, whereas he is only a symbol in a vision. To assert that the Son of Man who comes upon the clouds of heaven cannot, in Biblical tradition, be anything "but a manifestation of God in person" (p. 188), would be to assert that the revelation of the only-begotten Son equal to God was already given through Daniel, and that Jesus' coming serves merely to confirm it by deeds. But only the living person of Jesus can bring this revelation and enable us to conceive of the face-to-face presence of two beings who bear the divine name. The Son of Man in Dan. 7, 13-14 is led into the presence of the "Ancient of Days," who confers "sovereignty, glory and kingship" on him. How could a Jew visualize God in this position?
5. The Ethiopian version of the book of Enoch (Ch. 70-71) describes the arrival in heaven—in the capacity of Son of Man—of the patriarch Enoch, who was taken up from earth in ancient times. Could not the Christian community have used this as the model for Jesus' heavenly enthronement?
6. C. Colpe, *Theologisches Wörterbuch zum Neuen Testament,* VIII, pp. 404-406.
7. Colpe, *op. cit.,* pp. 435-444.
8. R. Bultmann, *The Theology of the New Testament,* Vol. I, pp. 28-30. For Bultmann, if Jesus "believed himself to be the Son of Man," that would mean he "understood himself in the light of mythology." See *Jesus Christ and Mythology,* p. 16. But Jesus never loses sight of the fact that the Son of Man is an apocalyptic personage. He merely affirms that this personage represents him.
9. Disheartening, too, is the incalculable and ever growing mass of studies published on this subject. C. Colpe's contribution in *Theologisches Wörter-*

buch zum Neuen Testament, VIII, pp. 403-481, synthesizes and enumerates them but would have to be supplemented with a list of the many pertinent articles written since it appeared in December of 1967. For a brief discussion of the problem, the reader is referred to H. Conzelmann, *An Outline of the Theology of the New Testament,* pp. 131-137, with its astonishingly bold criticism; or, for much greater subtlety and insight, to G. Minette de Tillesse, *Le secret messianique dans l'évangile de Marc,* pp. 364-367.

10. "Clearly the predictions of the parousia originally had nothing to do with the predictions of death and resurrection." R. Bultmann, *Theology of the New Testament,* Vol. I, p. 29. In a similar vein, but far more nuanced, is C. Colpe's view in *Theologisches Wörterbuch zum Neuen Testament,* VIII, pp. 446-447.

11. Without making a detailed analysis of John's theology of the Son of Man, one can, by simply looking at the texts, easily discern in it the language of the synoptics concerning the Son of Man, along with its typical associations: seeing (Jn. 1, 51; 6, 62), angels (1, 51), heaven (3, 13; 6, 62), glory (12, 23; 13, 31), power (5, 27). This is the traditional apocalyptic vocabulary, but we should notice how its application to the deeds in Jesus' life, by abolishing the difference of time found in the synoptics, simply spells out to the very last syllable the correspondences which they had already stressed. See S. S. Smalley, "The Johannine Son of Man Sayings," in *New Testament Studies,* 14 (1967-1968), pp. 278-301; R. Schnackenberg, "Der Menschensohn in Johannesevangelium," in *New Testament Studies,* 11 (1964-1965), pp. 123-137; O. Cullman, *Christology of the New Testament,* pp. 184-188.

12. See R. Bultmann, *History of the Synoptic Tradition,* pp. 151-152, and Heinz E. Tödt, *The Son of Man in the Synoptic Tradition* (Philadelphia: Westminster Press, 1965).

13. Between the Son of Man and Jesus, therefore, there is both identity and distance. To say, with R. Otto in *Reich Gottes und Menschensohn* (München, 1940), that "Jesus is the representative *(Funktionär)* of the Son of Man, acting and speaking in his name" is to give the consistency of a being to what is yet only a figure. E. Lohmeyer's subtle and complicated explanation in *Gottesknecht und Davidsohn* (Copenhagen, 1945), p. 126, likewise supposes between the one sent and the sender a relationship which none of the texts suggests: "Only Jesus can speak about the Son of Man, and he must speak about him as another; but because he has complete power to speak, his way of speaking about him establishes a link which borders on identity between the one sent who speaks and the supreme Judge, still hidden, who will judge the world." As R. Schnackenberg writes in *God's Rule and Kingdom,* p. 165, if we made two distinct persons out of Jesus and the Son of Man, the relation between them "would remain completely obscure."

14. In his *Der verborgene Menschensohn in den Evangelien* (Lund, 1955), E. Sjöberg has brought out the importance of the traditional apocalyptic *hidden-revealed* pattern in the evangelical view of the Son of Man. We find it worth stressing that this coupling does not only derive from a traditional pattern, but that the very nature of an apocalypse implies the dyad *celestial vision* and *terrestrial history.* What is original about Jesus is that with him, in contradistinction to ordinary apocalypses, fulfillment on earth precedes fulfillment in heaven. This is the sign of his unique condition: with him

comes the end of time.

15. A. Feuillet, "L'*Exousia* du Fils de l'homme," in *Recherches de Science religieuse,* 42 (1954), pp. 170-174; and J.-Dupont, "Le paralytique pardonné (Mt. 9, 1-8)," in *Nouvelle Revue Théologique,* 92 (1960), pp. 948-958. However, some exegetes wonder whether the statement concerning the Son of Man and his power—a statement which, in Mk. 2, 10, for example, seems to interrupt the narrative—is really original. They believe that *Son of Man* was added by the Christian community, which thus proclaimed that its power to forgive sins was in fact the power of the risen Son of Man. See J. Murphy-O'Connor, "Péché et communauté dans le Nouveau Testament," in *Revue Biblique,* 74 (1967), pp. 181-185. We must admit that Mark's account flows better without v. 10, but the explanation offered seems very complicated. It runs as follows: since the Jewish tradition concerning the Son of Man did not attribute to him the power to forgive sins, it is hardly likely that the Christian community deduced this power from the title *Son of Man.* We must therefore suppose, with H. E. Tödt, that the power was first seen in Jesus and that, as a consequence, he was then given the title. This argument is not too convincing. Why would the transfer be more natural in this direction than in the other? And if it is not natural, should it not be attributed to Jesus' creative power rather than to an invention of the community?

16. In most groupings of texts about the Son of Man, numbers 23 and 24 are placed in category B, with the announcements of the passion. This is a mistake caused by hastily proceeding to the content which is thought to be there, without paying sufficient attention to the form. These two texts, like those in the first category, do not refer to a precise event but describe a fundamental law of Jesus' mission.

17. F. Vielhauer, "Gottersreich und Menschensohn in der Verkündigung Jesu," in *Aufsätze zum Neuen Testament* (München, 1965), pp. 55-91.

18. G. Minette de Tillesse, *Le secret messianique dans l'évangile de Marc,* pp. 389-394.

11
Announcements of the Passion

The gospels underline, as a decisive turning point in Jesus' life, the moment when he began to announce openly to his disciples that he had to suffer and die, the victim of his adversaries. It was right after Peter's profession of faith at Caesarea: the revelation of the Messiah would be sheer illusion if one refused to accept his true face, which is doomed to hatred and death. This journey of Christ's toward his passion constitutes not only an oft-repeated theme from Caesarea till the last day but—especially in Mark and Luke—the very movement and structure of the narrative. In Mark, from Caesarea to the entrance into Jerusalem, three similar announcements punctuate, like a refrain, the steady advance which leads Jesus to his death: "The Son of Man has to suffer, die and rise again" (see Mk. 8, 31; 9, 31; 10, 33; and Table III, texts 2, 5 and 8, on p. 142). All three appear again in Matthew (16, 21; 17, 22; 20, 18) and in Luke (9, 22; 9, 44; 18, 31), but there the repetition does not have the same impact, because the narrative is much more developed and rich in various episodes and instruction. Aware of this loss, perhaps, Luke has compensated for it in an original way by building his narrative, starting from Caesarea, on the themes of the exodus (9, 31) and of the assumption (9, 51) which awaited Jesus in Jerusalem: the Lord's liberating exodus and his assumption into glory could not be accomplished except through his passion.

For the evangelists, it is an indubitable fact and a basic teaching that Jesus was aware both of the fate ordained for him and of its meaning. Today, we tend to wonder about this awareness, which, in our eyes, derogates from his humanity and the consistency of his life and death. If Jesus knows ahead of time everything that will happen to him, then everything is already over for him, and his passion is only a dreadful moment to be undergone, a dark tunnel whose end he already sees bathed in light. But this simplistic notion is not what emerges from the gospels: Jesus' view of his passion and his announcements of it are at once certain as to the fact, dependent on natural foresight and intuitions as to the unfolding of the event to come, and mysterious as to its significance. When we make allowance for literary devices and the composition of the gospels, Jesus' language in announcing his passion surely has a unique ring and import, and supposes a consciousness whose mystery transcends us. Yet this consciousness is that of a man, and we have access to it.

The first step is to catalogue the sayings where Jesus, in one way or another, predicts his passion. They are listed in Table III, on page 142. Not all equally authentic, these quotations often differ from one evangelist to the next, so that sometimes we have had to choose between them (texts 2, 9 and 11). The version we have chosen is not necessarily the surest, but it is the most significant for our purposes. Indeed, only an overall view of these texts allows us to ascertain their value and their implications. A critical assessment would show that some are certainly better authenticated than others; and, although we cannot undertake such a task here, we shall try to abide by its rules and findings. In this chapter, we shall contemplate only the first twelve texts, leaving the others for the study of the passion itself.

In the first two texts, a grouping seems to take shape immediately: the series of sayings which link the passion and the Son of Man (2, 3, 4, 5, 8, 10). This series, however, is not absolutely homogeneous, and we have to set text 10 apart. In the first five texts, the Son of Man must suffer and die: the accent is on the event, and this is truly an announcement. Text 10 also concerns the event, but here the accent is rather more on the Son of Man's mission and on Jesus' actual consciousness of it. Accordingly, we think this saying belongs in the series of statements about the Son of Man's earthly existence instead.[1] Leaving this text aside, we have the group of the five announcements (2, 3, 4, 5, 8). Three of them (2, 5, 8) are nearly identical, to the point of constituting three variants of one same initial formula; and we are inclined to believe that Mark repeated it purposely, with Matthew and Luke

Table III

ANNOUNCEMENTS OF THE PASSION IN THE SYNOPTICS

	Mt.	Mk.	Lk.	
1	9, 15	2, 19s	5, 34s	Surely the bridegroom's attendants would never think of mourning as long as the bridegroom is still with them? But the time will come for the bridegroom to be taken away from them . . .
2	16, 21	8, 31	9, 22	The Son of Man is destined to suffer grievously, to be rejected . . . and to be put to death, and to be raised up on the third day (Mk. and Lk.).
3	17, 9	9, 9		Tell no man about the vision until the Son of Man has risen from the dead.
4	17, 12	9, 12		Elijah has come already and they . . . treated him as they pleased; and the Son of Man will suffer similarly at their hands.
5	17, 22	9, 31	9, 44	The Son of Man is going to be handed over into the power of men; they will put him to death, and on the third day he will be raised to life again.
6			12, 49s	I have come to bring fire to the earth, and how I wish it were blazing already! There is a baptism I must still receive, and how great is my distress till it is over!
7			13, 32s	Today and tomorrow I cast out devils and on the third day attain my end. But for today and tomorrow and the next day I must go on, since it would not be right for a prophet to die outside Jerusalem.
8	20, 18	10, 33	18, 31	Now we are going up to Jerusalem, and the Son of Man is about to be handed over . . . and on the third day he will rise again.
9	20, 13	10, 39		The cup that I must drink you shall drink, and with the baptism with which I must be baptized you shall be baptized . . . (Mk.)
10	20, 28	10, 45		The Son of Man came not to be served but to serve, and to give his life as a ransom for many.
11	21, 37s	12, 6s	20, 13s	Finally he sent his son to them. . . . They seized him . . . and killed him.
12	21, 42	12, 10	20, 17	Have you never read in the scriptures: "It was the stone rejected by the builders that became the keystone. This was the Lord's doing, and it is wonderful to see"? (= Ps. 117, 22s, in LXX)
13	26, 12	14, 8		When she poured this ointment on my body, she did it to prepare me for burial.
14	26, 21	14, 18		Someone who has dipped his hand into the dish with me, will betray me (cf. Ps. 40, 10, in LXX)
15	26, 24	14, 21	22, 21	The Son of Man is going to his fate, as the scriptures say he will, but alas for that man by whom the Son of Man is betrayed!
16			22, 19	This is my body which will be given for you.
17	26, 28	14, 24		This is my blood, the blood of the covenant, which is to be poured out for many . . .
18	26, 29	14, 25		I shall not drink wine until the day I drink the new wine with you in the kingdom of my Father.
19	26, 31	14, 27		You will all lose faith in me this night, for the scripture says: "I shall strike the shepherd and the sheep of the flock will be scattered," but after my resurrection I shall go before you to Galilee.

taking up the same pattern afterwards.[2] If we add that texts 3 and 4 seem to presuppose the first declaration at Caesarea (text 2) and to have been written in this perspective, one could conclude that, out of the whole series, only the first text is original and reproduces Jesus' own words. But it is important to note that, even though one adopted this conclusion—which has been questioned by competent authors[3]—one would be wrong to infer from this literary fact an affirmation that tended to minimize as much as possible the connection Jesus made between his passion and the theme of the Son of Man. Even if the whole series contained only one saying directly from Jesus, it would hardly be reasonable simply to attribute all the others to a tendency in the evangelical tradition, as if this tendency could not be rooted in the lasting recollection of a language which Jesus himself fashioned and doubtlessly used more than once. When all the other announcements involve only one title each, there must be a reason for deliberately repeating *Son of Man*.

Among the six other announcements, three refer explicitly to the scriptures. The procedure is fairly close to that which makes him adopt the title *Son of Man*—with a notable difference, however: the Son of Man is an apocalyptic theme, essentially oriented toward a future revelation, whereas the references to the bridegroom (1), to the murdered prophet (7) and to the stone rejected by the builders (12) derive rather from a prophetic meditation based on the experiences already lived in Israel and about to be consummated in Jesus.[4] There remain three texts: on the one hand, two sayings of remarkable similarity and perhaps of identical origin—Jesus' reply to the sons of Zebedee concerning the cup and the baptism which await him (9), and his mysterious allusion, retained by Luke, to the fire and the baptism which he must undergo (6); and on the other hand, the parable of the murderous vinedressers (11). These three texts are precious: they are too enigmatic to have been invented later, and they certainly seem to afford us access to Jesus' very consciousness, to the sentiments which inhabit him as he contemplates what lies ahead. Nevertheless, they pose a few problems.

The parable of the murderous vinedressers, which is so telling in our gospel texts—especially in Mark (12, 6), where the addition of one word, "his *beloved* son," evokes the sacrifice of

Abraham and the love of the Father delivering up his only Son—was perhaps less telling in its early form. In the gospels, the Christian mind has given the characters of the original story a new transparency: the owner of the vineyard has taken on the features of Isaiah's God, who loves his vines (Is. 5, 1-2); the servants are the prophets; and the Son is the Messiah rejected by men and chosen by God. The allegory is manifest.[5] Most likely the original parable was not so obvious; but it is all the more precious because it presupposes in Jesus confident awareness of his personality and his mission, as well as extreme reserve in his way of revealing himself—something perfectly in keeping with his whole comportment. This parable is not meant primarily to highlight the secret of what he is, but to warn the instigators of the plot which is taking shape that they are in the process of committing an irreparable act.[6]

The two parallel texts about the fire, the cup and the baptism (6 and 9) have a unique accent which is noticeable especially in Luke and much more restrained in Mark and Matthew: that of a very brief confidence, but one heavy with emotion and anxiety. The difficulty of the bipartite saying in Luke (12, 49-50) derives at one and the same time from the relation between the two phrases "I have come to bring fire . . ." and "There is a baptism I must still receive . . ." and from their content. What is this fire or this baptism? What relation exists between them: between this fire which Jesus has come to kindle and which is not yet burning, and this baptism which he must undergo and which torments him?[7] His reply to Zebedee's sons is infinitely clearer, but this very clarity gives rise to problems. Is not the pairing of *cup* and *baptism* an obvious allusion to the two great sacraments and, therefore, a manifest anachronism in this dialogue, since the question could not have been formulated thus at the time? On the other hand, does not his promise to James and John, "The cup that I must drink you shall drink, and with the baptism with which I must be baptized you shall be baptized," suppose a prophecy introduced after the martyrdom of the two apostles?[8] These problems are real; but the solutions to them, though not always evident, can be solidly grounded. We have no proof that drinking the cup and undergoing the baptism necessarily mean a violent death nor, therefore, that this saying was devised later, after the martyrdom of

James and John. The correspondence between Jesus' cup-baptism terminology and that of the Christian sacraments of the Eucharist and Baptism is certainly striking, and Mark was probably aware of it. But that is not enough to prove that Jesus himself could not have established this link in the very context of the gospels—the pre-passion context—and without adverting to the practice of future communities. This language, at once suggestive and vague, is definitely in tune with the announcements of the passion.

From this rapid review of the texts, a few conclusions soon follow. For one thing, even though all these texts illustrate Jesus' awareness of going to a cruel death and a melancholy fate, not one of them presents this awareness as a reading from afar of the events to come. Even the three most precise announcements, those which reproduce the stages of the passion beforehand—the Son of Man handed over, put to death and rising again (2, 5, 8)—do not necessarily imply that, in order to formulate them, Jesus had to see the future scenario unfold. There are solid reasons to think that these three texts were redacted by authors who knew this scenario and were familiar with a passion narrative; but they are literary reasons, the same themes being repeated here and there. The language of Jesus as he appears in the gospels is not that of a seer deciphering a future in the process of unfolding before him, but that of someone sent by God, conscious of his mission and the outcome it entails and interpreting in this light the events which befall him and which, like everyone else, he sees headed his way. This general impression holds for all the other texts; and if we are inclined to suspect that the somewhat too pat sequel to text 8 was composed afterwards, the reason is not that the episode seems improbable but mainly that it is out of keeping with Jesus' customary style.[9]

These announcements, therefore, contain nothing that would keep Jesus from being a true man. "Jesus is an authentic man, and man's inalienable nobility is that he can—and even must—freely project the pattern of his life into a future of which he knows nothing. If this man is a believer, the future into which he casts and projects himself is God in his freedom and his immensity. To deprive Jesus of this opportunity and make him advance toward a goal which he already knows and which is distant only in time, would mean stripping him of his dignity as a man."[10]

And in point of fact, Jesus' reactions to the future are the same as ours: surprise and wonder at the centurion's faith, concern on seeing his disciples in the synagogue at Capernaum leave him one by one, anguish at the thought of the hatred that pursues him and bides its time. Nothing in the gospels warrants our imagining, behind this human face just like ours, another consciousness for which everything would already be over and done with. To invent, miraculously lodged in the infant of Bethlehem or the workman of Nazareth, a God with infallible perception who could already see the dawn of Easter, would be to introduce into Jesus two persons, two Christs, and dissolve him in myth. If, in Jesus, God is not the one who says "I," the one who stands amazed, who worries and is seized by fear, then Jesus is not God but only an impersonator. The Jesus of the gospels exists in real time—ours—and can leave it only by resurrecting. It takes him twelve years to achieve the proper distance with regard to his parents, and thirty years to become a man and to master the heritage of religious, human and professional culture—what the Jews called "wisdom" —which he needs so that his words and actions may truly convey our experience as men. Like us, he makes plans; and, like us, he sees them upset and thwarted. The moment he sets out to cure the centurion's servant, he is stopped with the protestation "Sir, I am not worthy to have you under my roof" (Mt. 8, 8). He follows Jairus home, where his young daughter is dying, but he allows himself to be delayed along the way by a sick woman (Mt. 9, 19-20). He decides to go away for a few moments' rest with his weary disciples; but when the crowds find him again, he forgoes the idea in order to give himself to them (Mk. 6, 30-34).

In Jesus' flexibility with regard to events and in his acceptance of the future as it gradually comes upon him, there is something completely different from an avowal of powerlessness and a determination to share our weakness; there is also—perhaps we should say "first of all"—the mark of his divine condition. We are the ones who, conscious of our limitations, have to devise plans and schemes to map out our future and protect ourselves from the risks that threaten us. We are the ones who conceive of divine omnipotence as a blueprint unrolled, or a process carried out, second by second, and think of our freedom as the power to throw the whole mechanism out of order. But this omnipotence we bestow on God is only a caricature; and the future which we believe we are placing in his hands is not the future, but only something past which we project before us. Bergson's insights always hold true: "Then, as the succession to come will end by being a succession past, we persuade ourselves that the duration to come admits of the same treatment as past duration, that it is, even now, unrollable, that the future is there, rolled up, already painted on the canvas. An illusion, no doubt, but an illusion that is natural, ineradicable, and that will last as long as the human mind. Time is invention or it is nothing at all." [11]

Such is Jesus according to the gospels. He speaks for the future, he announces the kingdom; he recruits for the future, he gathers disciples; he stakes his whole existence on the future, he will be himself only when the Son of Man appears. Nevertheless, he neither plans nor schemes. Not driven by caprice or impulse, he is always ready to serve because he is always himself. In all circumstances and regardless of what happens, he has within himself the wherewithal to react and reply. He may be taken unawares, but never caught unprepared. He may be assailed and mortally wounded, for he is infinitely vulnerable; but he is never more himself than when imprisoned and agonizing, never more open to men than the day he dies, rejected by all. To be so free in a world weighed down with so many servitudes—is this not to be God? Only the Creator is capable of accepting all beings in their reality like this, of taking things, events and men as they are, of judging them at their true worth, of forgiving and saving them. That is what Jesus does: he lays hold of people as they are—the incurably sick, the excommunicated sinners, the lost women, the overburdened hearts—and propels them forward: "Go, sin no more." He is the Lord of the future, not because he would hold some mind-boggling spectacle in reserve behind the curtain that shuts off our horizon, but because, at this present moment, from dead people crushed beneath their past he brings forth free men who conquer fear and are humbly prepared for any eventuality.

This unique and divine manner of dominating the future by letting it come to him appears with crystalline clarity in the announcements of the passion. By an astounding paradox, they show him mastering the future, conscious of what it is bringing and where it will lead him, and at the same time stripped of all his power and delivered up to the most fearsome might—the hatred of his enemies. Nothing better expresses this coincidence between his sovereign power and his utter powerlessness than his statements concerning the Son of Man who has come to be handed over to the cruelty of men. And we can understand why the gospels make a point of emphasizing and repeating this basic idea in sundry variants. For Jesus, identifying himself with the apocalyptic Son of Man who is to appear on the clouds of heaven means not only forestalling the future by announcing a hidden event, but placing himself at the close of that future as the one who, in Biblical terms, must judge it—that is, gather up the whole human adventure, bring together this immense epic, and give everyone his true place and his definitive countenance. The Son of Man on the clouds of heaven is the end of history, the coming of the kingdom, the Son restoring kingship to the Father so that God may at last be all in all (1 Cor. 15, 24-28). Now, this Son of Man is made precisely to be delivered up to the powers of the world and see them wreak their devices on him.

The force of these announcements does not reside in some divinatory power which might have enabled Jesus to outline beforehand a happening that could not be foreseen humanly. Not one of them derives its weight from this sort of sign; but all of them rest upon Jesus' consciousness of having received from God a unique role in the world, of being obliged to play it till its termination in a bitter and ignominious death, and of scrutinizing events and the people he meets for a gradual disclosure of the future that awaits him. While the assertions about the Son of Man are typical, the others exhibit the same content. In one way or another, they all invoke a figure from the scriptures—in other words, a figure sketched out by God—through which Jesus interprets his existence: he is the bridegroom who will be taken away (1), he is a prophet and cannot die outside Jerusalem since that is where he has been sent (7),[12] he is the Son and cannot escape the fate of the landowner's servants (11), he is the keystone on which God builds his work—an edifice that can rise only in a ravaged land (12; cf. Is. 28, 15-16), he must learn what is most frightful about the passage of God for sinful man: he must be baptized in this swirling torrent (9; cf. Is. 30, 27-28) and drink the dreadful cup where the horror of all the world's sins is distilled.

Not a single one of these images is secondary or marginal, not a single one merely conjures up a striking detail; on the contrary, they all express a unique and global view of the scriptures—not the kind of interpretation a skillful commentator would patiently construct by grouping themes, but a gaze which feels at home in this world and grasps it in its entirety. This spontaneous and, at the same time, radical vision of the Bible; this ease in establishing himself there and playing every role in it, so to say, from that of the prophet who speaks in God's name to that of the sinner who experiences his wrath—this is proper to Jesus. And this is what enables him to go to the inner meaning of the Bible, to the very limit of God's promises, to the final instant of the future.[13]

Jesus does not transpose into a dream this immediate and definitive reading of the scriptures, whereby he travels at a glance to the last moment of the future; nor does he act out in the world a role for which he has decoded the promptbook that was mysteriously concealed in the labyrinthine texts. He finds the scriptures in his everyday life, and he need only look and listen to notice events taking shape, opposition stiffening, plots hatching, and decisions being made. It takes no exceptional gifts to sense all this; in fact, even his disciples see the storm clouds gathering (Mk. 10, 32; Jn. 11, 8).

This antagonism cannot surprise Jesus, since he himself has provoked it: the positions he has taken have necessarily offended many people and given rise to violent reactions. Spurning the current interpretations of the doctors of the Law, calling Herod a fox publicly (Lk. 13, 32), denouncing the hypocrisy of kings who like to be hailed as benefactors (Lk. 22, 25) and driving out the merchants who were transacting business in the Temple (Lk. 11, 15-18) has created an instant coalition of formidable adversaries in every important milieu—business, politics and religion. Matters reach such a point that some wonder whether Jesus' vigor in confronting the establishment does not bespeak active sympathy for the religiorevolutionary movement of the Zealots.[14] And it is a fact that Jesus, who often violently attacked the scribes and the Pharisees, seems never to have said a word against the Zealots; however, he differs from them on too many essential points to be a sympathizer of theirs.[15] Still, although he does not question the legitimacy of the powers that be, he remains totally independent

with regard to them and judges their comportment severely. Such
independence necessarily exposes him to their suspicions and their
vigilance, for, in these restless and troubled times, they are constantly on the lookout and quick to react if they feel threatened.
Everyone senses it, and Jesus cannot possibly have any illusions.
And so he lives his last weeks under the watchful eyes of the
police. He knows it, because he foresaw it; he does nothing to
arouse them and, instead, avoids them as much as possible; but he
does not evade them once his hour has come. He is at the mercy
of a dastardly deed being planned by Judas.

Jesus is too perceptive not to see and follow this opposition
mobilizing against him, these threats growing clearer and sharper,
these decisions brewing. But he does more than follow them: in a
sense, we could almost say he precedes and provokes them, as if
the power of evil itself also depended on him and acted only in reaction to his initiative. Here, once again, Jesus gives rise to a
paradox. On the one hand, throughout his life he "went about
doing good" (Acts 10, 38), and not one of his actions justifies the
evil about to befall him. The fact that men cannot respond to his
goodness except by killing him is a sign of their wickedness. But it
seems as if this response—which comes from them alone, and not
from him—is elicited in them by his approach and his presence.

Thus, in the course of the gospels, we hear the words of the
Sermon on the Mount take on an ever harsher tone till they end
in pitiless condemnations. At the time of the Sermon, Jesus con-
tented himself with contrasting the behavior of the hypocrites,
who publicize their prayers and good works in the synagogues
and streets so as to be honored by men, with the attitude of the
disciples, who hope only to be seen by their Father (Mt. 6, 1-6).
But now, in the closing pages of the narrative and at the end of
his career, he tears aside the veil of anonymity and calls these
hypocrites by name: they are "the scribes and the Pharisees" (Mt.
23, 13.15.23.25.27.29);[16] he trains his listeners' eyes on these men
who do everything "to attract attention, like wearing broader
phylacteries and longer tassels, like wanting to take the place of
honor at banquets and the front seats in the synagogues, being
greeted obsequiously in the market squares and having people call
them Rabbi" (Mt. 23, 5-7). The Sermon on the Mount maintained a certain distance from the articles of the Law, but that

was in order to go to the very heart of it and map out the road which led it to its perfection. Now, Jesus' attacks against the scribes and the Pharisees denounce their aberrant interpretations, the deviations which falsify the Law and render it both unbearable and inoperative, omitting what matters most—justice and mercy (Mt. 23, 23; cf. 5, 7.20)—to heap up meaningless obligations and make people pay taxes on the grass in the fields.

Compositional techniques obviously account for some of the distance, on both sides, between the Sermon on the Mount and the indictment of the scribes and the Pharisees. In the Sermon, Matthew has included the whole positive aspect of Jesus' teaching; and in the discourse from his last week on earth, all the reproaches he used to level at these hypocrites. But the procedure certainly mirrors the contour of Jesus' career, from the enthusiasm attending the first steps in Galilee to the open hostility of the leaders in Jerusalem. And if, little by little, the conflict becomes irreconcilable, ending in the resolution by the Sanhedrin, the chief priests, the elders and the scribes to get rid of Jesus, their decision doubtlessly exposes the recesses of their hearts and the evil that dwells there, but it also reveals the ground on which the battle is being fought.

This ground is public and, from a certain point of view, political. Of course, political activity would hardly mean the same thing in Jesus' case as in that of a citizen in a modern state, and it is manifest that Jesus remains aloof both from the politicians in his country and from the political movements of his people: we cannot identify him with any party, and he supports none. But he takes the Sermon on the Mount seriously; he lives and makes others live what he says, and this logic causes him to meet and confront all parties. He does not challenge responsible authorities, but he judges them severely; he declares the rich unhappy and asks his disciples to give their possessions to the poor; he preaches forgiveness and associates with tax collectors and prostitutes; he places mercy above sacrifice and, ignoring the sabbath, heals the sick who come to him; he tells of a God who wants hearts that are free and entirely his, and he throws the merchants out of the Temple; he announces the coming of the kingdom and, although he disclaims any intention of seizing power, he can understand why his presence should stir up Jerusalem and create

panic in the administration (Lk. 19, 39-40). These are political
acts, not that they form part of a political program or are dictated by political objectives, but that they bring him face to face
with leaders and attitudes, forcing him to explain his position and
choose sides publicly. In this way, he demonstrates the implications of the Sermon on the Mount: they are not political in the
sense that the Sermon could launch an "evangelical polity" complete with its own special ends and means, but they are political
from the fact that, in a world where nothing escapes politics,
Jesus must assume political responsibility for his acts before the
political authorities. What is shocking is not Jesus' trial, but its
outcome. It is only to be expected that Jesus, inaugurating an
unheard-of life style that breaks with consecrated traditions,
should have to explain and defend himself. Nor did he shirk the
task: in fact, a good part of his teaching constitutes a vast plea
justifying his conduct. The tragedy is that his judges are incapable
of understanding him.

Through all Jesus' announcements, we see these ominous
forces leaguing together and looming on the horizon. There is no
need to follow all their plots; it is sufficient to feel their capacity
for hatred and their power for evil draw near. The most meaningful of Jesus' words are perhaps those which remain vaguest: suffering grievously and being rejected (text 2), being treated "as
they pleased" like Elijah [that is, John the Baptist] (4), dying in
Jerusalem like the prophets (7), falling into the hands of merciless
people who no longer have anything to lose (11). One word translates this frightful sensation of powerlessness and horror: Jesus
must be "handed over." Before it becomes one of the refrains of
the passion and is confirmed by the grim spectacle of Jesus being
tossed back and forth from Judas to the guards (Mk. 14, 44),
from the Sanhedrin to Pilate (Mk. 15, 1) and from Pilate to the
executioners (15, 15), the phrase *handed over*—which recurs oftener as the hour draws nearer—fully expresses what that hour can
mean for Jesus, who foresees it but cannot escape it: falling defenseless into the clutches of powers left free to do whatever they
choose. This is "the reign of darkness" (Lk. 22, 53), beyond his
worst imaginings.

Still, even though Jesus feels the horror and anguish of this
evil before it ever seizes him, it is not what his announcements are

concerned with. Evil is present there, with its boundless cruelty; but it neither directs the performance nor terminates it. The language of these sayings is perfectly clear: evil, human malice and the power of sin all have their due place there, and nothing softens their sinister features: there is no room for illusion, no vain hope to latch on to. Jesus has to know all that—not because of evil, but because he is a prophet, like Elijah and John the Baptist (texts 4, 7), because he is the Son of Man (2, 4, 5, 8, 10), the bridegroom of Israel (1), the keystone (12), the Son of God (11). This necessity always resides in the figure come from God, never in the maleficent power. However slight the nuance may seem, it is of capital importance and dictates the Christian view on evil in the world. Had Jesus said, "Men must lay hold of me, they must put the prophet to death, they must destroy the work of God," he would have been admitting that evil was stronger, and that he had lost all hope in mankind. If sin really has to do its work, then there is nothing for us but to avoid it, if possible, and Jesus can go back where he comes from. The only possible hope is that evil may eventually exhaust itself in victory, but it will exhaust itself only by ceasing to conquer, and it will cease to conquer only by destroying its victim. Evil is destructive; it cannot stop till it has nothing left to destroy. If sin has to do its work, humanity is lost.

But Jesus does not say—or even suggest—that sin has to do its work. Never for a minute does he give way to our instinctive reactions: "It's not surprising! That's how people are. That's how the Jews are. What do you expect?" Doing so would be refusing to forgive them, leaving them in their sin, and renouncing his role as witness to God's tenderness. "The Son of Man must be handed over" means that men are sinners and are going to commit a monstrous sin, but that, at the other end of their sin, they will rediscover their victim, the Son of Man gathering the saints together, the prophet, the faithful witness, the keystone at the peak of the New Temple. The whole reality of evil remains, the cruelty of sin, and its destructive force. The passion is not a nightmare, not a difficult moment to go through; it is the unleashing of sin upon the Innocent One. Jesus has to undergo this experience and endure this loathsome contact in order to rob sin of its secret power, its deadly venom.

When taken seriously, as a necessity arising from God and

not from evil, the announcements of the passion are announcements of victory. As is only to be expected, that victory is rarely described, for Jesus' combat would not be real if he were already gazing upon the victorious battlefield. His struggle has to be an agony (Lk. 22, 44). But its outcome is certain, and Jesus knows it. This is the perspective we must adopt when approaching the problem created by the references to his resurrection in some of the passion announcements. The explicit announcement of the resurrection occurs in four texts, all of which mention the Son of Man. It appears—in very similar terms, including the detail about the third day—in the three great quasi-parallel texts concerning the Son of Man rejected and handed over (2, 5, 8), and strongly contributes to the unity of impression given by these three texts, which begin identically and, after considerable variants, also end identically: "after three days to rise again" (Mk. 8, 31) and "after three days he will rise again" (9, 31; 10, 34).

It is often asked whether this mention of the resurrection, together with the three days, is not a later addition, as would have been quite natural in a Christian community where the resurrection and the third day were essential articles of faith. There are weighty considerations behind this question. For one thing, if Jesus really announced his resurrection in these terms, it is surprising that the message of the angels at the tomb does not allude to any such statement. In Mark, the angel's words, "He is going before you to Galilee; it is there you will see him, just as he told you" (Mk. 16, 7), refer us to an announcement placed just before the episode in Gethsemane and formulated in very vague terms with no mention of a date: "After my resurrection I shall go before you into Galilee" (Mk. 14, 28). It is also surprising that the three days appear in the relatively early announcements of the passion, and then do not appear even once in the announcements which become more numerous as the event approaches. It seems more likely that the mention of the third day is a Christian addendum.[17]

It is more difficult to come to a decision about the word *resurrection*.[18] In any case, we should not make it the key to Jesus' hope and to the promise he holds out to his followers. For the word appears only in a specific context, at the end of a sequence which more or less sharply outlines the stages of a passion, and it is obviously used to cap that sequence. Now, of all the announcements, these sequences are precisely the ones from which we cannot exclude the echo of events. The fact remains that, even if we had to relinquish the word *resurrection,* Jesus' affirmation would keep all its force and significance. As we have seen, all his announcements define a necessity in God's work, a fundamental trait of the personage he sends; and they are announcements of victory. This holds true for every one of these texts, without always being so explicit. It is manifest in all the sayings about the Son of Man. For the Son of Man cannot cease to be what he is in the apocalyptic tradition: he who appears in the heavens to inaugurate the kingdom of the saints and sit through the ages in the power and glory of God. If this Son of Man must suffer and die, his suffering and his death have to be only a road and not the goal. Unless he is there at the end of this road, beyond this passageway, he will never be the Son of Man; and, therefore, he cannot be such today.[19]

As glimpsed through these announcements, Jesus' consciousness possesses something unique but remains totally human, and it is accessible to us. For what is unique about it—the certitude of being at the center of God's work and realizing exactly what he expects and wants in the world—obviously supposes an immediate exchange, a direct confidence, but, at the same time, a progression identical with our own, an itinerary with two sides which complete one another but both belong to our world. Jesus sees his future and his passion from two points of view: a direct look at the men and events which surround him and affect him; and a second, reflex look, illuminated by the scriptures of his people, through which he interprets his life and explains his actions. His lucid observation of the world assures him that he will not escape the death being prepared for him. His certitude that he is at the end of the scriptures assures him that this death is the crown of God's work, the fulfillment of his promises, the salvation of men. At the heart of these two glances and these two certitudes, in the deepest part of himself, there resides that inexhaustible and inaccessible source, that light which is his whole being. It is what enables him, as he looks upon the world and men, to penetrate to the very core of them, to reach them as they are, to be directly at the center of their life. It is also what makes him inhabit the scriptures, not as a book for him to decipher, nor even as a precious experience for him to relive, but as his own fatherland, his own existence, the very story he is actually living. Now, these two worlds, not a feature of which escapes him—the world of men and events, the world of time which comes and passes, and the world of the scriptures, where God tells the story he is putting together—these are two domains both of which are accessible and intelligible to us. No doubt, we have a superficial view and a poor understanding of them, because of our weakness and our limitations; but they are within our scope, and we can find our way around in them. And when Jesus, in a single glance, lays bare the scriptures and goes to the very bottom of our hearts, we know that we cannot imitate him, even from a great distance, but yet can recognize his infallible lucidity. Like his conduct, his consciousness is coherent; it springs from a depth our eyes cannot fathom, but it shows us a true being; it is not a mythical construct, but a mystery which reveals and gives itself.

NOTES TO CHAPTER 11

1. See Table I, p. 125.
2. Analysis is difficult here, and the conclusions of the exegetes are quite divergent. See G. Minette de Tillesse, *Le secret messianique dans l'évangile de Marc,* pp. 374-380; G. Strecker, "Die Leidens und Auferstehungsvoraussagen im Markusevangelium," in *Zeitschrift für Theologie und Kirche,* 64 (1967), pp. 16-39; M. Black, "The 'Son of Man' Passion Sayings in the Gospel Tradition," in *Zeitschrift für die neutestamentliche Wissenschaft,* 60 (1969), pp. 1-8.
3. E. Lohmeyer, in *Das Evangelium nach Markus* Göttingen, 1967), p. 220, notes the originality of the third announcement in relation to Mark's account of the passion. Under "Païs Theou," in *Theologisches Wörterbuch zum neuen Testament,* V, p. 710, n. 459, J. Jeremias observes that, despite the visible stylization, all the details of this announcement agree with the regular practices of the time and could have belonged to the original announcement, even before the passion took place.
4. Often impugned, the authenticity of the allusion to the bridegroom's being "taken away" is well defended in V. Taylor's *The Gospel According to St. Mark* (London: Macmillan, 1966), pp. 211-212. A later addition could neither have invented this unexpected link between the theme of the bridegroom and that of his being taken away (which recalls Is. 53, 8) nor have preserved this subtlety in evoking it. It is more difficult to rule out the hypothesis that the use of Ps. 117 in text 12 reflects a habit of the Christian community, but neither is there any decisive reason why we may not think that the allusion to the stone goes back to Jesus himself. V. Taylor, *op. cit.,* p. 476.
5. The work of allegorization appears still more considerable when we compare the gospel versions with the version preserved in the Coptic text discovered in Upper Egypt in 1945. See J. Doresse, *L'évangile selon saint Thomas ou les paroles de Jésus* (Paris: Plon, 1959), text No. 65. It has been suggested that we should take this non-allegorized version, in which the example is what counts and not the characters, as the original form of the parable: "There can be no doubt that in the sending of the son Jesus himself had his own sending in mind, but for the mass of his hearers the Messianic significance of the son could not be taken for granted, since no evidence is forthcoming for the application of the title 'Son of God' to the Messiah in pre-Christian Palestinian Judaism." J. Jeremias, *The Parables of Jesus,* pp. 72-73. On the contrary, it seems that *The Gospel of Thomas,* far from being an early version, is a text which depends on Luke and systematically eliminates every possibility of allegorical interpretation, in order to safeguard the secret reserved to the initiates of this gnostic milieu. See X. Léon-Dufour, *Etudes d'Evangile* (Paris: Seuil, 1965), p. 312. See also the nuanced interpretation of Heinrich Kahlefeld, *Parables and Instructions in the Gospels,* trans. by Arlene Swidler (New York: Herder and Herder, 1966), pp. 72-84.
6. That is why this parable retains its full significance even if we admit—and the view seems certain—that "Son of God" did not constitute a title of the

Messiah in the pre-Christian Judaism of Palestine. See J. Jeremias, *op. cit.*, pp. 72-73.

7. A. Feuillet, "La coupe et le baptême de la Passion," in *Revue Biblique*, 74 (1967), pp. 368-370. See especially note 42.

8. A. Feuillet, *art. cit.*, pp. 356-391.

9. Still, we must not be dogmatic. Some very substantial authors deem that the second and third announcements contain original features exactly suited to the specific situation in which Jesus was, and that these announcements do not imply any exceptional type of knowledge. See Note 3 in this chapter.

10. H. Urs von Balthasar, *La foi du Christ* (Paris: Aubier, 1969), p. 181.

11. Henri Bergson, *Creative Evolution*, trans. by Arthur Mitchell (New York: Henry Holt and Co., 1911), p. 341.

12. Lk. 13, 31-33 is a difficult text. The relation between the two sequences "today and tomorrow . . . and on the third day" (v. 32) and "today and tomorrow and the next day" (v. 33) remains unclear. Why is the formula repeated twice, with this variation? Are we dealing with the same operation presented from different viewpoints in each verse: in 32, from an active viewpoint—that of the deeds Jesus performs; and in 33, from a passive viewpoint—that of the necessity which leads him to Jerusalem? Or are these two different and successive moments? And what does the link—*plèn*—between both sentences mean? Does it express opposition or add precision, like "Or, more exactly . . ."? The text has been studied in detail by O. H. Steck, *Israel und das gewaltsame Geschick der Propheten* (Neukirchen-Vluyn, 1967), pp. 40-47. Steck thinks that the whole of v. 33 is a creation of Luke's, in which he expresses his theology of the ascent to Jerusalem. In that case, one should not expect it to yield any testimony concerning Jesus himself on the eve of his passion. We cannot go over Steck's arguments here but only ask whether his conclusion is absolutely satisfying, since separating v. 33 from 31-32 leaves Jesus' answer incomplete. He has been advised, "Go away . . . because Herod means to kill you" (31), and the real answer comes only in 33: "I must go on."

If we endeavor to keep the text as it is and to find coherence in it, we must apparently stress the difference between the first answer, where Jesus speaks in the active voice about the deeds he is performing, and the second answer, where, starting from "I must go on," these deeds become the implementation of God's plan. There is obviously something abrupt in this progression, and well may it surprise us; but perhaps it accurately translates what is so basic and so essential in Jesus: the coincidence between his total spontaneity and his awareness of carrying out the work of Another. The text would then mean: "You may go and give that fox this message: 'Learn that today and tomorrow I cast out devils and finish curing, and on the third day will come my turn to be finished.' Nevertheless, today and tomorrow and the next day I must be on my way, since it would not be right for a prophet to die outside Jerusalem." We have here a twofold answer, according to two points of view: on the one hand, Jesus has not yet finished his work of casting out devils and healing, and very soon—on the third day—he himself will be near his end, finished. This is an initial answer, on the level of visible events: Jesus will soon go away. But on another level—that which directs Jesus' journey—he has already left: he left the moment he was called to Jerusalem to suffer the fate of the prophets. The second answer, moreover, can correct the first and bring it into focus: "I am staying only two days—or, more exactly, even during these two days, I am already on my way."

13. To us, this spontaneous synthetic view seems likeliest to hold a clue to difficult sayings like the one about the cup and the baptism. Our only reservation with regard to A. Feuillet's precious article "La coupe et le baptême de la Passion," in *Revue Biblique,* 74 (1967), pp. 356-391, concerns the overexplicit notion of solidarity which he tends to discover in these themes: "The cup Jesus has to drink must therefore refer to the divine chastisement he will undergo *in place of the guilty*" (p. 376); "If Jesus . . . did not hesitate to call his passion a baptism, that is because he and his apostles were familiar with a repentance rite called 'baptism' closely connected with sin, and because he intended *to relate his death and sin*" (p. 381). We have underlined the two phrases which cause us misgivings. Though it seems certain to us—and the article furnishes a solid demonstration of it—that the cup and the baptism refer to a redoubtable intervention by God with regard to man's sin, it is far less certain that Jesus reasoned in these terms. Feuillet recalls that Jesus and his followers were cognizant of John's baptism and the connection he established between sin and repentance. The fact is beyond question but is counterbalanced by another—namely, that this connection is not expressed here. Perhaps we would be closer to our text if we remembered that in giving the name *baptism* to the gesture he used to make with water over sinners, John himself saw therein the prophetic gesture given by God in order to allow man to pass through the baptism of fire which would strike the sinful world (Mt. 3, 11-12). When Jesus simply suggests that he is walking toward death, that this death will recall the fate scripture promises to sinners, and that nevertheless it is God's will for him, he is not yet constructing a theology of the redemption, but he is giving the impending event its full dimensions in the mystery of God and the abyss of sin, and is making it the principle of all subsequent theologies, from the explanations of the kerygma in the Acts of the Apostles to the reflections of Paul and the letter to the Hebrews.

14. S. G. F. Brandon, *Jesus and the Zealots, A Study of Political Factors in Primitive Christianity* (New York: Charles Scribner's Sons, 1968).

15. O. Cullmann, *Jesus and the Revolutionaries,* trans. by Gareth Putnam (New York: Harper and Row, Publishers, 1970), puts his finger on the basic point: "It is in any case certain that Jesus viewed the political conception of Messiah always as a temptation, and indeed as *his special temptation*" (p. 39; cf. also pp. 3-5 and 35). See also D. Flusser, *Jesus* (New York: Herder and Herder, 1969), pp. 84-88.

16. The expression "scribes and Pharisees" is a simplified way used by the evangelists to designate a more complex situation, which they can define in greater detail when necessary. See J. Jeremias, *Jerusalem in the Time of Jesus,* trans. by F. H. and C. H. Cave (Philadelphia: Fortress Press, 1969), pp. 233-245, 246-253. The scribes, or doctors of the Law, constitute a social class composed of men who, under qualified masters or rabbis, have pursued "advanced studies" in the discipline which embraced them all—the study of the Law. The scribes are "theologians," theorists. The Pharisees, on the contrary, are concerned with practice. Recruited from every milieu, they group themselves into communities (Jeremias, *op. cit.,* p. 247) in order to live the Law in all its purity. The evangelists' habit of naming them together

—"the scribes and the Pharisees"—derives from the fact that the leaders and the most influential members of these communities were scribes (p. 254), which is understandable, since they were considered specialists in the Law. But, just as there were many scribes outside the Pharisaic movement, so there were many pious persons who adhered to it without possessing the knowledge expected of scribes (pp. 258-259). In Mt. 23, Christ's sevenfold indictment of the scribes and the Pharisees is addressed to both groups together, whereas the parallel passages in Luke distinguish more clearly between two categories of reproaches (pp. 252-254).

We may sometimes be surprised at how relentlessly Jesus warns his listeners against the scribes and the Pharisees, and how unimportant he seems to consider the chief priests and the elders, the sacerdotal aristocracy and the lay nobility which, together with a certain number of scribes, govern the Jewish people under the supervision of the Roman governor (Jeremias, *op. cit.*, pp. 147-232, 235-267). It is because those notables are more preoccupied with political issues than with religious matters, and Jesus rarely meets them on his own ground. They appear, however, the moment they suspect him of trying to overthrow the established order—for example, when he routs the merchants who have set up shop in the Temple—and their language faithfully translates their mentality: "Who gave you authority to do these things?" (Mk. 11, 28). The scribes' usual question, on the contrary, concerns Jesus' demeanor and life style, and takes on the form of a discussion: "Why do you do that?" (Mk. 2, 18; 7, 5). See C. H. Dodd, *Historical Tradition in the Fourth Gospel*, p. 264, n. 4.

17. K. Lehmann, in *Auferweckt am dritten Tag nach der Schrift* (Freiburg-im-Breisgau, 1968), shows that "the third day" has theological significance first of all and is used to denote that the event marks a turning point in salvation history. On this view, it would be more natural for Jesus to have used the expression. But we would still have difficulty explaining why such an announcement is not echoed in the resurrection narratives.

18. Moreover, it is not identical in Mk. 8, 31; 9, 31; 10, 34 (*anastènai:* to get up again) and in Mt. 16, 21; 17, 23; 20, 19 (*egerthènai:* to awaken). Matthew has doubtlessly adopted the accepted terminology (cf. 1 Cor. 15, 4; Acts 3, 15; 4, 10; 5, 30; 10, 40).

19. We should note Jesus' three statements on being apprehended: "This is your hour; this is the reign of darkness" (Lk. 22, 53), "This is to fulfill the scriptures" (Mk. 14, 49), and "Am I not to drink the cup that my Father has given me?" (Jn. 18, 11). These are the three components of his consciousness: men and events, the scriptures, and the Father.

12
Awaiting the Son of Man

In presenting himself as the Son of Man and announcing that he would die and return in the likeness of man, Jesus was not only formulating a capital statement about his person and his role in the advent of God's kingdom, but was also opening an absolutely new era in the march of time and introducing a radically original element into the history and the figure of mankind. Since he was going to die as a man and reappear in a celestial form, invested with all-embracing power, two possibilities existed: he would return either immediately after his death or some time later. Taken by themselves, the announcements of the passion would seem to support the first hypothesis. Apparently, none of them anticipates any appreciable lapse of time between Jesus' death and the coming of the Son of Man. As we have just seen, it is not certain that the words which foretell the resurrection distinguished it, at first, from the apparition of the Son of Man. Only one text—that in which the bridegroom's attendants see him taken away, snatched from their friendship (Mk. 2, 20)—seems to suggest an interval after Jesus' death, but it never even mentions his return. We may ask ourselves whether all these texts do not presuppose that Jesus' death is going to set off a chain of events which will culminate in the apparition of the Son of Man. Even if this process must take a little while, the delay will be negligible, filled with happenings that already belong to a different time from ours and to what we call the end of the world. This eschatological perspective does not seem to be contradicted by any of the passion announcements. Furthermore, it is perfectly natural in the mentality and atmosphere surrounding Jesus, and we find it again in the first Christian communities, where the parousia of the Lord was considered imminent.

Yet, even though all these announcements are compatible with the hypothesis that the passion will be followed almost immediately by the parousia, not a single one imposes such a view; and this fact should make us think twice, since the normal tendency would be to stress the passion-parousia sequence or at least the brevity of the delay. But a cogent reason obliges us to conclude that Jesus, in distinguishing between his death and the coming of the Son of Man, was contemplating not only two aspects or two moments of the same event but two separate, though closely related, events. It is the way Jesus speaks to his disciples about their future—a future which they will have to live, after his death, apart from him. This future is the object of his so-called eschatological teachings.

Although the announcements of the passion form a series which, in its diversity, is sufficiently consistent and homogeneous to make them difficult to ignore, they nevertheless occupy only a modest place compared with the considerable development given, in Jesus' teaching, to the eschatological themes of the coming of the Son of Man, the judgment of the world, the expectation of that day, and the proper way to live meanwhile. It is true that these themes, instead of appealing to us, disconcert us. We feel far removed from this apocalyptic language, these grandiose but unreal visions, this violence which seems either intolerable or unnecessary; and we stand aside, prudent and yet ill at ease, refusing to yield to a fear which strikes us as puerile and taking shelter in an indifference which is equally unworthy of a man.

Still, we cannot ignore such a sizeable portion of the gospels and deem it valueless. And if, through scorn or fear, we refuse to approach this domain, then we gravely mutilate the person of Jesus, depriving it of essential traits and condemning ourselves to understanding nothing of his existence. For, in Jesus' mind, these enigmatic visions, these rather incoherent images, these dazzling and at the same time simplistic epitomes not only depict that final event, the last day of our world, but embrace the entire future, his and ours.

Until his death and for the time left him to live on earth, Jesus can fashion himself an idea of his future out of his human experience. In order to know what it means to die, to die the victim of evil, to die at the hands of ruthless adversaries, to die through fidelity to his mission, he need only open his eyes, feel the hatred mounting around him, remember the prophets and saints among his people, and listen to his own heart telling him whence come his suffering and his strength. But what will happen after his death? And what does he know about that future, which has not yet been born? Is he carrying it even now as his own future, as the development of his own life? Does he contemplate it from a distance, like some vast spectacle?

As obscure as the eschatological passages may be concerning many details, they are perfectly clear on two points: Jesus affirms that, being the Son of Man, he is the Lord of the future, that all the ages will reach completion with his coming, and that the whole content of human history will find its meaning and its fulfillment in that hour. However, he sheds no special light on the concrete unfolding of this history. The only point on which he becomes specific is the destruction of Jerusalem and the Temple (Mk. 13, 2.14). But he does not speak of it as if, from afar, he could already see Titus' armies besieging and storming the city in the year 70. To describe the event, he has only the enigmatic image of the prophet Daniel announcing "disastrous abomination . . . on the wing of the Temple" (Dan. 9, 27);[1] and when he weeps over Jerusalem, "encircle[d] . . . and hem[med] . . . in on every side" (Lk. 19, 43), with her children "dash[ed] . . . to the ground" (19, 44), he does not have to see the catastrophe of the year 70 but only know what the siege and capture of a city is like.[2] Such is the only event Jesus posts beforehand in future history. He does so in the manner of the prophets, not as a vision unfurling before his very eyes, but as the ineluctable accomplishment of the present which he is now living. If Jerusalem, which had been chosen to welcome the Messiah, disregards her vocation, the reason is that she harbors within herself a destructive force from which even Jesus has been unable to save her.

Apart from this announcement, all Jesus' statements concerning the future leave it shrouded in vagueness and only broadly outlined with images from the present and the past: there will be wars, earthquakes, famines (Mk. 13, 7-8), the calamities of any age. The spiritual conflicts will become exceptionally intense, but their setting is the traditional theatre of persecutions—

"sanhedrins . . . synagogues . . . governors and kings" (Mk. 13, 9)
—which is so familiar to Jesus. Even the most acute crises exhibit no new features and can only be suggested by comparisons:
"In those days there will be such distress as, until now, has not
been equalled since the beginning when God created the world"
(Mk. 13, 19). The strictly apocalyptic images of stars losing their
brightness and universes crumbling belong no more to this history
but to the ultimate event, the coming of the Son of Man (Mk.
13, 24-27). Jesus can clearly demarcate what pertains to future
history and is "not yet . . . the end" (Mk. 13, 7) from "the end"
itself (Mt. 24, 14), which no longer pertains to history but to
God's definitive act, to the advent of the Son of Man and the
coming of the kingdom. Just as the future is not vividly painted
but only sketched on the basis of the present, so neither is the end
vividly painted but only suggested through apocalyptic symbols.

This presence of the future in the eschatological passages—of
the real future, which has not yet arrived and which Jesus himself
cannot define beforehand—this difference between what is still in
time and the end of that time, indicates that, for Jesus, history
would continue after his death and that an interval would separate his departure from the coming of the Son of Man. And if the
distinction between the images of the future and those of the end
seems strained,[3] there is a decisive proof: the fact that Jesus anticipates for his followers a period during which he will be separated
from them. The essential purpose of what we commonly call "the
eschatological discourse" is to prepare the disciples for that
period.[4] And this purpose appears even more clearly if we compare this eschatological discourse with an analogous discourse
recorded only by Luke and dealing with the day of the Son of
Man (Lk. 17, 22-37).[5]

Both have several points in common: the emergence of
pseudo-messiahs (Mk. 13, 21; cf. Lk. 17, 23), catastrophes to escape from (Mk. 13, 15-16; cf. 17, 31-32),[6] but especially the sudden, worldwide coming of the Son of Man, appearing before all
nations the way lightning flashes from one part of heaven to the
other (Lk. 17, 24), and sending angels "to gather his chosen . . .
from the ends of the world to the ends of heaven" (Mk. 13, 27).

But these similarities cannot conceal profound differences.
The discourse on the day of the Son of Man is a warning, like the

prophets' warnings about the day of the Lord (Amos 5, 18-20; 2, 13-16; Is. 2, 6-21; Jer. 30, 5-7; Zeph. 1, 2-16). Like the day of Yahweh for Israel, the day of the Son of Man will be a catastrophic surprise, swooping down on people unawares. Just as "in Noah's day . . . people were eating and drinking, marrying wives and husbands" (Lk. 17, 26-27) and they all perished; and just as "in Lot's day people were . . . buying and selling, planting and building" (17, 28) and they all perished, so will it be the day the Son of Man appears: no one will expect it, no one will have prepared for it, and each one's fate will depend on what he is at that moment: "On that night two will be in one bed: one will be taken, the other left; two women will be grinding corn together: one will be taken, the other left" (7, 34-35). This is the tone of prophetic warnings; this is the announcement of a dire event that is no longer just an episode in history—like the fall of Samaria or Jerusalem, in which God intervenes through the kings of Assyria and Babylon—but an event that transcends history and is prefigured by cataclysms like the Flood, a direct action of God. From this viewpoint, nothing is really historical, everything is eschatological; the discussion concerns only the end of history, not the future. The point of contact with history is the personage of the Son of Man. He who announces his coming is the Jesus who warns this generation, so that it may hear and be converted. Strictly speaking, we cannot deduce anything from this page as to what Jesus thought about the future of the world after him. All he says is that this future opens onto the coming of the Son of Man.

The eschatological discourse is entirely different. Here the future and eschatology are both envisaged; history and the end of history, without being confused, are reunited and placed end to end, like parturition and birth (Mk. 13, 8), like winter and summer (13, 18-29). But here eschatology appears only at the close, and the gist of the discourse concerns the period of preparation, a period filled with what makes up history. In these lines, it seems but a web of calamities: wars, natural disasters, hatred among men—crowned by the worst misfortune of all, the destruction of Jerusalem. This grim outlook doubtlessly derives from the time at which Jesus evokes the future—a few days before his death, facing a city controlled by his adversaries (Mk. 13, 3); and he cannot separate his destiny from the destiny which awaits this proud capital, these great buildings (13, 1-2). But above all, through his own fate, Jesus is thinking of that of his disciples; and if he presents the future to them in such somber colors, that is because his words now are an encouragement and a call to hope. Earlier, images of catastrophies held over the heads of indifferent men the threat of the day when the Son of Man would manifest his power. Here, the message is that the disciples, deprived of Jesus' presence and exposed to all the hatred he himself has known, have to wait faithfully and patiently, through the most tragic situations, for the coming of him who will not fail to reappear. In a word, the discourse on the day of the Son of Man is addressed to an undependable and unreceptive audience, in order to summon them to conversion; and the eschatological discourse is addressed to disciples, to very close disciples, in order to advise them of the trials which await them and of the strength with which God will fill them to await the end.[7]

This is why the first discourse speaks only of surprise, as if there were nothing to be done, whereas the eschatological discourse contains precise instructions, such as not giving way to fear (Mk. 13, 7), not confusing Christ with the imposters who will spring up (13, 6), not worrying beforehand about what to say in times of persecution (13, 9-13), not linking one's fate with Jerusalem's (13, 14-16), and not falling asleep while awaiting the Master's return (13, 33-37). All these admonitions go to make up a cohesive attitude, strongly marked by the impending trial, by the danger of succumbing to it and yielding to the simpler reactions: the wording is always negative—"Do not . . ."—because the first impulse would be to surrender to fear, worry, credulity, the herd instinct, and the easy way out. But here the threats come from outside, they are alarming, but they cannot prevail against the inner strength of the Holy Spirit, which will animate the disciple (13, 11); and all their might will last but a while and then disintegrate when the Son of Man appears: one need only stand firm to the end (13, 13). These storms announce peace as surely as the new leaves on the fig tree announce summer (13, 28-29).

As outlined in the eschatological discourse according to Mark, the comportment of a disciple does not constitute a parenthesis in the gospels, a fleeting glimpse into the future, which is quickly sealed up again. While certain topics—such as the fate of

Jerusalem or the promise of the Holy Spirit—appear solely in this context, the lessons Jesus teaches and the conduct he requires form part of what we could call his constant theme at this stage of his existence. This fact comes out, perhaps, in a series of parables which all center around a person who is absent and the way people connected with him react to his absence. These are the parables of the doorkeeper (Mk. 13, 33-37), the conscientious steward (Mt. 24, 45-51), the ten bridesmaids (Mt. 25, 1-13), the talents (Mt. 25, 14-30), and the royal pretender (Lk. 19, 12-27). Clearly, Matthew and Luke have added these parables to the eschatological discourse and, just as clearly, they think of the absent protagonist as the Son of Man, and the servants as his disciples. It is sometimes said that this grouping around the themes of the Son of Man is artificial, and that these "parousia parables" must originally have been "crisis parables" meant for the religious leaders of Israel.[8] Through a rather natural tendency to allegory, names would have been attached to the various characters, so that the "master" became Christ. But such a process would be secondary: the purpose of these parables, initially, was to warn the Jewish people and particularly its leaders that the hour of reckoning was drawing near and that their administration would be probed. We must not shrug off this view. It is apparent, for example, that the parable of the murderous vinedressers (Mk. 12, 1-11), in which the central character is a landowner who has gone abroad, does not refer to Jesus' parousia but to the option which the leaders of the people are currently making. And the eschatological discourse itself, by tacitly linking Jerusalem's fate with the attitude it has adopted toward Jesus, attests that he was conscious, at this time, of representing the divine visitation (Lk. 19, 44) and of forcing his people to make the crucial choice.

Nevertheless, these positions seem quite rigid. Dodd's—and he does not conceal the fact—are not unrelated to his personal theory of a "realized" eschatology, which makes Jesus' death and the coming of the Son of Man coincide totally;[9] and those of Jeremias shy away from allegory, perhaps excessively. In any case, the word *crisis* does not seem best suited to characterize these parables. They do not confront anyone with a choice, but rather warn those who have already chosen their master and know him, not to fall asleep, not to be disheartened by the wait or seduced by interlopers disguised as their master. The themes of the eschatological discourse and of these parables fuse and complete one another. In a language which remains peculiar to the gospels and bears the stamp of Jesus, these are Christian themes —those of Paul's first letters, of vigilance and discernment: "We should not go on sleeping . . . but stay wide awake and sober" (1 Thess. 5, 6) and "Think before you do anything—hold on to what is good and avoid every form of evil" (1 Thess. 5, 21-22). There is also the theme of absence and return. The point of all these parables is the instant of the master's return and the encounter that follows. From this point of view, the parable of the murderous vinedressers, which some would want to incorporate into this series, does not belong there. Granted that it is aimed at the Jewish leaders and postulates the master's absence, still there is no return because there has never been any contact between him and the workmen.[10] Jeremias is right in guarding against the temptation to allegorism which would identify the pretender who is detested by his subjects (Lk. 19, 11) or the harsh master (19, 22) with the Son of Man. But it is perfectly natural for Jesus, just before leaving his followers and letting them shift for themselves, to have them weigh the gravity of their responsibilities and to fix their gaze on the hour when they will have to render an account.

If it is true that the eschatological discourse assumes a period when Jesus will have vanished and his disciples will continue to live under his influence, if their comportment is to remain stamped by the experience they have shared with him, if the Holy Spirit is promised them so that they may bear witness to their Master (Mk. 13, 9-11), and if his word is to subsist and stay living among them while events crowd one another out and heaven and earth pass away (13, 31), then we have to say that Jesus, at the moment when he sees his people's fate being sealed and is leaving his followers amid that people, opens up a future to them—in other words, makes them his Church. The word *Church* does not appear at this time in any of the evangelists, and that is a good sign, for it proves that they did not try to identify the Christian community which they knew with the little group assembled on the Mount of Olives. But a group of people gathered together in Jesus' name (13, 13) and by that very fact distinguishing themselves from other men and even their own kin, to the point of being exposed to hatred and death in order to be faithful to that name (13, 12)—this is precisely what the Church will be. Not the Church delineated in advance like an architect's plan, not even an institution organized around a program with bylaws; and yet an original figure which already bears a name—that of Jesus—and which cannot be just one sect among others within Judaism or a mere figure of the world as it goes. At this date, the figure is still only prophetic, and Jesus sees his future take shape only through his actual experience and that of the prophets, his predecessors. He knows simply that he is in the process of giving birth to it and that he will find it again when he returns as the Son of Man.

When will "all these things" (Mk. 13, 4.30) happen? The prediction remains vague—purposely, no doubt; but, for the evangelist, who has constructed his discourse within the framework of this private lesson,[11] it certainly embraces a whole future, from the event which inspired the disciples' question, the destruction of the Temple, to the crowning event, the arrival of the Son of Man. It takes in the whole of history to come, until its close. But Jesus asserts he is ignorant as to that close; and his ignorance is not a weakness or a privation, but the consequence of what he is. He is the Son, and the only one who can claim that title. At the instant he is speaking, he is greater than all men and higher than the angels; and yet he does not know either "that day or hour" (Mk. 13, 32).[12] The significance of this statement is considerable: at the very moment he affirms his unique position in the world and his exclusive relationship with God, Jesus declares categorically that he does not know the date of the most important event in all of human history: the day it must come to an end. This is tantamount to saying that he cannot describe beforehand the course of that history and the chain of events it will comprise. His admission explains his way of speaking about that future, on the basis of his actual experience. It leaves intact and emphasizes all the more the certitude he possesses at this very moment—before his resurrection—of being the Son of Man who will come to terminate that history. Divine certitude and human awareness are here seen as perfectly compatible.

This declaration of ignorance, which very soon proved scandalous—the parallel text in Lk. 21, 33 discreetly glosses over it—is received with gratitude nowadays as a precious testimony of the humanity of Jesus. Still, we are tempted to question its worth, since, in practice, it apparently did not prevent him from envisaging a very brief delay between his departure and the coming of the Son of Man. Indeed, a series of statements by Jesus seems to presuppose that he was expecting the end of history soon and was preparing his disciples for it.[13] We would spontaneously group them around a refrain: "I tell you solemnly, before this generation has passed away all these things will have taken place" (Mk. 13, 30). Ironically, this affirmation is followed, two verses later, by his solemn declaration of ignorance (13, 32). With two such statements, both equally clear, it seems we have to choose one or the other. But on what basis should we make our choice?

A modest solution, but one that faces up to the complexity of the problem, consists in admitting that the evangelical tradition contains data which are difficult to reconcile. Although Jesus' habitual way of speaking seems to indicate that he expected the kingdom and the Son of Man to come in the near but unspecified future, an isolated text here and there mentions a time limited to that actual generation. No doubt, the early Church itself "was uncertain how to fit these awkward pieces neatly into the eschatological discourse of Jesus." [14]

For others, such as Jeremias, these inconsistencies and clashes between texts should not surprise us: they carry out an authentic revelation of God, of a God who can modify his plans and allow for men's supplication and his own pity: "On the one hand, God has ordained the path of history; he has fixed the moment for the final happenings to break forth. The measure of sins is filled to overflowing, and unimaginable destruction threatens. Then God takes pity on those who are doomed to die. He erases the date he has already set, postpones the catastrophe, and gives them one last chance to do penance. On the other hand, God has established the measure of afflictions, of eschatological tribulations, for those last days. But the result is that the final satanic assault would shatter all human resistance, and no one could stand fast. Then, once more, God has pity and cuts short the sufferings of the eschatological period. . . . How are both things possible? How can he, being God, change his mind and alter his plans? Is not God immutable? Has he corrected a mistake? To that we must reply: the Good News knows nothing about a God with an inflexible will. Jesus' Father is not an immovable God: he is a God of grace." [15]

We can easily see how evangelical this explanation is, how very close to Jesus' own words; and we, too, utterly reject an impassive God. But this God who revises his agenda, this God with successive programs, relinquished and adjusted—is he truly the God of the Gospel? He is still a God patterned on human models: a God who changes by renouncing his original intention, who advances in broken segments and zigzags. He may be a superior architect, never short of ideas and methods; but he is not God the creator, always respecting reality and things as they are, yet never bound by the past, always faithful to his promises, and capable at each instant of creating a new universe.

Moreover, we must not forget the strong note of imminence and urgency that necessarily enters into the language of eschatology, along with "the themes of exhortation, aspiration, hope and vigilance." [16] At one and the same time, the last things are the most remote and the most important, and they are always present this very day. We must beware of confusing Jesus' expectation and his teaching: he awaits the kingdom and the coming of the Son of Man with immense hope and could not do so unless he felt their nearness, but he uses the rigorous language of affirmation to teach his ignorance. [17]

Perhaps this language, while sensing the truth, lacks that very quality of rigor. There is in Jesus something which, deriving from expectation and sentiment, would necessarily remain indefinite and "conjectural," [18] and something which pertains to teaching and certain truth; and opposing them is rather infelicitous. True, Jesus adopts the language of imminence to speak about the kingdom and the coming of the Son of Man; but, on his level, it is absolutely accurate. On the eve of his death, the only future for him is the kingdom of God; and this kingdom comes at the end of his life: it will be there when he has given up his life—in a few days, a few hours. And since this kingdom is God's seizure of the entire universe, "in this man's consciousness, however paradoxical that may seem to us, his journey toward death has to coincide with the journey of heaven and earth toward their end. . . . Let historical time continue to run its course after his human death; he outstrips it by going toward the kingdom, where he regains and transcends all earthly possibilities. Thus, when he sees his own end and the end of the world coinciding, we must not suspect confusion in the text, but precise theological language. . . . For even during his own journey toward the unknown hour when the Father comes to him, Jesus must, in virtue of his mission, go to the very end of that journey which leads created and sinful humanity to the day of the God who is coming." [19]

Concerning his own future, Jesus can speak only in the language of imminence; concerning the future of mankind, he speaks in two ways and, as it were, on two levels. On the one hand, he knows that, for his disciples and their contemporaries, the future will extend beyond his own death, and he fixes no time for this duration, since he cannot, before his resurrection, "know times or dates that the Father has decided by his own authority" (Acts 1, 7). This is human language. Designed for men, it is necessarily inadequate to describe the future positively, but it states exactly what men cannot know. On the other hand, Jesus declares to those who understand him that "before this generation has passed away, all these things will have taken place" (Mk. 13, 30), and that "there are some standing here who will not taste death before they see the kingdom of God come with power" (Mk. 9, 1). The word *generation* in these formulas has a precise meaning we should not overlook: it is not directly a chronological term signifying the portion of mankind living on earth in Jesus' day, between 20 and 30 A.D.; it denotes "this" generation, the portion of mankind to whom Jesus is speaking, those whom his message has reached, all those who, because he crosses their path, have to take a position for or against him. This is undoubtedly a temporal category, since all this occurs at a given moment within time; but, primarily, it is a religious category: the totality of men who have at the same time met Jesus. It is literally true that this generation, destined to see Jesus' death and play a role in it, will also see the coming of the kingdom, since his death is to mark the first instant of this coming. That is exactly what Jesus, in a few days, will tell the Sanhedrin assembled for his trial: "You will see the Son of Man . . . coming with the clouds of heaven" (Mk. 14, 62). To the end of time, these words will remain true: for all generations which, throughout history, are joined by Christ, the kingdom of God has come and is offered to anyone who welcomes it, and the Son of Man reveals his glory.

Notes to Chapter 12

1. Only Luke has judged it necessary to name Jerusalem (Lk. 21, 20). In Daniel, this phrase alluded to the profanation of the Temple altar by the statue of Baal Shamaïm, the Syrian equivalent of Zeus Olympios, under Antiochus Epiphanes. Under a prophetic form, Jesus announces the destruction of Jerusalem, the religious capital. See G. Minette de Tillesse, *Le secret messianique dans l'évangile de Marc*, pp. 427-428.

2. It is probable, moreover, that v. 43 echoes Is. 29, 3 and that v. 44 echoes Ps. 137, 9: "A blessing on him who takes and dashes your babies against the rock!" The most cruel image in the Old Testament—a cry of hatred from the exiles in Babylon—becomes, with Jesus, an outpouring of emotion and pity.

3. It is true that, on the level of imagery, the distinction is not absolute: the same apocalyptic metaphors can signify the course of history and its end—for example, "the beginning of the birthpangs" (Mk. 13, 8). But, as a matter of fact, this image, which extends from the beginning to the end, supposes duration.

4. The eschatological discourse properly so called consists of Chapter 13 in Mark. Surprisingly, Mark's composition here seems more solid than that of the two other synoptics. To the instruction delivered when the Twelve were sent out in Galilee, Matthew has linked words which refer directly to their mission (Mt. 10, 17-22 = Mk. 13, 9-13). This is surely an anachronism, since that mission did not entail the possibility of their being persecuted but only ill received (Mk. 6, 8-11). Luke more or less follows Mark, but with many differences (Mk. 21, 5-36).

   The construction of Mk. 13 has recently been examined by J. Lambrecht, *Die Redaktion der Markus-Apokalypse. Literarische Analyse und Strukturuntersuchung* (Rome, 1967). The author has summarized and presented his analysis in a work published under the direction of I. de La Potterie, *De Jésus aux évangiles: Tradition et rédaction dans les évangiles synoptiques* (Gembloux, 1967), Vol. II, pp. 141-164. Lambrecht's studies shed light on the scope and skill of Mark's redactional labors and, at the same time, weaken the hypothesis that Mark utilized an earlier apocalypse which was later completed with Christian passages. See Willi Marxsen, *Mark the Evangelist*, trans. by Roy A. Harrisville et al. (New York: Abingdon Press, 1969), pp. 161-166. Concentrating entirely on the structure of the discourse, however, Lambrecht purposely relegates to the background all problems of content and of "Jesus speaking" (*art. cit.*, p. 162).

5. Matthew has incorporated this discourse into the eschatological discourse (Mt. 24, 26-28.37.41). On the other hand, he has transferred to the mission discourse (Ch. 10) Christ's later instructions to the disciples in view of persecution. (See the preceding note.) Actually, at the time of the first mission, Christ was speaking only of a passing situation, a temporary absence, a preaching identical with his; he did not mention persecution, but only the refusal of some to welcome and listen to his disciples. In particular, he said nothing about the Holy Spirit.

6. This theme is altogether germane in Mark, where it belongs to historical time and suggests that Jesus' disciples must distance themselves from Jerusalem; but it seems rather alien to the purely apocalyptic context of Luke.

7. The evangelists strongly emphasize that this discourse was addressed to the disciples. According to Mark, in fact, it was Jesus' answer to a question put to him privately by Peter, James, John and Andrew (Mk. 13, 3). Mark undoubtedly has his reasons: these four disciples were the first to be called (Mk. 1, 16-19). In any case, their presence, as in the house of Jairus (5, 37), at the transfiguration (9, 2) and in Gethsemane (14, 33), indicates an important revelation concerning the very person of Jesus. See G. Minette de Tillesse, *Le secret messianique dans l'évangile de Marc*, p. 242. True, Lk. 17, 22 introduces the discourse with the words "And he said to the disciples . . ." but the formula remains vague and could be a mere editorial transition. Besides, it does not square with the substance of the discourse, which, like those of the prophets, is addressed to the whole nation.

8. C. H. Dodd, *The Parables of the Kingdom* (London, 1936), pp. 154-174. J. Jeremias, *The Parables of Jesus*, pp. 48-66.

9. C. H. Dodd, *op. cit.*, p. 154.

10. C. H. Dodd, *op. cit.*, p. 124, and J. Jeremias, *op. cit.*, p. 74ff, show how this parable reflects the situation on the large Galilean estates which often belonged to strangers. Quite different is the case of the master who comes back home during the night, or of the bridegroom and his retinue. Even the parable of the talents, where the issue is management rather than human relations, gives prime importance to the moment the master returns. M. Didier, "La parabole des talents et des mines," in *De Jésus aux Evangiles, Tradition et rédaction dans les évangiles synoptiques* (Gembloux, 1967), Vol. II, pp. 248-271.

11. J. Lambrecht, "La structure de Mc. XIII," in *De Jésus aux évangiles, Tradition et rédaction dans les évangiles synoptiques* (Gembloux, 1967), Vol. II, pp. 145 and 164.

12. B. M. F. van Iersel, in *Der Sohn in den synoptischen Jesusworten* (Leiden, 1964), pp. 117-181, has shown that, unlike the title *Son of God,* which derives from a particular language and milieu, the formula *the Son* has to come from Jesus himself.

13. They have been listed by J. Jeremias in "L'attente de la fin prochaine dans la parole de Jésus," which appeared in E. Castelli's *L'infaillibilité: Son aspect philosophique et théologique* (Paris: Aubier, 1970), pp. 184-195. See also A. Voegtle, "Réflexions exégétiques sur la psychologie de Jésus," in *Le message de Jésus et l'interprétation moderne*, pp. 41-113.

14. R. Schnackenberg, *God's Rule and Kingdom*, p. 212. Starting from basically the same principle, A. Voegtle, *art. cit.*, pp. 94-95, attempts to determine, with regard to each of these *logia*, how much interpretation and sometimes deformation the original saying may have undergone when transmitted and included in a particular context. His analyses are extremely valuable, and his conclusion seems well founded to us: "Jesus revealed the meaning of his death and the new constitution of the salvational and Messianic community only to the Twelve. To them alone would he have mentioned an explicit— but not positively determinate—interval between his death and the parousia. Accordingly, the *logion* of Mk. 13, 30 par. can be inserted without difficulty into Jesus' temporal perspective, precisely if this verse is taken as a predic-

tion that the Temple will be destroyed before the contemporary generation disappears—a prediction made to the Twelve."

15. J. Jeremias, *art. cit.,* p. 194.

16. B. Rigaux, "La seconds v̇enue de Jésus," in *La venue du Messie* (Bruges-Paris: Desclée de Brouwer, 1962), p. 198.

17. *Ibid.,* p. 190.

18. *Ibid.,* p. 198.

19. H. Urs von Balthasar, *La foi du Christ* (Paris: Aubier, 1968), pp. 182-185.

13
The New Covenant

Jesus is anxious to celebrate the Passover with his disciples before going to his death. To know that his hour has come, he does not even need special lights. As a reading of the gospels shows, it is above all in Judas' heart and behavior that Jesus sees the plot take shape. But before "the reign of darkness" begins (Lk. 22, 53), before he is "handed over" to his enemies (Mk. 14, 10-11), and while he still remains master of his words and deeds, Jesus wants to take advantage of this paschal meal to do something extraordinary: he himself gives his body and his blood, he institutes the new covenant. The Last Supper is not only the final announcement of the passion, the last opportunity for him to demonstrate that he knows what is going to happen to him and why: it is a creation in which Jesus himself gives its meaning to the death he will undergo.

The gospel accounts of the Last Supper raise several difficult problems which have not all been definitively solved. First, there is a problem concerning the date. Did Jesus celebrate the paschal meal at the same time and under the same conditions as everyone around him in Jerusalem, as the synoptics suppose?[1] Did he, as John's chronology affirms, anticipate this meal by one day, in order to signify that, from that first night, he was embarking upon the sacrifice which would be accomplished on Calvary the next day, at the hour when, in the Temple, the lambs destined for the evening meal would be slain?[2] Would he not have celebrated the Passover on Tuesday evening, according to the ancient calendar followed by the Essenes of Qumran?[3] Be all that as it may, one point is beyond question: "The Last Supper would still be surrounded by the atmosphere of the Passover even if it should have occurred on the evening before the feast." [4]

The most complex question is posed by the palpable differences in the several accounts of this last meal. There are three versions: Paul's (1 Cor. 11, 23-26), Luke's (22, 15-20), and the one found, with a few slight but significant variants, in Matthew (26, 26-29) and in Mark (14, 22-25). Though the differences between Matthew's and Mark's texts on the one hand and Paul's on the other are manifest, they lie within the range of what can be expected from two independent liturgical traditions developing a common primary outline parallelly in two different milieus. Luke's text is more enigmatic. It comprises two moments: the first (22, 15-18), where Jesus speaks of the Passover meal he has longed to eat with his disciples, then gives them a cup to share; and the second (22, 19-20), where he gives them the bread, saying, "This is my body," and then the cup, calling it "the new covenant" in his blood, which will be poured out.[5]

To explain Luke's structure, with its two successive panels, two theories have been proposed. According to H. Schürmann, these panels represent two independent and complementary traditions, which the evangelist placed end to end. The first—and, no doubt, the more ancient—sees the Last Supper as a farewell meal during which Jesus announced his coming victory in the kingdom. The second—added later, but also going back to the Lord—shows how Jesus made this paschal meal a eucharistic meal, how he completed his testament with the gift of his body and blood destined for death.[6] Father Benoît, always a bit wary of categorical affirmations and overly rigid views, prefers "to see in these verses the result of a redactional construction by Luke himself, who combines the traditions of Mark and Paul to produce a skillfully balanced diptych in which the Jewish Pasch is opposed to the Christian Pasch, the lamp and the cup of the ancient rite (v. 15-18) giving place to the bread and the cup of the new (v. 19-20)." [7]

Schürmann's hypothesis is a bolder piece of criticism that seeks to discover the genesis of our texts, the successive stages of tradition. Appealing and often fruitful, this method is sometimes fragile. That of Father Benoît, who hardly ever departs from the text or forgets the personality of the author he is discussing, is doubtlessly surer, but perhaps timid at times. Since we feel incapable of choosing between these two methods, it will suffice if we retain what each holds as certain.

To begin with, there is the link between Jesus' last meal and the Passover—a link which Jesus himself doubtlessly wanted to establish. At any rate, the gospels make this last meal a paschal meal. Jesus is anxious to "eat the passover with [his] disciples" (Mk. 14, 14) and sends two of them ahead to prepare it. The details of the Last Supper "can be easily reinserted in the framework of the Jewish Passover rite."[8]

The piece of bread dipped into the sauce and handed to Judas, the preliminary ablutions which have become the washing of the feet, the blessing over the bread and the cup, the explanations by the head of the family concerning the significance of the various dishes, the singing of the Hallel: all this—which, in the perspectives of the Christian eucharist, takes on a new meaning and a new dimension—already had a meaning in the traditional structure of the paschal meal.

From all these correspondences, which are not fortuitous, there emerges a very clear and deliberate intention, whose amplitude we must measure. Not only does Jesus take advantage of a particularly solemn festival meal to make it his farewell and associate the memory of himself with this last meeting, but he transforms this meal profoundly and thus gives it a new significance.

To transform it, he begins by living it and celebrating it according to the time-honored rite. Now, this rite is essentially familial. Originally a nomadic feast and perhaps more ancient than Moses, the Pasch was connected, not with a sanctuary, but with families and clans.[9] Even after the Deuteronomic reform and the dominant importance assumed by the Temple in Jerusalem, the feast of Easter continued to be celebrated by small groups within the home. In fact, this feature is what stands out at the Last Supper: Jesus gathers the Twelve for a meal marked at once by the intimacy of a group profoundly united around him, by the gravity of the hour, and by the import of the actions he performs. The ritual he follows is not the detailed and solemn ritual of the Temple and large assemblies, but the informal ritual of a father surrounded by his family, of a friend welcoming his guests. Of the Pasch itself and the glorious memories it conjures up, the evangelists make no mention: what interests them, what seems to have filled Jesus' mind and heart, is the meal and what he is going to make of it: "I have longed to eat this passover with you before I suffer." [10] Whereas the paschal theology of the lamb and of the unleavened bread soon becomes explicit in Paul (1 Cor. 5, 7) and is basic in John (Jn. 19, 34-36), it seems not to have influenced the synoptics' account of the Last Supper—a fact which inclines us to trust them when they make this meal the Pasch celebrated by Jesus and his apostles.

What is certain, in any case, is that this meal is more than a farewell meal. Even according to Schürmann's reading—which takes Lk. 22, 15-18 as the earliest account of the Last Supper, before the details in the complementary account in v. 19-20—this meal possesses for Jesus an extraordinary consistency, as it were, to the point of constituting the pole of his most ardent longing. And the words he utters as he passes his cup around explain that longing. By this unusual gesture—for, customarily, the head of the family gave the signal to drink by simply bringing the cup to his lips first, after having rendered thanks—Jesus makes the cup a personal gift to his disciples. The eucharistic words explain just what this gift consists in: the bread broken and shared is the body which will be handed over; the cup passed from hand to hand is the new covenant in the blood which will be poured out (Lk. 22, 19-20).

Before even probing the meaning of the words to see what Jesus wants to make them signify, we must pause to consider the actions that accompany them. Words are heavy with meaning, but, as they are handed down, they may lend themselves to new interpretations; whereas gestures mold an image that is much more difficult to alter. Jesus' gesture is that of giving, and what he gives is a meal—not only the material for a meal: the food to be eaten and drunk at it; but its substance: the sharing of it. Jesus does not point to the bread on the table and say it is his body; rather, he takes it in his hands, breaks it and distributes it, and—while so doing—says, "This is my body." [11] His body is this piece of bread; but it is also this piece shared and distributed, since the body itself is given only because, at this instant, it is delivered up to death.

There is in this gesture something of the gesture of the prophets, and there is more. By associating his body and blood with the bread and wine which the guests will consume, Jesus obviously means to signify his death and his disappearance. But prophetic gestures are not purely symbolic: they already possess real efficacy when received in faith. John's baptism was not simply an expressive image of the purification sinners longed for; it was a gesture "come from heaven" (Mk. 11, 30), like a first step taken by God enabling those who would receive it to pass unscathed through the baptism in the fire and the Spirit which would renew the earth. There was something in John's baptism, therefore, which could be called sacramental: a true link with that ultimate event, the day of the Lord. There is infinitely more in the actions performed at the Last Supper. Here, the event remains prophesied, because it is not yet consummated; but it is not prophesied from without, by a confidant initiated into this secret and entrusted with announcing it. If it is true that, for some time now, Jesus has been establishing a necessary link between his own death, the coming of the Son of Man and the advent of the kingdom, his gestures at this moment are perfectly coherent: realizing that he is doomed to die so that the kingdom of God may come, he forestalls the hour when he will be incapable of anything except letting himself be led, and now freely delivers himself up to death. A prophetic gesture, this, and more than prophetic; not so much a matter of prescience as of his word pledged and kept. For Jesus is speaking about his own destiny and knows that he has the power to set it in motion. The ancient eucharistic formula in St. Paul— ". . . on the same night that he was betrayed, the Lord Jesus took some bread . . . and he said, 'This is my body, which is for you' " (1 Cor. 11, 23-24)—admirably translates this coincidence between the gesture of those who will lay hands on Jesus and his own gesture in giving himself up, and stresses the priority which Jesus retains. Appreciating the implications of this coincidence, the gospel narratives underline the presence, at the Last Supper, of the disciple who was about to hand Jesus over to the chief priests (Mk. 14, 18-20) and Jesus' complete awareness of what was going on.

The actions at the Last Supper are more than prophetic, once again, not only because they are performed by him who is to come as the Son of Man, but because they already belong to the end. Beyond this final meal, there is only the kingdom and the heavenly banquet. More clearly than ever, Jesus affirms the certitude which marked all the announcements of his passion: there is, if not exact coincidence in time, at least a necessary dependence between his death and the coming of the kingdom. For him, anyhow, there is only one future beyond his death—the coming of the kingdom; and this future, like the kingdom of God, cannot but embrace the entire world. And this future is already prefigured and posited by the meal to which he invites his disciples. After his death, he will meet them again in the kingdom, amid the intimacy and joy of a friendly meal. He cannot give more than he gives this evening; but in giving his body and blood, loving his own "to the end," as John says (Jn. 13, 1—RSV), and going to the very limits of love, he also goes to the very end of time—to what we call the end of the world, for, although "historical time continues to run its course after his human death, he outstrips it by going toward the kingdom, where he regains and transcends the possibilities of a terrestrial future." [12]

Is he conscious of this, or are we making him say things that would have greatly surprised him? Even if our language is not quite the same as his, his is explicit: until his last breath, he identifies his future with the coming of the kingdom and the advent of the Son of Man, and gives it the dimensions of the universe. However, he sees this future only in prophetic fashion and through his present experience, without ever so much as outlining it. But already his actual experience leads him to the end of this future and the close of this history. For if he loves his own "to the end," not only does it mean that he loves to the maximum, to the point of "lay[ing] down his life for his friends" (Jn. 15, 13), or even that there cannot be a greater love than this in the future, but it is also proved in the experience which he lives at the Last Supper and in this meal. Sitting before him at the same table and dipping into the same dish with him is the man who was once his friend (Mt. 26, 50) and is now about "to hand Jesus over" (Mk. 14, 10). That verb, *to hand over,* strikes the most tragic note in the announcements of the passion: the horrible sensation of falling defenseless into savage hands (Mk. 9, 31; 10, 33; 14, 10); and there, behind Judas, Jesus sees everything that awaits him: all the hands pouncing at him, all the hatred gloating over him, all the baseness poured out on him. This is indeed the end: never will

God give men a more precious gift than that of his beloved Son (Mk. 12, 6), and never will men respond with such a refusal. God has used his last resort, and men are putting up the utmost resistance. Neither gift nor sin can possibly go further: future ages will never see a new situation comparable to this.[13]

Now, this is the situation which Jesus reverses by delivering himself up to the death fated for him, by turning betrayal into the gift of his life for those he loves. Thus, despite appearances, sin is no match for Jesus: it may put him to death, but it will only succeed in making this death a victory for him who has already, with full consciousness, offered his life as a gift.

But did Jesus do all this consciously? To put it in words, of course, we have had to quote John here and there; but although he adds a special nuance of tenderness, he says nothing which is not already contained in the simple words spoken over the bread and the cup: "This is my body which will be given for you . . . my blood which will be poured out for you." When Jesus gives his life like this and gives it under such conditions—beleaguered by unrelenting enemies, and yet radiant with overpowering generosity— how can we doubt that his secret is anything but love? And when, from the inception of his public teaching, he has called himself the witness of the kingdom which is coming, and, from the first announcement of his passion, has presented it as the victory of the Son of Man, how can we be surprised that, at the instant he is handed over to death, he should make of his death the first moment of the kingdom? If his thinking is consistent and his awareness of his mission has not forsaken him, he naturally wants to go to the very end and give meaning to his death. If he claims to know why he is in the world, he must also know why he is dying. And if he does not tell us, we shall never know. We have no right to proclaim that Jesus Christ saves us by his death unless we hold this certitude from him. Without this connection, without this communication which comes to us from him, nothing warrants our saying that he died for us or that his death has any meaning for our life. God may perhaps save us from our sin, but then that is his business and we do not know how: it is not by Jesus Christ.

Such is the primal meaning of the eucharistic words. They attest, if we may venture to say so, that Jesus lives his death in advance, that he lives it in the presence of his disciples, and that he bestows it on them as a gift. Shall we say that the experience is fictitious and remains imaginary because no one—be he the Son of God—can live beforehand the wrenching from the world and the loss of self which are the essence of death, this annihilation which seems wholly to engulf us? No doubt, it will take the resurrection, and especially the meals eaten together again, for the disciples to be sure that Jesus spoke the truth when living his death in front of them. In this light, nevertheless, we see the importance of the meeting, at the Last Supper, between "the man who betrays" and the one who delivers himself up. For, in the traitor who hands him over, Jesus sees all his accomplices, the instigators of the plot, the more or less immediate accessories, the confederates ready to play their part, and the countless crowd of mute witnesses, uneasy and paralyzed. Such is the humanity that sin produces: a monstrous complicity of hatred, fear, cowardice and cruelty; a complicity that excludes no one—neither the Twelve, who are going to abandon him, nor Peter, who, without realizing it, is already prepared to deny him (Mk. 14, 27-31). This is what Jesus is living through at the Last Supper when he takes the bread and the cup. It is not yet the physical instant of death, and he still has to suffer an atrocious agony, but all the actors are on stage, ready. Jesus will not escape from them, he is lost, he cannot expect anything from them. This is the solitude of death, the solitude of the criminal rejected by society. If, at this hour, Jesus is capable of giving his disciples his body and blood, it can only be by surmounting this mortal abyss, by making of his impending death the very moment in which he comes to forgive and seek out those who reject him. From that comes the extraordinary note of tenderness and intimacy which, in the fourth gospel, imbues Jesus' words at the Last Supper: it is as if he were beyond his death: he has lived and forgiven all the evil he will undergo.

Though this note is not conveyed by the synoptics, it is certainly implied in the eucharistic words. These, moreover, are brought into sharper focus by explicit allusions to major themes to the same effect in the Old Testament: the evocation of the suffering Servant in Isaiah, and that of the new covenant.

As always, when dealing with literary references consisting of literal or virtual quotations, exegesis has a right to ask whether these references do not come from subsequent interpretation in

Christian communities rather than from Jesus himself. It is true that allusions to the suffering Servant are noticeably more numerous in the Acts of the Apostles than in the gospels, and this is a sign that early Christian thinking liked to refer to this prophetic page in order to justify the scandal of the passion.[14] By comparison, the gospel allusions are far less frequent. There will always be a question as to whether the close of Jesus' speech in Mk. 10, 45—"The Son of Man himself did not come to be served but to serve, and to give his life as a ransom for many"—with its definite allusions to Is. 53, 10.12,[15] is a deliberate theological composition or a spontaneous outpouring from Jesus, who knew this great text so well that he could echo its language in the simplest manner. Even if we cannot escape the impression that most of those who refuse to ascribe this sentence to Jesus are complying with the presupposition that his consciousness remains inaccessible to us, we must admit that we have only probable arguments to counter with and that conclusive proof is impossible.[16]

On the other hand, it is very difficult, without doing violence to the texts, to strike out from the words of institution the particulars which make Jesus' gesture a sacrifice and a covenant[17]—a sacrifice from the moment the body is given or the blood is shed *for* "many" (Mt. 26, 28; Mk. 14, 24); a covenant sealed in "my blood" (Mt. and Mk., *ibid.*), present in "this cup" (1 Cor. 11, 25; Lk. 22, 19). The formulas are not identical and not always in the same place: some concern the bread, others the cup or both elements. There are traces of two traditions—three, perhaps, if we follow Schürmann—and, furthermore, one tradition has influenced the other. The prehistory of these texts is assuredly most complex. But the fact remains that they all suppose the twofold theme of sacrifice, with a life given *for* others, and of covenant, this latter, moreover, always being associated with blood—that is, with sacrifice.[18]

Covenant and sacrifice mean a gesture made once and for all, opening a new era and giving it its character and its meaning. A covenant exists only if it is definitive, and it can be sealed only by a definitive event—a death. Jesus gives his life so that at last the covenant between God and his people may come into being. At the same time, he makes of his death, of the life he will place in his Father's hands, the starting point of a new life for mankind.

He is going to die and disappear so that, from this humanity which condemns him to perish, there may arise a holy people. This people is, first of all, the group of disciples with whom Jesus shares his last meal, as shown by Paul and Luke: "This is my body which will be given for you" (Lk. 22, 19; 1 Cor. 11, 24); but it is also the limitless multitude of mankind, as shown by Mark and Matthew: "This is my blood . . . which is to be poured out for many" (Mt. 26, 28; Mk. 14, 24).[19] If we believe that Jesus intended to make his death the origin of this covenant, we have no reason to suspect that, with these *for*'s, the texts introduced a later theology of expiation or substitution.[20] What Jesus does, he does for these people: no mode of expression could be more natural. This gesture, therefore, is inseparable from the future which it inaugurates. Governed by the covenant, this future is a future in the world. The eucharistic gesture institutes the life style of a disciple of Jesus in the world. And this life is modelled on that of Jesus; it is the realization of the gospel program. Thus Jesus' existence, the life he has led, takes on its full meaning. Had his mission consisted merely in putting an end to a world that was damned, by raising it up to God in one sweep with a single gesture of forgiveness, the world would have ended immediately. But then there would have been no need of his coming to live this human life and illustrate what it is to be a child of God in the world, since there would have been no one to live such a life after him. Had his salvific act consisted in bringing human existence to a more or less rapid close, what would have been the nature of the salvation of something destined to disappear so soon? It would have meant, not transforming, but obliterating an irreparable ruin. Unable to draw anything good from man, God would have been uprooting and transplanting him elsewhere, sheltered from evil. That would not have been salvation, but, in a change of metaphor, a contest abruptly terminated to prevent disaster.

The covenant of the Last Supper is something quite different from a simple divine pardon abolishing the past. It is an experience founded on that of Jesus which is drawing to a close: an existence lived in our world, in the darkest part of it, at the very hub of sin and opposition to God, under the constant cloud of death, but lived in filial joy, under the gaze of the Father and in the love of a friend for his friends. It is still human existence, but an existence that has been saved.

This covenant is enduring: no one can destroy it, no one can replace it with another. After Jesus, those who claim to come in God's name can only be false messiahs: "Many will come using my name and saying, 'I am he' . . . And if anyone says to you then, 'Look, here is the Christ' or, 'Look, he is there,' do not believe it" (Mk. 13, 6.21). Beyond this covenant, only one event is possible: the coming of the Son of Man. When leaving his followers, Jesus bequeathes to them this twofold perspective: a covenant to be lived on earth according to his example, and the expectation of his coming as the Son of Man. He makes his last meal both the foundation of this covenant to be lived each day and the pledge of his coming on the last day, of the banquet in the kingdom. This twofold perspective rests on the two aspects of the event he himself is in the process of living and bringing about: it is an initial and basal event, the beginning of a new era; and, at the same time, it is the final event, the consummation of the world in the founding of the kingdom of God. By leaving this last meal in the hands of his followers and asking them to reproduce it after his death, Jesus gives them a triple gift: the death he will suffer, the kingdom into which he will introduce them, and the life they will lead between his death and his coming. That life is not only a certain span in the time allotted to mankind; it is a covenant, a life transformed and profoundly stamped by the initial event till its consummation at the end of time; it is what the Church today calls a "sacrament."

Jesus does not use this word, which, in the Church, will barely antedate St. Augustine and St. Ambrose. Neither does he speak of "mystery," as will the Fathers of the first centuries when they want to describe the gesture he is performing. Instead, he speaks of "covenant," and this is a word his disciples can understand, but he utilizes it while accomplishing a gesture they could never have imagined. He performs this radically new gesture and leaves it in their hands; but, by characterizing it as a gesture of covenant, he gives them the means of expressing if not of explaining it. Whether he himself says "new covenant," as Paul and Luke suggest, or whether he simply designates his blood as "the blood of the covenant," according to the untranslatable Semitic expression in Matthew and Mark, matters little at bottom: this, of necessity, is an absolutely new covenant, from the moment it is sealed with an unprecedented gesture and by God's Messiah. Whether or not Jesus explicitly evokes Jeremiah's promise announcing a new covenant in which God would personally plant his Law and the knowledge of himself deep within his people's heart (Jer. 31, 31-34), it is clear that in leaving to his followers, at the moment he is about to penetrate into God's world, the most telling sign there could possibly be of his close and familiar presence, he gives them access to that world in a mysterious but absolutely real fashion.

If Jesus made the eucharistic gesture the gesture of covenant, there is no cause to doubt that he is its author. The determining reason which keeps theologians like Bultmann or Conzelmann from admitting that Jesus himself could institute the Christian eucharist, is that, for them, the account of the Last Supper—even in the most ancient version, that of Paul—is related to what they call "sacrament." Now, "sacrament" is the introduction into Christianity of a foreign body imported from the pagan world of the Greek mystery religions. A "sacrament" is a rite, representing and reproducing a primordial supraterrestrial event, in which the initiates, by virtue of the mystery, are snatched from the forces of perdition in our world and reintroduced into the divine world of salvation. But this world of forces is only a pseudospiritual vision inherited from ancient myths and perpetuated by natural man's inveterate penchant for mythologizing and objectivating authentic spiritual experience. Paul and John will need very strong faith to demythologize this mythic conception of a sacrament.[21]

That Jesus did not share these conceptions, but that the words at the Last Supper presuppose them, would have to be proved. Now, these words seem to be explained sufficiently by the notion of covenant—a notion which it would be quite natural for Jesus to reflect upon at this time. From the very beginning of his activity, he based his teaching on the Law, like an in-depth reading that approached it earnestly and brought out its full significance. He has finished speaking now, but his work is not over. If he has not spoken in vain, if his words are capable of inspiring faith, if men can bear testimony to his Gospel, he now has to impart consistency to what he has done and set up in the world a visible expression of what he can do. A covenant—this reality which is familiar to the entire Jewish people, this reality which implies at one and the same time an enduring and visible form, a community gathered together, life shaped by a law, a spiritual relationship between God and man, together with knowledge and personal commitment—a covenant seems most fitting at the stage Jesus has reached when death comes. For a covenant is also an event, a decisive moment on which a whole future depends; it is a single event at the outset, and yet permanent, perpetually actualized, as long as there exists a community that is aware of its origin. God's covenant with his people was not only the initial episode on Sinai with Moses' generation, but a daily reality for all the generations of Israel: "It was not with our fathers that Yahweh made this covenant, but with us, with us who are here, all living today" (Deut. 5, 2; cf. 27, 9; 29, 9-12).[22]

What actualizes a covenant is at once the fidelity of God who has bound himself, the faith of the community which continues to welcome him and respond to his word, and also—as the visible form of this faith—a rite, a sacred act. Not all myths are necessarily false and not all rites are necessarily vain, even among pagans. But in Israel, God showed what he was doing, the myth became a slice of history, the rite was able to express an authentic meeting, the rite which instituted the covenant really laid the foundations of an experience of God for this people down through the centuries. Still, it was only a question of a slaughtered animal, of an unimportant death. Reflecting on the mysterious and disturbing episode involving Isaac, the Jewish mind had already sensed the inadequacy of such sacrifices, the need of transcending them, and the impossibility of doing so. We know that in Jesus' day Judaism was drawn to the figure of Isaac,[23] and we see evidence of this feeling in the gospels (Mk. 1, 11; 9, 7; 12, 6). If Jesus wants to reveal the meaning of his death, if he wants to stress the link between his death and the work he is completing—and nothing is more human or more natural than to want this—the sacrifice of covenant affords him an expressive framework. But it also enables him to highlight the unique character of his gesture. In this covenant, everything comes from him: its charter is his Gospel, he himself has introduced his disciples into it, he has lived it in their presence till the end, he is faithful to it to the point of dying for it. If he gives his life now, if he offers up his body and blood, the covenant he thus establishes does not rest upon a rite, however solemn and significant, but upon his own death, and upon his certitude of being accepted and received by God in his capacity as victim—that is to say, for the people to whom he has given himself.

To his disciples he leaves something like a rite: words to pronounce, gestures to reproduce. Man cannot do without rites, without actions through which, by means of a few great symbols, he expresses his most profound experiences, the faith of the community in which he speaks to God. So it is that Jesus gives his followers a few words and gestures. But, if we may say so, these rites are reduced to a minimum, to the barest essentials of ritual: they are the religious acts which used to accompany festive meals, and they are stamped both with the gravity of the faith and the thankfulness they express, and with the familial joy that brings a happy group together around a table. That the eucharistic rite presents such a simple form, at once firm and free, is unquestionably due, not to some general mistrust with regard to ritual—at least, there is no reason to think so—but above all to the fact that, here, the ritual derives its value solely from him who performs it. It is the act of Jesus sacrificing his life, the utterance of Jesus offering up his body and blood, that give value to his words and gestures. And if, of all sacramental rites, this one and this one alone is properly intangible, that is because it expresses the essence of the Christian sacrament, whose rites are simply the expression of the Church's faith, but whose reality is the active presence of Christ offering his life to his Father for his followers.

Jesus, however, makes a point of putting this bread, which is his body, and this cup, which is that of his blood, into his disciples' hands. The insistence on the word *take* (Mk. 14, 22) proves that the nascent Church sensed the importance of that act. In this mysterious form, Jesus truly entrusts to his own his sacrifice, his entire person, as molded by the life he is winding up and the death he is assuming. He thus produces in the world a reality which is not different from himself, since it consists in his person, his gift, his life and his death, and which nevertheless possesses this extraordinary character of existing outside of him, in the community of his disciples, in the act they repeat, in the bread and the cup they hold in their hands. These acts are performed by him, they have no other content but him and, without his living presence, they would be mere empty rites; still, they are effectuated by men and are susceptible of taking on very diverse forms with time and distance, provided men always make them mean what Jesus is doing this very evening. Such is the Christian sacrament, the total sacrament, which consists at one and the same time in the gift of Jesus laying down his life for his followers, in the faith of the community he has constituted, and in the actions by which this community receives and transmits his gift.

At the instant Jesus rises from table to plunge into the dark night of his passion, he has really finished telling his own what he had to tell them, and performing those gestures which depend upon him. There is nothing left to do now but let the crushing burden he has taken up descend upon him, and, till his dying breath, keep his promise to give them his body which will be handed over and his blood which will be poured out. More than ever before, everything depends on him alone, and yet everything is left in the hands of men: "This is your hour; this is the reign of darkness" (Lk. 22, 53). Until that darkness has exhausted its power and Jesus has fulfilled the pledge made at the Last Supper, the Last Supper itself will remain in abeyance, so to speak—not unavailing and ineffectual, but as yet still prophetic and incomplete. Besides, the community to which he has entrusted the Supper is scattering and seems to be dissolving: it no longer subsists except in him, in the prayer by which he gathers it together (Lk. 22, 31-32). So that it may take shape again and know that its Lord is in its midst, Jesus has to rise and collect his dispersed flock (Mk. 14, 28; 16, 7). So that the prophetic words at the Last Supper may become reality till the end of time, he has to die and commit his spirit into God's hands (Lk. 23, 46). Then stripped of all limitations and received by the Father in his glory, everything he is, his body, his life, his words and his deeds carry the power of the Spirit to the very ends of the earth and the very close of history (Acts 2, 33). From his side opened eternally, from his body delivered from death, are born the Church and the sacraments (Jn. 19, 34; 20, 22).

NOTES TO CHAPTER 13

1. J. Jeremias staunchly defends this position in *The Eucharistic Words of Jesus*, trans. by Norman Perrin (New York: Charles Scribner's Sons, 1966), pp. 15-88. See P. Benoît, "Note sur une étude de J. Jeremias," in *Exégèse et théologie* (Paris: Cerf, 1961), Vol. I, p. 240.

2. This is the solution which P. Benoît seems to prefer. See his "La date de la Cène," in *Exégèse et théologie*, Vol. I, p. 260.

3. A. Jaubert develops this hypothesis in *The Date of the Last Supper* (Staten Island: Alba House, 1965). Critical reaction has varied, being quite favorable in some instances but, on the whole, rather reserved. See P. Benoît, "La date de la Cène," in *Exégèse et théologie*, Vol. I, pp. 255-261; X. Léon-Dufour, "Autour des récits de la Passion," in *Recherches de science religieuse*, 48 (1960), pp. 489-495.

4. J. Jeremias, *The Eucharistic Words of Jesus*, p. 88.

5. An additional difficulty comes from the fact that an important family of manuscripts, sometimes called "Western," omits the end of v. 19 and all of v. 20. For a long time, many exegetes preferred this short text, thinking that it represented an archaic form of the evangelical tradition, in which the Last Supper would originally have been only a farewell meal prefiguring the banquet in the kingdom, and in which the only strictly eucharistic word, preserved in v. 19a, would have concerned the bread (supposing that v. 19a was not introduced afterwards, under the influence of the later, parallel accounts of Paul and Mark). This position is losing ground today, and most exegetes agree that the long text, being more difficult to explain, is doubtlessly the original one. See P. Benoît, "Le récit de la Cène dans Lc 23, 15-20," in *Exégèse et théologie*, Vol. I, pp. 163-203; and "Note sur une étude de J. Jeremias," *ibid.*, pp. 240-241.

6. H. Schürmann has presented his investigations in a little volume which should have a wide audience. It has been translated into French under the title *Le récit de la dernière Cène* (Le Puy: Mappus, 1966).

7. P. Benoît, "Les récits de l'institution de l'Eucharistie et leur portée," in *Exégèse et théologie*, Vol. I, p. 211.

8. P. Benoît, *op. cit.*, p. 215.

9. H. Haag, "Pâque," in *Dictionnaire de la Bible, Supplément*, VI, 1127-1128, 1132. According to Roland de Vaux, *Ancient Israel: Its Life and Institutions*, trans. by John McHugh (New York: McGraw-Hill Book Company, Inc., 1961), p. 488, "Before the institution of the monarchy, the Passover may well have been a common feast celebrated at the central sanctuary of the tribal federation. . . . It certainly had been a tribal feast before the settlement. But the settlement led to a loosening of tribal bonds, and to a decentralization of cultic worship; and so the Passover became a family feast." Nevertheless, it never lost its character as a feast of the "beginning of Israel's history as a people" (p. 493), and it retains this character even today. See A. Neher, *Moïse et la vocation juive* (Paris: Seuil, 1956), p. 129.

10. That is why, in order to give meaning to this meal and to the eucharistic words, it is not absolutely necessary to see the paschal meal in it. H. Haag,

"Páque," *op cit.,* 1147; N. Füglister, "Passah," in *Sacramentum Mundi,* 3, p. 1040.

11. Although they belong to different traditions, the text in Mk. 14, 22: "Take it, this is my body," and that in Lk. 22, 19: "This is my body which will be given for you" converge. Luke's formula stresses the giving, while Mark's stresses the receiving; but both gestures go together, and this gift is essential.

12. H. Urs von Balthasar, *La foi du Christ,* p. 185.

13. Be it well understood, we are not concerned here with measuring the gravity of the sins committed during the passion or the culpability of each of the actors, but with understanding how Jesus' situation leads him to the very limits of man's ability to sin and God's power to forgive.

14. The reader may wish to consult the table of quotations drawn up by J. Dupont, "L'utilisation apologétique de l'Ancien Testament dans les discours des Actes," in *Etudes sur les Actes des Apôtres* (Paris: Cerf, 1967 [Lectio Divina, 45]), p. 281. However, it is important to note that the identification of Jesus with the suffering Servant, after occupying a very large place in early Christology, drops into the background in later Christology, particularly in Paul's. Its reappearance in the gospels must, therefore, result from a distant memory. See O. Cullmann, *The Christology of the New Testament,* pp. 73-78.

15. "To give his life" = Is. 53, 10.12; "as a ransom" = 53, 10; "for many" = 53, 12. But "to serve" *(diakonein)* does not hark back to Is. 53, 11 *(douleuein).*

16. A. Feuillet, "Le logion sur la rançon," in *Revue des sciences philosophiques et théologiques,* 51 (1967), pp. 365-402, builds a good case in favor of the arguments for authenticity, which are very strong. In support of Feuillet's observations concerning the importance of the idea of expiation in the Judaism of those times, we would further mention the place it allotted to the theme of Isaac bound hand and foot and to his expiatory value. See J. E. Wood, "Isaac Typology in the New Testament," in *New Testament Studies,* 14 (1967-1968), pp. 583-589.

17. H. Conzelmann, in *An Outline of the Theology of the New Testament,* pp. 55-59, believes that the two themes of sacrifice and covenant are fairly closely related and that, even if not primitive, they must have a common ancient origin. This position strikes us as very reasonable and solid. We would only take exception to his conclusion, where he denies that this origin could be Jesus himself because "it is clear that for Jesus [the words of institution] cannot have a Hellenistic, sacramental sense" (p. 59). This argument rests on a debatable identification between "Hellenistic" and "sacramental."

18. Must we add to these two themes a third which would tie them together— that of the suffering Servant giving his life for many? O. Cullmann, *The Christology of the New Testament,* pp. 64-65, insists that we must, basing his argument chiefly on the mission entrusted to the Servant of reestablishing the covenant between God and his people (Is. 42, 6; 49, 8) and on the very name *covenant* which God gives his Servant (49, 8). See H. Schürmann, *Le récit de la dernière Cène* (Le Puy, 1966), p. 31. While deeming this position very probable, one may nevertheless maintain a certain reserve and point out that, even if it were proved that Jesus did not identify himself with the Servant, his manner of offering his body and blood in this language of sacrifice and covenant suffices to give his actions a

decisive significance, that of an eschatological and foundational event.

19. The current English versions of the Bible all translate "for many," but some older versions carried "for the multitude" [Tr]. "The multitude" (Hebrew: *harabbim*) is a Semitism which is often equivalent to "the whole." In Rom. 5, 15, Paul describes as "so many" *(hoi polloi)* those whom he will call "everyone" *(pantas)* in Rom. 5, 18. And it is significant that for the Semitic expression "to give his life as a ransom for a multitude" the purer Greek of 1 Tim. 2, 6 substitutes "Christ Jesus, who sacrificed himself as a ransom for them all." See A. Feuillet, *art. cit.,* p. 374.

20. The phrasing used by C. H. Dodd, *According to the Scriptures* (London: Collins, Fontana Books, 1965), p. 123, ". . . this representative character of expiatory sacrifice is intrinsic to the whole idea of such sacrifice" is perhaps too conceptual in its language; but, all questions of wording put aside, one point is clear: a sacrifice always has a purpose and seeks the "good" of those *for* whom it is offered.

21. See R. Bultmann, *The Theology of the New Testament,* Vol. I, pp. 133-152. According to him, Paul found the eucharist, in its properly sacramental form—that is to say, conceived of as a mysterial communion with the body and blood of the Lord—in the Hellenistic communities (*op. cit.,* pp. 148-150). Since this form could not have originated in the first Palestinian communities, it cannot go back to Jesus. H. Conzelmann follows the same line of reasoning in *An Outline of the Theology of the New Testament,* p. 59. Bultmann thinks that the original formula said only, "This is my body, this is my blood," and that the explanation in terms of a covenant is a subsequent addition. Though it is quite true that the mention of the covenant constitutes an addition in regard to the bare formula, we wonder whether the formula could mean anything by itself and whether an explanation was not required from the start. As we said earlier, perhaps it is impossible to prove that Bultmann's cutting is unjustifiable, but we can show that a less arbitrary reading also possesses its own coherence.

22. See G. Von Rad, *Old Testament Theology,* Vol. I, trans. by D. M. G. Stalker (New York: Harper and Row, 1962).

23. J. E. Wood, "Isaac Typology in the New Testament," in *New Testament Studies,* 14 (1967-1968), pp. 583-589.

14
The Son and the Father

"That Jesus is the Christ, the Son of God" is the fundamental Christian affirmation, and the gospels were written to prove it. This purpose is stated explicitly in John (Jn. 20, 31), but it stands out just as clearly in the three other gospels. In their several ways, they all demonstrate how, through his life, his deeds and his words, Jesus revealed himself to be the Son of God. For Mark, the Gospel is "the Good News about Jesus Christ, the Son of God" (Mk. 1, 1),[1] and this revelation culminates in the assertion by the Roman centurion who saw how Jesus died: "In truth this man was a son of God" (Mk. 15, 39). In Matthew the importance of the theme is underlined by the number of texts in which Jesus is called the Son of God, and God is called the Father of Jesus.[2] Such references are less numerous in Luke, who has deliberately omitted several cases typical of the synoptic tradition, but the silences and the tone peculiar to this gospel show that it intends to give an extremely rich and thought-provoking picture— at once precise and mysterious—of the relations between the Son of God and his Father.[3] This insistence on the part of the evangelists accords with Paul's message (1 Thess. 1, 10; 1 Cor. 1, 9; 15, 28; 2 Cor. 1, 19; Gal. 1, 16; 2, 20; 4, 4.6; Rom. 1, 3.4.9; 5, 10; 8, 3.29.32; Eph. 4, 13) and has fixed the Christian profession of faith for the ages.

Nevertheless, behind this capital and comprehensive datum, there appear two major facts which should help to understand it better. First, this formula does not occur in the earliest New Testament professions of faith; and second, we are not sure it was expressed in these terms by Jesus himself. "Here," it will be said, "is a new blow leveled at traditional beliefs!" and, according to their mood, some will revolt at the scandal, while others gleefully jettison these last pieces of a burden they still find too heavy. Both will be wrong: these two facts testify to the fidelity of the gospel tradition, to its understanding of what the revelation of God in Jesus Christ is; and, if we can see right, they give us access to the supreme moment of this revelation, to Jesus' final hours.

It is a fact, first of all, that the most ancient professions of faith do not call Jesus "Son of God." Indeed, it seems that the oldest formulas of the Christian faith have been preserved for us in the "missionary discourses" which the first half of the Acts of the Apostles places on the lips of Peter (Ch. 2, 3, 4, 5, 10) and Paul (Ch. 13). All these discourses are built on the same pattern, more or less developed according to circumstances, and all reflect a stage of Christian thought and expression which seems deliberately archaic—more primitive than the theology of Paul, for example. Accordingly, it is natural to consider them the echo of the earliest Christian preaching.[4]

Now, a striking feature of these discourses is precisely the archaic tone of their Christology. They give Jesus various titles, several of which have been widely used since—such as "Christ" and "Lord," whereas others never really became current—such as "Servant" of God (Acts 3, 13.26; 4, 27-30), "Holy One" and "Just One" (3, 14; 7, 52; 22, 14), "Leader" and "Savior" (5, 31; 3, 13; 13, 23). In this fairly broad repertory, the title "Son of God" appears only twice, each time on Paul's lips: in the sentence that sums up his early preaching as a convert (9, 20) and in his discourse in the synagogue at Antioch in Pisidia (13, 33). Taking these texts literally, we would be led to conclude that "Son of God," without necessarily coming later, was only one title among others at first and carried no very definite meaning. Unquestionably, it would denote a special relationship with God, but that could be a particular mission or some Messianic function. From there to divine personality is a long step.

There also seems to be a long step between Christian usage and the words of Jesus. For, according to the three synoptics, never once did Jesus expressly say he was the Son of God, never once did he even utter the title applying it to himself. His most explicit declaration—during Caiaphas' questioning before the Sanhedrin—is a mere reply whose phrasing avoids the designation in the charge and whose tone, at least in Matthew, suggests deliberate ambiguity: "The words are your own" (Mt. 26, 64), which can mean "I'm not forcing you to say so" or, just as well, "If you insist on putting it that way."

Shocking as these observations may seem, they are actually enlightening and reassuring. They prove that the basic formulas of the Christian faith do not come from the iterating of words heard and repeated, from a lesson Jesus would have made his disciples learn so that they in turn might engrave it in the memory of their hearers. In all likelihood, the title "Son of God" in the New Testament is a Christian creation, and Christians themselves originally discovered this way of referring to Jesus.[5] The essential point is to know how they found this expression and whence they derived the certitude that it said exactly what Jesus was. If we can possibly retrace the intellectual process whereby men thought they could, in their own language, say who Jesus was by calling him the Son of God, as well as the initial experience through which they received this certitude from him, then we shall doubtlessly be able to understand what the revelation of God in Jesus Christ is—that mysterious communication by which the person of Jesus, living with men and unveiling his secret to them, made them capable of receiving and expressing him. At the same time, no doubt, we shall discover the path that will preserve us from mythologizing Jesus. If we can ascertain that this path is rational, definable and discoverable by the intellect, but, at the same time, that it originates in the spiritual experience of faith in God and his Son, then we shall have found, from its birth, Christianity as it has always wanted to be and has always presented itself: an access to God made immediate through faith in Jesus Christ, and a communicable and inviolable acknowledgement of belief in the person of Jesus Christ Son of God.

We must therefore posit—what is more likely by far—that the title "Son of God" was neither assumed in this form by Jesus himself nor immediately and spontaneously adopted by the first Christian community to express its faith in the Messiah whom God had just given it, as would doubtlessly have been the case had this title been a current name in Judaism for the expected Messiah. In other words, we must presuppose a process, the evolution of a question and of thought, between the first experience of belief in Jesus within the Church, and the moment when this title became, for all Christians, the most common and authoritative expression of their faith. But we shall then have to ask—and this is the supreme question—what this expression corresponds to: is it only the more or less felicitous translation of an experience these Christians have lived together, a powerful way of voicing their belief, or the echo in them of an original experience to which their faith has given them access—the very experience of Jesus?

If the most ancient Christian formulas do not call Jesus the Son of God, it is not that they entertain doubts about the scope of his work, the faith placed in him, or even the importance and meaning of the personage he is. From the very first day, as far back as we can hear the Church speak, she declares that in Jesus God fulfills all his promises, makes the world undergo a profound change, and introduces man into a radically new experience: that of the Spirit, of forgiveness, and divine power. From the very first day, she holds up before men the image of Jesus, of his life, his death, his resurrection and his actual power in those who cleave to his name, and proclaims that without him she would not have been born and would be nothing. Now, whenever she speaks of Jesus, whenever she strives to give him a name that defines his work and expresses what he is, this name expresses a unique relationship between Jesus and God: "God has made this Jesus . . . both Lord and Christ" (Acts 2, 36); ". . . the Holy One, the Just One . . . the Prince of life . . . God raised him from the dead" (3, 14-15); "God . . . had foretold . . . that his Christ would suffer" (3, 18); "God raised up his servant" (3, 26); ". . . the name of Jesus Christ the Nazarene . . . of all the names in the world given to men, this is the only one by which we can be saved" (4, 10-12); ". . . your holy servant Jesus whom you anointed . . . stretch out your hand to heal and to work miracles and marvels through the name of your holy servant Jesus" (4, 27.30); "By his own right hand God has now raised him up to be leader and savior" (5, 31); "God has appointed him to judge everyone, alive or dead" (10, 42).

The most salient feature about this series is perhaps the possessive. The titles given to Jesus are diverse and denote various aspects of his action, but they all say that this action is God's and that, in order to accomplish it, God uses this personage who belongs to him and on whom he relies completely. Even though the possessive is not always explicit, it is present everywhere, and, if the shape of the sentence permitted, we would say "his Holy One and his Just One" or "his Leader and his Savior" as naturally as "his Christ" or "his Servant." The experience of early Christianity confirms both that Jesus exercises his power immediately in the community which bears his name, by filling it with his Spirit, and that the secret of this power lies in the unique bond which binds him to God: "Now raised to the heights by God's right hand, he has received from the Father the Holy Spirit, who was promised, and what you see and hear is the outpouring of that Spirit" (2, 33).

To express this bond, the Christian faith early used the word *Son,* which very quickly became general and concentrated in itself all the relationships the oldest titles could suggest. Insofar as we can retrace a history about which so little information has come down to us, several factors seem to have contributed to the genesis of this formulation. First of all, because Jesus' resurrection and the outpouring of the Spirit showed he was the promised Messiah, it became quite natural to identify him with the royal personage in the coronation psalms. Ps. 110, 1 announced that the Messiah would be exalted and made to sit at the Lord's right hand; and Ps. 2, 7, on the day of his coming, presented him to the nations as the Son designated by God: "You are my son, today I have become your father." Even though the identification of the Messiah and the Son had not been emphasized in contemporary Jewish tradition, which carefully protected the image of the true God from anything that could evoke the divine begettals and apotheoses of paganism, it seems clear that the Christians, liberated from such scruples by the very figure they had seen living among them, promptly exploited these parallels.[6] Another path which likewise led to stressing Jesus' filial mission was the importance the first Christians attached to the figure of the Servant of God announced in Isaiah. This is one of the titles most frequently given to Jesus in ancient texts. Now, the Septuagint usually translates *servant* by the Greek word *païs,* which means *child* as much as *servant.*[7] The shift from *païs* as *child* to *huios,* which means *son,* is quite normal and is attested in both the Old and the

New Testament.[8] To call Jesus the Son of God, therefore, was not to make him a sort of hero endowed with superhuman powers, as in pagan mythology; on the contrary, it was to carry the concept of servant in Isaiah to its logical conclusion, to underscore the aspect of personal relationship (already so pronounced in the prophet) between God and the personage whom he had chosen and to whom he was entrusting his purpose and his work.[9] Lastly, the study of the Old Testament has recently yielded a third meaning for "Son of God," one which clearly reappears in early Christology. We are referring to the equivalence set up between being a son of God's and belonging to the world above, the world of divine holiness. "Saints" and "sons of God" can become synonymous, denoting persons who live close to God and reflect his holiness.[10] Now, by resurrecting Jesus, God exalted him and made him sit at his right hand amid his glory and holiness. Such, from the beginning, is the substance of the Christian message: "This news is about the Son of God who, according to the human nature he took, was a descendant of David; it is about Jesus Christ our Lord who, in the order of the spirit, the spirit of holiness that was in him, was proclaimed Son of God in all his power through his resurrection from the dead" (Rom. 1, 3-4).[11]

From many viewpoints, then, the process that ended by substituting "Son of God" for the various names by which early Christian thinking had sought to designate Jesus and qualify his work, possessed its own logic and coherence. Nevertheless, the fact that it compelled recognition so fast and so completely, and that it furnished Johannine and Pauline reflection with an inexhaustible source of meditation, prayer and action as well as a norm of life and faith, was due, not to its logic or its force, but to its truth. "Son of God" became Jesus' essential title, not because it was more felicitous, more evocative or more precise, but because it expressed far more exactly the experience lived by the witnesses and because it said exactly what Jesus was. Originating later than others perhaps, it supplanted them all because it chimed with the very language of Jesus and allowed the Church, when voicing her own faith and her own thinking, to repeat in her way the word she had received from her Lord.

For, although "Son of God" is probably a Christian creation, its content does not derive from its past history but from the object it contemplates; and although Jesus undoubtedly never uttered the phrase as it stands, it echoes words which were certainly authentic and through which, at a few crucial moments, he permitted his profoundest secret to break through: he is the Son. Such moments are rare: the synoptics record only two—the hymn of jubilation: "No one knows the Son except the Father, just as no one knows the Father except the Son" (Mt. 11, 27; Lk. 10, 22); and the declaration of ignorance at the end of the eschatological discourse: "But as for that day and hour, nobody knows it, neither the angels of heaven, nor the Son, no one but the Father only" (Mt. 24, 36; Mk. 13, 32)—two texts whose authenticity seems well guaranteed both by the unique character of their content, which would have been difficult to imagine, and by an inimitable style.[12]

Even words as spontaneous as these can spring from a definite mode of expression and a tradition. We have underlined the affinity between "the Son" and "the Son of Man":[13] both appear in an apocalyptic atmosphere, in connection with angels, secrets and revelations. These remarks are beyond discussion and suggest that, to speak about the Son, Jesus utilizes a phraseology which is familiar to him—that of the Son of Man. But the differences are no less striking, and, if anything, are more significant, because they show exactly why he speaks here, not about the Son of Man, but about the Son. For what Jesus says about the Son is different from what he says about the Son of Man. The Son of Man is always in the process of doing or undergoing; he has a life to live, a destiny to accomplish; he is *en route* to his hour, and becomes himself only in his future. The Son, on the contrary, is wholly present here; he is not defined by his action or his passion, but by what he is, by the bond that unites him with the Father, by their reciprocal gaze. Even if he does not know everything the Father knows, it matters little: he is the Son.

Though spontaneous like everything Jesus says, his statements about the Son of Man are generally deliberate; they constitute a teaching and form part of a program which Jesus makes it his mission to present. Conversely, his statements about the Son are neither prepared beforehand nor justified by explanations; they spring from a particular moment and a concrete situation, and afford a glimpse of a consciousness which was present and alive and has nothing to do but exist. While all these features appear in the two examples from the synoptics, they are particularly arresting in the rather more numerous Johannine formulas. They do not result from any set purpose, but simply state a fact.

The fact is, then, that Jesus is "the Son." The whole force of this word is that it has meaning only in relation to the Father and can be applied only to one person. The Son cannot be other than one, and he cannot be the Son other than to the Father. But, at the same time, this force makes a formidable demand: lest this word remain a hollow sound, lest it be lost in the multitude of pseudo-revelations and secret names mysteriously communicated to a few initiates, what it expresses has to be lived, and Jesus has to show forth as the Son he claims to be.

The moment he appears, as we have seen, the moment he starts talking about the kingdom of God, the moment he brings the Father's generosity to the poor and his forgiveness to sinners, Jesus speaks and lives like the Son he is. And, in the opinion of the evangelists, this must have been perceptible to anyone with eyes to see, for they show Peter at Caesarea acknowledging his belief in the Christ given by God. Yet, for them, the decisive moment in this revelation is the passion. Beyond a doubt, the passion was a tremendous crisis for the disciples, and nothing less than the resurrection could confirm their faith for good and all. But if, according to the gospels, the resurrection is what founds belief by making Jesus appear in his power, the passion is what enables us to say who this risen Jesus is. For, once risen, he does not have much to say and reveals nothing new about what he is: he refers his disciples to what he used to tell them before he died, and he sends them forth into the world. If the resurrection proves anything, it proves the truth of what he had said till then, without managing to make himself understood; it unveils the meaning of what he had done, without yet being able to explain it. The risen Jesus brings proof that he is exactly what he claimed to be, what he died for. The revelation of Jesus Christ was not completed and did not take on its configuration before the resurrection, but it was integrally expressed, in words and in deeds, the moment he drew his last breath. Otherwise, we would have the right to consider it a myth. If this revelation were delivered to us by someone who had risen and come from another world to tell us about a new universe he has just discovered, our faith would be only blind acceptance of unverifiable statements. But the risen Jesus comes back solely to assure us that he is always the same, that everything he said was true and that it holds good for all peoples of all times.

Of all his words and all his deeds, the last are the most meaningful and weighty. The evangelists have garnered them with special care, so that the account of the passion is the most fully developed portion of the gospel narratives[14] and the richest in many ways: topographic and chronological details, the unfolding of the facts, and doctrinal and spiritual substance.[15]

Now, according to the four gospels (each of which nevertheless pursues its own viewpoint here more than ever), an essential theme—not to say the central theme—of the passion is the question of knowing who Jesus is. This is the object of all the cross-examinations, this is the refrain of all the insults and contumely, this is the trilingual inscription nailed to the cross, this is the response of the Roman officer. We cannot make sense out of these accounts if we disregard this axis. For the gospels, the answer is, "Jesus is the Son of God, and he was put to death for having so maintained." John's gospel agrees with the synoptics on this point: " 'We have a law,' the Jews replied, 'and according to that Law he ought to die, because he has claimed to be the Son of God' " (Jn. 19, 7). According to Matthew, Mark and Luke, the Sanhedrin condemned Jesus to death for having replied affirmatively to Caiaphas' question: "Are you the Christ, the Son of God?"

It is certain that the gospels give this formula its Christian meaning here and intend precisely to emphasize that the acknowledgement of Jesus Christ, the Son of God, is addressed to him who was condemned and crucified. But if the formula carries its Christian meaning, how could it possibly mean the same thing on the lips of Caiaphas, and what could Jesus' answers mean since the questions put to him were equivocal in the first place? Is the whole debate over his identity, though inserted into the passion narrative, only a later figuration, a dramatizing of Christian belief?

Let us observe, first, that the gospel account of this debate is perfectly in keeping with Jesus' entire comportment. Neither here

nor elsewhere does he himself pronounce the title "Son of God."
He merely acquiesces when it is given him—and, even then, only
with reservations: refusing, according to Luke, to answer the Sanhedrin's question about the Messiah, or, according to Matthew,
answering only by making the questioner responsible for the formula: "The words are your own" (Mt. 26, 64). At any rate, Jesus
and his judges agree on one point: the whole issue is to know who
he is; and there is no misunderstanding: what they call blasphemy
is for him the plain truth.[16] Judging from the texts, what is blasphemous for the Jews and capital for Jesus is the fact that he calls
himself the Son of God. Perhaps the gospels have summarized in
a few simple words a dialogue which was probably more subtle
and sinuous, like those recorded by John. In fact, they take pains
to suggest such complexity by linking to the title "Son of God"
those of "Christ" and "Son of Man." In the end, "Son of God"
is the one which polarizes both the scandal of those who reject
him and the adoration of those who believe.[17]

And, indeed, this is the title that best expresses the meaning
which Jesus, having reached his final hour, gives to his work, his
life and his death. If he is in the hands of the authorities, inter-
rogated like a culprit and already treated like a criminal (Mk.
14, 48-49), this is no accident, no mistake, but the logical outcome of a line of conduct he pursued to the bitter end. Without
casting doubt on the legitimacy of the religious and political leaders, he so freely criticized their performance and so categorically
recalled the sovereign exigencies of God, the priority of the
wretched and the sinful, the price of reconciliation and forgiveness, and the precariousness of vested interests, that all the authorities—chief priests, doctors of the Law, elders and Roman
commanders—felt threatened and so joined forces to eliminate him.

It would be useless, furthermore, to ask the gospels to fix the
ultimate blame in Jesus' trial and death. If there is one thing God
alone can know, it is the choice each conscience made at that
time. The whole message of the New Testament consists in proclaiming that this choice is not irreversible, and not one voice
heard in the gospels claims to be that of the supreme judge.
Besides, the evangelists themselves do not paint an absolutely
identical picture of Jesus' trial.[18] All relate, if not two successive
trials, one Jewish and one Roman, at least two court appearances

and two death sentences. For Mark and Matthew, the session of the Sanhedrin is the principal trial, and Pilate's sentence is only an indispensable formality quickly obtained as the chief priests barter Jesus' death for Barabbas' pardon. On this view, the trial is primarily a religious matter, and the essential question is the one Caiaphas asks: "Are you the Christ, the Son of God?" John's account reads quite differently. For him, this primal question is no less important; in fact, it is so important that it lies at the bottom of every discussion in which Jesus confronts the religious leaders of Jerusalem (Ch. 5, 7, 8, 9 and 10), and precisely because it has already been settled in their mind do they decide on the death penalty (Jn. 10, 33; cf. 19, 7). But, for John, the real trial is the Roman one, held to determine whether Jesus claims kingship and is thus a threat to Caesar's power.[19] A political question, this directly concerns the representative of Rome, Pilate, who, despite his dodging, is forced to resolve it. Willy-nilly, the death sentence comes from him, and he stands responsible for it. John's viewpoint does not contradict Mark's and Matthew's but is vaster and more complex. Luke, by simplifying matters perhaps, presents a coherent scenario: Jesus' death is the result of a coalition among all his enemies, the Jewish leaders, Herod and Pilate (cf. Acts 4, 27).

If we attach more importance to the Mark-Matthew version, we shall be inclined to stress the responsibility of the Sanhedrin.[20] But if we consider how singularly "right" the tone of John's account is, how skillfully he conveys the complex relationships between the Jewish leaders and their Roman rulers, and how much audacity it took to publish—under Domitian or even Nerva or Trajan—a chronicle so apt to awaken the suspicions of Rome, we shall be inclined to follow the fourth gospel.[21] In that case, the political trial assumes its full importance, and the ultimate responsibility rests on Pilate.[22] This historical point possesses some significance, and we must be careful not to minimize the role which the pagans played in Jesus' death. Still, it would be superficial of us to exploit John's data one-sidedly, since he makes it clear that the Jews are just as responsible. For the New Testament, for the Acts of the Apostles and for Paul, Jews and pagans are equally culpable and have no right to pin their own guilt on each other.

Moreover, we would be misreading the whole of the Good

News and, in the first place, the message of the passion narratives if we sought there the yardstick of human responsibility. The entire passion is the work of God, whose victory consists precisely in turning all the evil mankind can commit into a revelation of love and forgiveness. That is a matter for the Son of God.[23]

Such is the meaning of Jesus' agony in Gethsemane: at the beginning of the passion, this page—the darkest and most appalling in the whole story—was written to show that what is about to happen results entirely from the dialogue which has taken place between God and Jesus.[24] Now, this dialogue is a meeting between the Father and the Son: "Abba (Father)! Everything is possible for you. Take this cup away from me. But let it be as you, not I, would have it" (Mk. 14, 36). It is one of the rare instances when the evangelists let us hear Jesus speak his native tongue,[25] and the only time he calls God "Father" in that language. Without being extremely common, this appellation was not unknown either in the Old Testament or by the Jews of Jesus' day. But "Abba" is not only "Father"; it is the familiar term children use to name their father. "With the help of my assistants," writes J. Jeremias, "I have examined the prayer literature of Late Judaism —a large, rich literature, all too little explored. The result of this examination was that in no place in this immense literature is this invocation of God as *abba* to be found. . . . *Abba* was an everyday word, a homely family-word, a secular word, the tender address of the child to its father: 'Dear father.' No Jew would have dared to address God in this manner. Jesus did it always, in all his prayers which are handed down to us, with one single exception, the cry from the cross: 'My God, my God, why hast thou forsaken me?'; here the term of address for God was prescribed by the fact that Jesus was quoting Psalm 22:1." [26]

What is unique about the scene in Gethsemane is that it yields us both a firsthand confidence from Jesus, a direct example of his filial reaction, and a carefully planned theological composition. In several respects, the episode evokes the transfiguration[27] and, like it, constitutes a "theophany": God is there, very close, and Jesus stands before him. Unrecognizable on Mount Tabor, so radiant was his face with the inner glory that filled him, Jesus is now disfigured by anguish and terror. Here as there, everything takes place between God and him: a secret is shared, which three apostles are invited to witness—"Listen to him," "Wait here, and keep awake"—but which they cannot comprehend. And, on both occasions, this secret is basically the same: the dread cup of the passion.[28]

What appears here does not differ from what the whole gospel account presupposes. From the very beginning, whenever he spoke about the kingdom which was coming, and as he went seeking out sinners, Jesus was manifestly indwelt by a presence, led by an experience, testifying to an initiative: God. God, with his secret, with his purposes and choices, was the immediate source and the perfectly clear meaning of his activity and his mission. Gethsemane affords us a glimpse of this permanent meeting between Jesus and God. In his human distress, in his appeal to the friendship of his disciples, Jesus discloses to them his profoundest mystery. The harrowing hours he will go through, everything the cup symbolizes, the torrent of hatred and cruelty and baseness loosed against him, the sight of what sin is making out of Jerusalem and can make out of humanity, his powerlessness to reach men, all the horror of the passion—this is the subject of the exchange between the Father and the Son.

On this debate hangs the destiny of the world. For the Father, everything is possible; he is not subject to any fatality—not even sin; other solutions remain open to him. Jesus goes forth to his passion, not because sin is stronger and he must bow to its law, but because God has chosen this means to triumph over sin, and because he has chosen it for his Son. Jesus has to will it, and the Father cannot compel the Son; but the Son, however horrible his repugnance, cannot will anything other than the Father wills. Until he says "Yes," the passion cannot begin, because it does not yet have meaning. Gethsemane gives it that meaning, and the successive episodes of the trials and the crucifixion will spell it out and explain it.

Now, indeed, Jesus' identity must be made known, and he will no longer hide. When Caiaphas and Pilate, after trying to ascertain what he has said or done and what crimes he can be accused of (Mt. 26, 59-61; Jn. 18, 19-21.35), are both driven to ask him, each in his own way, the crucial question: "Are you the Christ, the Son of God?" (Mt. 26, 63), "Are you the king of the Jews?" (Mt. 27, 11; Jn. 18, 33), Jesus finally speaks out. This is the only question he deigns to answer, the only one that still has meaning, because he has never really said much about it. His words and deeds are common knowledge, and there are enough witnesses to report on them (Jn. 18, 20-21). But his identity he has never yet revealed openly. Whenever the question has been brought up—whether by the perspicacity of his adversaries (Mk. 1, 25.34; 3, 12), the blind enthusiasm of the crowds (Jn. 6, 14), or the still unstable faith of his disciples (Mk. 8, 30; 9, 9)—he has vigorously pushed it back into the shadows. Until he reaches the end of this task, he cannot call himself the Messiah or the Son of God without exposing himself to all sorts of misinterpretations: if he be the Son of God, let him take advantage of his status to turn stones into bread (Mt. 4, 3) and life into a dream, to throw himself from the parapet of the Temple (4, 6) and become master of men.

At this moment, all the titles Jesus claims—Messiah, Son of Man, Son of God—can have only one meaning: referring him to God. Proclaiming oneself the Christ was not necessarily blasphemous, provided one performed deeds showing that God was actually intervening; but Jesus no longer has a single disciple at his side to support his cause. Speaking about the Son of Man as if one were to incarnate this figure could be tolerated, as long as one produced signs indicating that the kingdom of God would come soon; but now Jesus is unable to work the least sign, either for himself or for others (Lk. 23, 9.39). To claim kinship with God at this point, when he is doomed, when all his activity has ended in utter failure, when nothing remains of his endeavors, and his words bounce back as a barren echo—this is sheer madness. And, indeed, the unfolding of the passion, as the gospels saw it, shows how empty were all Jesus' claims. The scenes of ignominy prove the worth of this Christ-Prophet,[29] this alleged king of the Jews. And the gibes hurled at him on the cross bring out the basic issue: to know whether or not Jesus can invoke a relationship with God which sets him apart and makes him answerable to none but God: "Save yourself! If you are God's son, come down from the cross!" (Mt. 27, 40; cf. 27, 43). In this perspective, the cry "My God, my God, why have you deserted me?" (Mt. 27, 46) takes on a meaning we would not dare imagine. It is not just the avowal of atrocious suffering, of unfathomable distress;[30] it is like admitting defeat, and now his adversaries have only to take possession of him. Their victory is total: the whole matter has turned out better than they dared dream; neither on earth nor in heaven does anyone stir: this man was, therefore, not the Son of God.

And yet, "this man was [the] Son of God" (Mk. 15, 39).[31] And it is the passion, it is this death which completes the revelation of him. Since Gethsemane, since Jesus has, as it were, lost the initiative, since he has ceased speaking except in reply to the questions of his judges, the commiseration of the women or the request of his companion, since he is captive and bound, he converses with God. He most certainly does not cut himself off from men: during the whole passion, we shall not find in him a single word of condemnation, a single gesture of aloofness, a single movement of withdrawal; and this attitude, at once so natural and so incomprehensible, says more eloquently than "Father, forgive them" (Lk. 23, 24) how vast is the forgiveness that fills his heart. But what he has done is stop speaking to men, since he no longer has anything to tell them. Now he is turned toward God—but no longer needing to bear witness to him or asking to be championed before men. This is very different from prophets and martyrs: they die to give testimony, they invoke him for whose name they suffer, they proclaim his excellence and grandeur. Jesus no longer speaks about God, but to him. And a painful dialogue it is; all we know of it, till his last breath, is the anguished supplications in Gethsemane and the cry that rose from the cross into the void. But it is also a dialogue in which the Son truly reveals himself. For Jesus to cleave to God amid this horror and emptiness, and keep his eyes fixed on him though he deprives him of all defense, all protection and all joy, there has to exist between God and Jesus a bond invulnerable to any attack, an unshakeable trust, a certitude stronger than death. Now, at the end, exhausted and crushed, Jesus does not need to turn toward God, for he has never left him: he is the Son.

Such is the Son whom God resurrects—the one whom he desired to see in the face of man, the one whom he has been awaiting since Bethlehem and whom the passion brings to him now.

NOTES TO CHAPTER 14

1. Even if the longer version, with its explicit mention of "the Son of God," is not original—which remains a possibility, for the shorter version seems more "difficult" to accept—it "agrees perfectly with Mark's message." G. Minette de Tillesse, *Le secret messianique dans l'évangile de Marc*, p. 353.

2. Jesus is called the Son of God eighteen times in fourteen passages, and God is called the Father of Jesus twenty-four times in eighteen passages. See A. George, "Jésus Fils de Dieu dans l'évangile selon saint Luc," in *Revue Biblique*, 72 (1965), p. 185.

3. A. George, *art. cit.*, pp. 206-209.

4. This view, which for a long time was rather widespread, has recently been challenged. Some contemporary exegetes think that these discourses embody Luke's theology first and foremost and that the contribution—if any— of ancient sources and documents is indiscernible. See E. Haenchen, *Die Apostelgeschichte*, Kritisch-exegetischer Kommentar, 10th-edition (Göttingen, 1956); U. Wilckens, *Die Missionsreden der Apostelgeschichte. Form und traditionsgeschichtliche Untersuchungen* (Neukirchen Kreis Moers, 1961). However, an exegete of the caliber of J. Dupont is not convinced by their arguments and holds that these discourses go back to very ancient documents. J. Dupont, *Etudes sur les Actes des Apôtres* (Paris: Cerf, 1967 [Lectio Divina, 45]), pp. 127-128, 145-155.

5. "No evidence is forthcoming for the application of the title 'Son of God' to the Messiah in pre-Christian Palestinian Judaism." J. Jeremias, *The Parables of Jesus*, p. 73. Similarly, O. Cullmann, in *The Christology of the New Testament*, p. 274, states: "No known ancient text definitely calls the Messiah 'Son of God.' " Passages like Ps. 2, 7 and 2 Sam. 7, 14 certainly held out this possibility and largely contributed to orienting the expectation of the Messiah in that direction; but it seems that the fear of suggesting physical generation, according to the interpretations current in pagan milieus, always kept Judaism from presenting the Messiah simply as the Son of God. See E. Lohse, *Theologisches Wörterbuch zum Neuen Testament*, VIII, pp. 361-363.

6. C. H. Dodd, *According to the Scriptures*, pp. 31-35. J. Dupont, *Etudes sur les Actes des Apôtres*, pp. 265-267, 291-297; *Idem*, "Filius meus es tu. L'interprétation de Ps. 2, 7 dans le Nouveau Testament," in *Recherches de Science religieuse*, 35 (1948), pp. 522-543.

7. W. Zimmerli, *Theologisches Wörterbuch zum Neuen Testament*, V, pp. 675-676.

8. Wis. 2, 13-18: "[The virtuous man] calls himself a son of the Lord [*païs*]. . . . Let us see if what he says is true. . . . If the virtuous man is God's son [*huios*], God will take his part." What appears to be one and the same person is called *païs* in Mt. 8, 6, *doulos* in Lk. 7, 2, and *huios* in Jn. 4, 16.

9. See J. Jeremias, *Theologisches Wörterbuch zum Neuen Testament*, V, pp. 698-709; C. Maurer, "Knecht Gottes und Sohn Gottes im Passionsbericht des Markusevangeliums," in *Zeitschrift für Theologie und Kirche*, 50 (1953), pp. 1-38; G. Minette de Tillesse, *Le secret messianique dans l'évan-*

gile de Marc, pp. 344-346.
10. G. Minette de Tillesse, *op. cit.,* pp. 348-351. To this use of the title, the author connects the divine proclamation addressed to the king on his coronation day: "You are my son . . ." (Ps. 2, 7).
11. See M.-E. Boismard, "Constitué Fils de Dieu (Rom. 1, 4)," in *Revue Biblique,* 60 (1953), pp. 5-17.
12. B. F. M. van Iersel, *Der Sohn in den synoptischen Jesusworten* (Leiden, 1964), pp. 117-161.
13. E. Schweizer, *Theologisches Wörterbuch zum Neuen Testament,* VIII, pp. 372-375. We find the same apocalyptic climate in 1 Cor. 15, 28, when "the Son himself will be subject in his turn to the One who subjected all things to him."
14. For a presentation and synthesis of the historical, literary and theological problems raised by these accounts, see X. Léon-Dufour, "Passion," in *Dictionnaire de la Bible, Supplément,* VI (1960), 1419-1492; see also the commentary on the texts in P. Benoît, *The Passion and Resurrection of Jesus Christ,* trans. by Benet Weatherhead (New York: Herder and Herder, 1969).
15. Mt. 26, 63; Mk. 14, 61; Lk. 22, 67-70. Each gospel presents its own version. Luke's, in particular, distinguishes very sharply between the question concerning the Christ, which Jesus avoids answering, and the one concerning the Son of God, which he answers categorically. But these slight differences do not detract from the overall agreement.
16. As we consider Jesus' declarations before the Sanhedrin, it is not so easy to specify wherein lay the blasphemy properly so called which the judges alleged. In itself, neither claiming to be the Messiah nor pretending to the title of son of God nor even identifying oneself with the Son of Man constituted a direct affirmation of divinity. See P. Lamarche, *Christ vivant* (Paris: Cerf, 1966 [Lectio Divina, 43]), pp. 150-155. Father Lamarche thinks that this affirmation of divinity results from the conjunction of the texts: a Messiah seated at God's right hand in heaven, in the place destined for the Son of Man, cannot be anything but a divine personage. In full agreement with this line of interpretation (which is keenly aware of the impasse reached by a literal analysis of the texts taken separately although they constitute a whole), we would go even a little further: from a simple analysis of these words and formulas, which all come from the Old Testament and therefore necessarily exclude any identification with the transcendent God, it is evident *a priori* that we could never draw a strict affirmation of divinity. The blasphemy properly so called can arise only from the content Jesus gives to words which, by themselves, necessarily had a limited and finite sense. Recent essays highlighting the "celestial" traits of the Son of Man in the pre-Christian tradition are thought-provoking. See, for instance, A. Feuillet, "Le Fils de l'Homme de Daniel et la tradition biblique," in *Revue Biblique,* 60 (1953), pp. 170-202 and 321-346. They nevertheless entail an uncrossable boundary: if this personage really possesses divine traits, without on the other hand being a literary personification of God and his action (as is the personage called Wisdom, for example), he sets himself up before God as an equal—which is obviously unthinkable.
17. It is difficult to determine to what extent the gospel narrative reflects the progress of this trial. To those who object that the report cannot be based on

the evidence of eye-witnesses, we reply with P. Benoît: "It would be enough for a Nicodemus, a Joseph of Arimathea, members of the Sanhedrin, to have given an account of what happened. Besides, it is naïve surely to imagine that the secrets of an assembly can be kept. Human nature is not like that; even if they are not supposed to, men talk." P. Benoît, *The Passion and Resurrection of Jesus Christ,* p. 109. With that said, and the fact and theme of the trial established beyond doubt, it is clear that the evangelists themselves do not claim to be giving any more than a meaningful condensation in a few lines: the equivalent of a memorandum.

18. Concerning the different problems raised by Jesus' trial, see P. Benoît, *The Passion and Resurrection of Jesus Christ,* pp. 79-151; *Idem,* "Le procès de Jésus," in *Exégèse et Théologie* (Paris: Cerf), Vol. I (1961), pp. 267-315; Vol. III (1968), pp. 243-250.

19. C. H. Dodd, *Historical Tradition in the Fourth Gospel,* pp. 112-115.

20. This is the tendency represented, with many qualifications, by J. Blinzler, *Le procès de Jésus* (Tours-Paris: Mame, French translation, 1966).

21. C. H. Dodd, *op. cit.,* p. 115.

22. O. Cullmann, *Jesus and the Revolutionaries* (New York: Harper and Row, 1970), pp. 31-33, believes that "Jesus was condemned by Pilate as a political rebel, as a Zealot."

23. "We do not believe that analyzing the documents in the case presented in the gospels can reveal 'the true motives which led to Jesus' condemnation and, therefore, indicate who was really responsible for it' (P. Benoît); from the viewpoint of the accounts themselves, these 'motives' are so unfathomable that the evangelists suggest God was the author of the drama." P. Bonnard, *L'évangile selon saint Matthieu,* Commentaire du Nouveau Testament (Neuchâtel: Delachaux et Niestlé, 1963), Vol. I, p. 388.

24. P. Benoît, *The Passion and Resurrection of Jesus Christ,* pp. 21-23, agrees with K. G. Kuhn, "Jesus in Gethsemane," in *Evangelische Theologie,* 12 (1952-1953), pp. 260-285, who believes that Mark's narrative derives from two earlier accounts, one of which stressed the person of Christ and the hour of the Son of Man, while the other stressed the example he gives his followers. Kuhn attempts to seek out a third version, attested by Luke and John, characterized especially by Jesus' distress and the strength given him from above. P. Benoît thinks rather that Luke and John, each in his own way, developed one of the two traditions. See P. Benoît, "Les outrages à Jésus prophète," in *Exégèse et Théologie,* III (1968), p. 262.

25. *"Talitha koum"* (Mk. 5, 41); *"Epphata"* (7, 34); *"Eloi, Eloi, lama sabachtani"* (15, 34).

26. J. Jeremias, *The Lord's Prayer,* trans. by John Reumann (Philadelphia: Fortress Press, 1964), pp. 19-20. D. Flusser, *Jesus,* pp. 93-95 and n. 159, would modify this statement: "Jeremias could not find 'Abba' used to address God in Talmudic literature; but considering the scarcity of rabbinic material on charismatic prayer, this does not tell us very much." The remark is pertinent, and the examples Flusser adduces, in which wonderworkers who were almost contemporaneous with Jesus and were described in chronicles as "sons of God" declare that we should call God "Abba," are infinitely precious. They bespeak a truly filial faith, capable of perceiving a profound kinship between the confidence of a child in his father and that which God expects from us. But if these wonder-workers dare apply *Abba* to

God, they do so only after a reasoning process and a comparison based on the *abba* of children. In Jesus, the word leaps forth spontaneously and requires no justification.

27. "Then he took Peter, James and John with him" (Mk. 14, 33 = Mk. 9, 2); "He . . . found them sleeping . . . and they could find no answer for him" (Mk. 14, 40; cf. Mk. 9, 6; Lk. 9, 32).

28. A. Feuillet, "La coupe et le baptême de la Passion," in *Revue Biblique,* 74 (1967), pp. 371-377.

29. P. Benoît, "Les outrages à Jésus prophète," in *Exégèse et Théologie,* Vol. III, pp. 265-268.

30. Ps. 22 ends with the joyous certitude of salvation, and we would be misapprehending the import of Jesus' cry if we reduced it to the first words of the psalm, which are quoted to indicate the content of his prayer on the cross. If the evangelists retain only these opening words, the cruelest and most shocking, that is because they want to show that Jesus' agony was horrible and that God himself seemed absent. Still, we must not read into this text the anguished cry of damnation. The damned cannot say "my God," since, for them, he is only a stranger. Jesus' most profound distress remains a prayer.

31. One sometimes sees the translation "This man was a son of God." Though perhaps it comes closer to the statement of the Roman officer ("This was a great and good man," Lk. 23, 47), there is little probability that it renders the text exactly. Grammatically, the absence of the article before "son of God" proves nothing: it is always omitted when the attribute precedes the verb. See M. Zerwick, *Graecitas biblica,* 4th edition (Rome, 1960), pp. 171-175. And, in Mark, the profession of faith in Jesus, Son of God, is certainly the echo of the revelation which constitutes the fundamental theme of his whole gospel. G. Minette de Tillesse, *Le secret messianique dans l'évangile de Marc,* p. 358.

Index